*Key Issues*

# KEYNES
## Contemporary Responses to the General Theory

*Key Issues*

# KEYNES

## Contemporary Responses to the General Theory

Edited and Introduced by
### Roger E. Backhouse
University of Birmingham

Series Editor
### ANDREW PYLE
University of Bristol

ST. AUGUSTINE'S PRESS
SOUTH BEND, INDIANA

© Thoemmes Press 1999

Published by
St. Augustine's Press
South Bend, Indiana, USA

ISBN
Paper: 1 890318 28 0

*Keynes*
Key Issues No. 21

*Library of Congress Cataloging-in-Publication Data*
Keynes : contemporary responses to the general theory /
    edited and introduced by Roger E. Backhouse.
        p.    cm — (Key Issues; no. 21)
    Includes bibliographical references and index.
    ISBN 1-890318-28-0
    1. Keynes, John Maynard, 1883–1946. General theory of
employment, interest and money. 2. Keynesian economics.
I. Backhouse, Roger. II. Series : Key Issues (Bristol, England);
no. 21.
HB99.7.K364   1999
330.15'6—dc21                                          99–39475
                                                            CIP

Printed in Great Britain by Antony Rowe Ltd, Chippenham.

# CONTENTS

## III. SPECIALIST ACADEMIC JOURNALS

# INTRODUCTION[1]

*The General Theory of Employment, Interest and Money*, by John Maynard Keynes, published on 4 February 1936, was, with little doubt, the most important and influential contribution to economics in the twentieth century. The mythology of the 'Keynesian revolution', which has its roots in the book's dramatic first chapter, is of Keynes having brought down a 'classical' orthodoxy, providing for the first time a theoretical explanation of how persistent unemployment could arise, and how deficit-financed government expenditure could be used to restore full employment. 'Keynesian' policies were believed to be the main reason why the capitalist world experienced such a prolonged period of prosperity following the end of the Second World War. These myths have long since been stripped away – there was much more variety within 'classical' economics than Keynes implied, the case for public works policy was made well before the 1930s, in Sweden and in the United States, and it has been argued that post-war prosperity owed little to Keynesian policies. On top of this, the 1980s and 1990s saw a major assault on the theoretical basis for Keynesian economics. Yet, even after all this, it remains the case that the *General Theory* made an unparalleled and permanent mark on the way the problem of unemployment has been conceived and analysed.

The reception of the *General Theory* has probably no parallel in the history of economics, the appearance of the book immediately generating intense excitement. Symptomatic of this is the fact that at Harvard, a group of students (who turned out to be crucial in the spread of Keynesian ideas in

---

[1] There are several reviews of the reviews of the *General Theory* (Harris, 1984; Klein, 1952; Skidelsky, 1992, chap. 16). Though none is comprehensive in its coverage, all are good and I have therefore not sought, in this Introduction, to go over ground covered by them. Though not a review of the reviews, Moggridge (1992, chap. 23) provides a detailed discussion of some reviews, notably those by Keynes's colleagues Robertson and Henderson, and Keynes's reaction to these. I leave the reader to follow up these references.

the US) arranged for the book to be available to them immediately on its publication in the UK. Only a decade later, in a set of surveys of contemporary economics commissioned by the American Economic Association (Ellis, 1948), Keynes was, by a long way, the most frequently cited economist. Paul Samuelson, one of the leading American Keynesians, claimed that virtually no economist under the age of 50 was immune to the appeal of Keynesian ideas. This dramatic reception of the book was reflected in the number of reviews published. By the end of 1936, just eleven months after publication, over 125 English-language reviews had been published,[2] many of them substantial essays by the period's leading economists, and the flow of reviews did not cease then.

There were several reasons for the book's reception.[3] Perhaps the most important is that Keynes was a well-known public figure – so well-known, indeed, that cartoonists regarded him as instantly recognizable, not needing to be named. His *Economic Consequences of the Peace* (1919), in which he had denounced the peace-makers at Versailles, had been a bestseller. In addition, he was a respected academic at the leading British university, and had been actively involved in politics and public life during the 1920s and 1930s. He was a frequent contributor to the press. A further reason for the level of interest in the book was that it was widely known that Keynes was working on a book for which he made great claims. In 1930, he had published *A Treatise on Money*, in two volumes. At this stage, he had already acquired a reputation as one of the world's leading monetary economists, but had yet to publish a definitive work on the subject. His *Tract on Monetary Reform* (1923) had its origins in a series of articles in the *Manchester Guardian* and was, as its title implied, a tract rather than a systematic academic work. But not only was the *Treatise* very critically received,[4] no sooner was it published than Keynes announced that he was dissatisfied with it and that he was starting afresh on a new book. Though detailed discussions

---

[2] I have a list of 104 reviews, and it is certain that there are ones that I have not discovered.

[3] The literature on the background to the *General Theory* is too voluminous even to attempt to list it. Good introductions are the biographies of Moggridge (1992) and Skidelsky (1983 and 1992). Much shorter introductions are found in Moggridge (1980), Skidelsky (1996) and Blaug (1990).

[4] For a review of the reviews, see Dimand (1988).

of the text were confined, by and large, to a small group of Cambridge colleagues, the *General Theory*, unlike the *Treatise*, was extensively discussed before its publication. Finally, on top of all this, the book opened with a dramatic appeal to over-throw an entrenched orthodoxy, inviting the reader to join with him in this task. This was an appeal that caught the imagination of many in the rising generation of economists.

Though the *General Theory* was immensely successful, many economists found its arguments hard to understand. Indeed, it has been argued that a certain level of difficulty was an essential ingredient in its success. The reason was not that Keynes failed to explain what he was trying to do – this was made very clear in his dramatic, one-page opening chapter. It was that Keynes was arguing in a style that was unfamiliar, introducing many new (or apparently new) concepts and developing on a wide range of theoretical arguments. Economists found the new ideas hard to grasp, and hard to relate to the way they had previously thought about the problem of unemployment. The result of this was that there were many reviews that sought to explain what Keynes was actually saying – to translate his ideas into terminology and language that made sense. Of these, the most successful was John Hicks's 'Mr Keynes and the "classics" ', published at the beginning of 1937. The 'IS-LM' model, as it has come to be known, that Hicks proposed has been so successful that, for many economists, it has become Keynesian economics. It has become impossible to view the *General Theory* except through the lens of Hicks's interpre-tation.[5]

In the hands of economists such as Franco Modigliani and Don Patinkin, Hicks's analysis of unemployment in terms of a simultaneous equilibrium of the markets for goods and money was integrated into a theory of general competitive equilib-rium. The conclusion was reached that unemployment could, in principle, be cured if money wages were flexible: if they fell in response to high levels of unemployment, the system would move towards full employment. It was agreed, however, that this process might take an unacceptably long time, and hence that government policy might be required to alleviate the situation. According to this view, though Keynes was wrong to

[5] The history of the IS-LM model is discussed in Young (1994).

argue that his theory was more general than the classical, it dealt with the case that was relevant in practice.

This interpretation, the so-called 'neoclassical' synthesis, was, however, challenged. Amongst the critics of the neoclassical synthesis, many have drawn attention to chapter twelve of the *General Theory*, in which Keynes argues that long-term expectations are determined by habits and conventions, not by rational calculation of the future, for there is no basis on which rational calculations can be made of, for example, the probability of a European war twenty years hence. This is the theme on which Keynes focused when, in 1937, he published a reply to his critics in the *Quarterly Journal of Economics*. The fundamental flaw in classical economics, he argued, was that it abstracted from the fact that we know very little about the future. This was the key message of the *General Theory*. It stands in seeming contrast with the stable equilibrium of the IS-LM model. From this the conclusion is drawn that the IS-LM model misrepresents Keynes's fundamental message. Against this, is the fact that Keynes expressed his admiration for the papers in which the IS-LM model was developed (see Moggridge, 1992, p. 595; Skidelsky, 1992, p. 614).

The reviews collected here all date from 1936.[6] The prime reason for this was a practical one: there had to be some cut-off point, and the end of 1936 is one that is easy to apply. But it also means that we are looking at reactions to the *General Theory* that antedate 'IS-LM' – views of Keynesian economics that are untainted by the Hicksian interpretation. Looking at these early reviews means we can see how economists responded to Keynes before their perspective had been altered by Hicks.

In examining these reviews, the main focus is on the many very substantial reviews of the book published in academic journals. However, it is also valuable to see how the *General Theory* was viewed in reviews aimed at a more popular audi-

---

[6] Unfortunately, constraints on space mean that not even all the reviews from 1936 can be included here. In selecting reviews for inclusion, priority was attached to including reviews from newspapers and non-academic journals, as these are comparatively hard to obtain. Reviews that are reprinted in Lekachman (1964), which is widely available, are not included. Even with these excluded, it was still necessary to leave out some reviews in academic journals and to reprint only selections from some of the longer ones.

ence, for it is unusual for an academic work to be so widely reviewed.

The challenge to the 'classical' orthodoxy was a recurring theme in reviews in newspaper reviews. Amongst the newspaper reviews we find headings such as 'Mr Keynes Bombards a Citadel'; 'A Daniel Come to Judgement'; 'An Economic Bombshell'; and 'The Blunders of Economics'. Keynes's message, expressed clearly at the beginning of the book, that he was overthrowing a long-established orthodoxy, had clearly got across. A. Wyatt Tilby (*The Observer*, in a review that was widely syndicated) commented that economists were never convinced by evidence, but that if only one or two of the hares Keynes had started took refuge in the temple of orthodox economics and raised a dust, he would have achieved his purpose. A. L. Rowse, a historian, was far more specific in that he argued that there had been a trend in economics, led by 'the London School', including Lionel Robbins and T. E. Gregory, away from the real world. He saw this unreality of mind as having been the root cause of the subject's loss of prestige.

Reviewers also picked up Keynes's argument that the cause of unemployment was a shortage of demand for goods as a whole and that the cure for unemployment was to spend more: that saving impeded growth. Keynes's argument that, though there were much more rational things to do, unemployment could be alleviated by building pyramids, or even by burying money in the ground and then paying men to dig it up again, attracted much comment. They also turned, in large numbers, to the chapter in which Keynes offers 'Concluding notes on the social philosophy towards which the general theory might lead' – the notion that prosperity and ever-falling rates of interest might lead to the euthanasia of the rentier.

But if Keynes was seen as having written a book that was of fundamental importance, reviewers were quick to point out that it was a difficult book. It was described as technical theory, not for laymen, introducing new and unfamiliar concepts. Hartley Withers, a financial journalist, went so far as to suggest that a translation was required!

Can he not be persuaded to get some student who knows what he means and can and will write in the vulgar tongue – which Mr Keynes can do so well himself when he is in the

mood – to produce a translation of this volume which might
be so valuable if it could be understood?

(Hartley Withers, *The Sunday Times*, 23 February 1936)

Others said that the final judgement had to be suspended
pending the verdict of those qualified to understand its arguments. But if the book was difficult, it was also cheap. Reviewer
after reviewer commented on the price of only 5s.[7] T. S. Ashton
even managed to provide what was presumably intended as a
light-hearted link between this and what Keynes was saying in
the book.

> The book is published at five shillings. Its size and form seem
> to justify a price three or four times that amount. What
> should be done with the balance 'saved'? Clearly economists
> who are convinced must not seek to hold it in liquid form.
> If they cannot find an investment perhaps they will pay
> labour to carry away their libraries of 'Principles' and make
> a bonfire. For this would have the same beneficial effect as
> the pyramid-building and digging for hidden money com-
> mended by Mr Keynes as alternatives to his own plan.
> (T. S. Ashton, *Manchester Guardian*, 24 February 1936)

One reviewer got it exactly right. 'By putting the book forward
at such a price, Mr. Keynes is saying in effect: "This is no
ordinary book. It is a book that *has* to be understood because
it really matters. It marks an epoch in economic thought" ' (G.
D. H. Cole, *New Statesman and Nation*, 15 February 1936).
If this was Keynes's strategy in setting his price, it was a
great success. (His books were published by Macmillan, but
at Keynes's own risk, so he set their prices.)

But if reviewers outside the academic economics journals
were overwhelmingly enthusiastic, there were instances of
strong criticism. One was Montague Fordham, who made fun
of Keynes's frequent changes of mind, sometimes, he alleged,
in the middle of a book. He went on to criticize Keynes for
being guilty of the same 'abstractionism' that characterized
orthodox economics: 'it is as if a Seventh Day Advent Baptist,
having seen the fallacy of his particular teaching, hurries off
to become a Plymouth Brother' (Montague Fordham, *GK's
Weekly*, 26 March 1936). A realist outlook, going below the

---

[7] In Britain's pre-decimal currency, there were 20s. to £1.

surface, was called for. A sceptical stance was taken by R. C. K. Ensor, a historian, whose concern arose from the fact that Keynes's theoretical conclusions supported policies that he (Keynes) had long since been advocating. Keynes's conclusions would have been more impressive, Ensor contended, had he proved results that he found unpalatable. The low esteem in which economics was held, Ensor argued, arose because economic theory had come 'to seem too capable of proving anything that the economist favours' (R. C. K. Ensor, *The London Mercury*, April 1936).

Such criticisms, however, were mild in comparison with that of the communist *Daily Worker*. In its review, under the heading 'What *Does* Mr. Keynes Want – Poison Gas??' Henry Douglas criticized Keynes for failing to discuss Marx, and for producing 'hard suggestions in line with the necessities of British imperialism' (*Daily Worker*, 8 April 1936). Keynes, the reviewer contends, wants 'efficiency and freedom' but disguises the (Fascist) implications of his argument using 'a modern variety of literal mysticism'. His conclusion,

> Which 'reality' does Keynes want – Olympia and the poison-gas of Abyssinia, the end of Bloomsbury and all culture – or the flowering of new life (and full employment, his objective in this book) in the Soviet Union?
>
> (Henry Douglas, *Daily Worker*, 8 April 1936)

Other reviews from the political left were less extreme, though even among the more academic reviews, the Soviet Union received the odd favourable mention. A. L. Rowse, for example, used the existence of a planned economy in the Soviet Union to suggest that Mises and his followers were completely out of touch with reality in suggesting that a planned economy could not exist.

Evan Durbin (*Labour*, April 1936) took issue with what he described as Keynes's 'short and curious' defence of capitalism. One by one he rejected Keynes's arguments for capitalism – that it would deflect impulses of cruelty and domination into the industrial sphere; that a falling interest rate will result in a more just income distribution; and that private enterprise means competition and an appropriate distribution of resources rather than combination, monopoly and exploitation. Low interest rates may cure unemployment but what, Durbin asked, would prevent the outcome being yet another boom which subsequently collapsed? This attitude presumably reflects the 'Austrian' theories of the cycle held at LSE by Hayek and Robbins. G. D. H. Cole, another socialist, noted that Keynes's argument about the euthanasia of the rentier was separable from the rest of his analysis. It was not for this that Keynes would be remembered, but for his having demonstrated 'the falsity, even from a capitalist standpoint, of the most cherished practical "morals" of the orthodox economics' (namely that cutting wages would cure unemployment), and for having constructed a theory of capitalism 'so clearly nearer to the facts that it will be impossible for it to be ignored or set aside' (G. D. H. Cole, *New Statesman and Nation*, 15 February 1936). In a review published much later in the year, A. L. Rowse agreed with Cole's appraisal of the *General Theory* as 'the most important theoretical economic writing since Marx's *Capital*' (A. L. Rowse, *Nineteenth Century*, September 1936). He saw the book as completely vindicating Labour Party policies, and conjectured that it was to hide this that the *Times* had published such a short review. It was, he suggested, impossible to give an adequate account of Keynes's argument in a very short space.

The book was reviewed by two future Labour Cabinet ministers. H. A. Marquand (who held various ministerial positions in Attlee's government, culminating in that of Minister of Health) saw the book as continuing arguments about the business cycle first advanced in the *Treatise on Money*. He emphasized the importance of assuming that the economy was operating at less than full capacity, adducing evidence that, even in 1929, the US economy was working at no more than 80 per cent of capacity. Yet in the end, Marquand reserves judgement on the book, waiting for the outcome of the counter-attack from more orthodox theorists. Douglas Jay (President of the Board of Trade under Harold Wilson), on the other hand, is more positive about the book. He is much more confident than Marquand in his criticisms. He makes the point that the implications of an increase in fixed investment (which raises employment) are very different from an increase (implicitly an unintended increase) in stocks, which may reflect a fall in demand and employment. He also criticizes Keynes for placing excessive emphasis on investment relative to consumption. The logical implication of the *General Theory*, Jay argues, is not simply that monetary policy should be used to sustain investment, but that direct measures should be taken to maintain consumption.

An LSE response to Keynes is found in Arnold Plant's review. He disputed Keynes's claim that the classical economists did not allow for unemployment, suggesting that if Keynes were to re-read J. S. Mill he would find there an explanation of how 'errors due to imperfect foresight' might cause departures from full employment. Plant also found many similarities between Keynesian and orthodox theory (such as the marginal efficiency of capital). Overall, his conclusion was that the differences arose 'more in the field of policy than of analysis' (Arnold Plant, *Fortnightly Review*, 1936). This minimizing the differences between Keynesian and orthodox economics is also to be found in H. D. Henderson's review, where he describes the *General Theory* as 'a real and much-needed contribution to short-term economic analysis' (H. D. Henderson, *The Spectator*, 14 February 1936). But the classical theory had always admitted, as Plant also pointed out in his review, that unemployment might arise during a trade depression. Henderson focused on the determination of the rate of interest as the key difference between Keynes and the classical theory, claiming that Keynes had failed to make out his case.

These very sceptical, though respectful, reviews, stood in stark contrast to two reviews written by a young Cambridge economist, Austin Robinson. Though Keynes might, Robinson admitted, be using stones taken from an earlier building, he was trying to build something totally new (E. A. G. Robinson, *The Economist*, 29 February 1936). 'With the old', Robinson contended, 'it will not be a popular book'. To the young, on the other hand, it would be 'a testament' (Austin Robinson, *The Cambridge Review*, 21 February 1936).

As an illustration of how the *General Theory* offered material for reviewers with different interests to pick on very different parts of the book, the review in the Catholic journal, *The Tablet*, discussed Keynes's objections to Ricardianism, but in an unusual way. The Ricardian doctrine of *laissez-faire* was described as 'a curious form of animism' which 'history may yet record .. as a ghastly perversion of the Christian doctrine of Providence'. It also took up Keynes claim that interest is 'the reward for abstinence from liquidity'. Whereas most economists reviewing the book took this as making a technical point about interest depending on demand and supply of liquidity rather than saving, *The Tablet*'s reviewer suggested Keynes's claim was based on 'a new and specious claim to *lucrum cessans*', for which there was no basis in either equity or morals.

*The Christian Century*, in contrast, contained a review by a prominent Chicago economist, Henry Simons. He expressed himself in strong agreement with Keynes's criticism of much orthodox monetary policy, and with the charge that orthodox economists often make 'bad applications of their relative-price analysis' by abstracting from monetary disturbances when such abstractions are inappropriate. However, he took issue with the nature of Keynes's attack on orthodoxy.

> If the attack upon orthodoxy is misdirected, it is also indiscreet. Not content to point out the shortcomings of traditional views, Mr. Keynes proceeds to espouse the cause of an army of cranks and heretics simply on the grounds that their schemes or ideas would incidentally have involved or suggested mitigation of the deflationary tendencies in the economy. The fondness for a labor theory of value may be pardoned as mere intellectual dillettantism; but the author might adequately have criticized economists for their neglect of monetary problems without endorsing mercantilism, *autarchie*, social credit, stamped money, fantastic government spending, the single tax, underconsumption theories and usury laws. The reviewer is not inclined to be more generous toward monetary orthodoxy than is Mr. Keynes. But the sophistical academic leg-pulling which he perpetrates in this volume, however delightful and entertaining in its proper place, should not be done publicly in times like these, least of all by persons of Mr. Keynes' repute.
>
> Readers should be warned against the presumption that the author has eschewed advocacy of practical expedients in favor of objective analytical inquiry, and cautioned against hasty or credulous acceptance of analysis, arguments and critical judgements which are always highly sophisticated and often merely sophistical.
>
> (Henry C. Simons, *The Christian Century*, 22 July 1936)

Though others were much less critical than Simons, North American reviewers greeted the book with more reservations than their British counterparts. Howard Barger (*Nature*, 9 May 1936) compared the book with Keynes's *Treatise on Money*, pointing out that though the *General Theory* grew out of the *Treatise*, it was in no sense a 'mere' revision of it. His criticisms of the *General Theory* were that it was not always the weakest parts of the *Treatise* that it tore to pieces; that Keynes's arguments about the instability of investment (which Barger contended was the key judgement separating Keynes from the Ricardians) were not sufficiently well supported; and that the multiplier process might not converge. His verdict was that on fundamental questions, the *Treatise* remained a safer, if less ambitious guide. Maxwell S. Stewart (*The Nation*, 15 April 1936) criticized Keynes for assuming the same 'flexible or semi-flexible economic system' as the economists he criticized. Keynes, he argued, ignored the trend towards 'rigidity in our economic structure' caused by the emergence of gigantic corporations and trade associations. Similarly, Virginius Coe (*The Canadian Forum*, 1936) criticized him for overlooking 'the ubiquity of monopoly'. Horace Taylor (*New Republic*, 29 April 1936) doubted the generality of Keynes's theory: 'it is apparent that he is concerned primarily with British conditions and British policies.' Furthermore, in view of the 'highly abstruse and mathematical' presentation, Taylor thought the book would not add to Keynes's popular prestige.

However, not all North American reviewers were quite so sceptical. Fabian Franklin (*Saturday Review*, 4 April 1936) is perhaps best described as neutral. He did criticize Keynes, but for falsely claiming that his fundamental ideas were extremely simple. Franklin argued that the ideas of the classics, concerned only with the distribution of output between landowners, capitalists, entrepreneurs and wage-earners, were much simpler. It was a matter of 'keen regret' that Keynes had not made his ideas more accessible. Montgomery Butchart (*The Criterion*, September 1936) was much more sympathetic in arguing that the praise the book had received was deserved, but claimed that the book had not gone far enough. Keynes's 'revolution in economic theory' had gone but 'half a turn'. Unemployment, Butchart claimed, was a sign of 'the triumph of industry', the solution to which was not re-employment, but the provision of a minimum level of income irrespective of whether someone was in employment.

The reception of the *General Theory* in the specialist journals was rather different. Not only were reviews longer and more technical, but they focused on different issues. There were long, and detailed discussions of Keynes new terminology in which savings were identically equal to investment (though he could still talk of them, in places, as unequal); of the determination of the rate of interest (whether Keynes's claim that it was determined not by saving and investment, but by the demand for liquidity was either justified or incompatible with classical views); of whether reductions in money wage rates would raise aggregate demand; and of other technical points. The one reviewer who stands out in providing an interpretation of the *General Theory* that amounts to a new theoretical perspective, was Hicks, who saw Keynes's greatest contribution as lying in his method of dealing with expectations. This is an idea that Hicks developed in *Value and Capital* (1939) with his concept of temporary equilibrium, in which the equilibrium of the economic system is dependent on expectations of the future. If these change, the whole equilibrium changes.

Whilst all bar one reviewer (Beckhart, *Political Science Quarterly*, p. 602, who thought the book likely to remain 'but an interesting exhibit in the museum of depression curiosities') considered it an important book, it was subjected to strong criticism. Enthusiasm was generally muted, Harris (1948, p. 29) going so far as to say that not a single enthusiastic review had come to his attention. Whilst Adarkar's review (*Indian Economic Review*) is a clear exception, comparing Keynes's book with those of Adam Smith, Ricardo, Marshall and Pigou (*The Economics of Welfare*), Harris's remark is a fair comment on the Anglo-American reviews. A possible explanation, from another leading American Keynesian, is that neither Keynes nor his followers understood the full implications of the book's theoretical arguments. This might explain why even those who might be termed Keynes's disciples, were muted in their criticism. Many reviewers (notably Lerner, in the *International Labour Review*, who sought to explain the book in simpler, more traditional language) provided expositions of Keynesian ideas rather than judgements, just as if they were still trying to absorb its message. Champernowne (*Review of Economic Studies*) provided an algebraic account of some of the main propositions. Even Harrod (*Political Quarterly*), later a biographer of Keynes and an enthusiastic Keynesian, was non-committal on the book.

Where the 'popular' reviews focused on Keynes's chapter on the social philosophy implied by the general theory, this received far less attention in the specialist reviews. One who did take up the idea was Schumpeter (*Journal of the American Statistical Association*), who poured scorn on it.

> The less said about the last book the better. Let him who accepts the message there expounded rewrite the history of the French *ancien régime* in some such terms as these: Louis XV was a most enlightened monarch. Feeling the necessity of stimulating expenditure he secured the services of such expert spenders as Madame de Pompadour and Madame du Barry. They went to work with unsurpassable efficiency. Full employment, a maximum of resulting output, and general well-being ought to have been the consequence. It is true that instead we find misery, shame and, at the end of it all, a stream of blood. But that was a chance coincidence.
>
> (Schumpeter, *Journal of the American Statistical Association*, p. 795)

Another to take up this theme was Emil Lederer (*Social Research*, 1936), who saw several parallels between Keynes's ideas in the last chapters of the *General Theory* and Marx.

Many of the critical reviews were to be expected. Pigou, selected as the main target for the *General Theory*'s attack on 'classical economics', quite reasonably objected to this treatment. By describing Pigou's *The Theory of Unemployment* (1933) as the only detailed account of the classical theory, Keynes was able to claim that faults in that book were faults in 'classical economics'. But if Pigou protested his innocence, Keynes could argue that Pigou had not followed the logic of the classical system and hence ought to have been guilty. Either way Pigou lost. The habit of presenting his own ideas in a matrix of sarcastic comment was something Keynes had learned, Pigou suggested, in his immensely successful *Economic Consequences of the Peace* (1919). Pigou's response was that 'Einstein actually did for Physics what Mr. Keynes believes himself to have done for Economics . . . [Einstein] did not, in announcing his discovery, insinuate, through carefully barbed sentences, that Newton and those who had hitherto followed his lead were a gang of incompetent bunglers' (*Economica*, p. 115).

The Harvard reviewers, Taussig, Leontief and Schumpeter were all critical of the book. Where Keynes saw himself as throwing off the Ricardian approach, Schumpeter saw him as guilty of the same methodological short-cuts as Ricardo: skirting problems through artificial definitions, and offering as general scientific truth advice that is meaningful only in a specific historical situation. Taussig and Leontief confined themselves to critiques of specific assumptions underlying Keynes's argument, and though they were respectful towards the book, they clearly regarded his conclusions as, at best, unproven.

This attitude contrasted with the much more favourable attitude of the Chicago economist, Jacob Viner. Of Keynes's many reviewers, Viner was the one to whom Keynes chose to reply in detail. Viner's colleague at Chicago, Simons (discussed above), though sympathetic towards parts of Keynes's argument, was overall very critical. In contrast, the two reviews in *Social Research*, by Emil Lederer and Hans Neisser, were much more respectful, more like the British reviews. The review in the *American Economic Review*, the official journal of the American Economic Association, gave no hint that the book was particularly important, and after an exposition of some of the book's main contentions, Hardy has a paragraph where he takes issue with these, and reaches the opinion that Keynes's argument assumes its conclusion.

Particularly interesting are the two reviews by Alvin Hansen (then at Minnesota, though he soon moved to Harvard) who became perhaps the leading advocate of Keynesian economics in America. His first review (*Yale Review*) was very critical. He predicted that the *General Theory* would fare no better than the *Treatise* – in other words that it would be a failure. The theory of unemployment equilibrium presumed a rigid economy, perhaps one dominated by monopoly, with little technological innovation. Hansen regarded it as open question whether a situation of technological stagnation had been reached, with institutional arrangements impeding any tendency towards full employment, but he contended that accepted theory was quite able to explain this. By the time of his second, more widely read, review in the *Journal of Political Economy*, however, Hansen was more sympathetic towards the *General Theory*. He still accused Keynes of sophistry, and found technical faults in the argument. On the other hand, he now saw the economic order as in a state of transition – half flexible, half rigid. Though he did not see this as having been provided by Keynes, a 'new economics' was needed, The *General Theory* provided important ideas, improved theoretical constructs and at least one brilliant chapter that could contribute towards such a new economics.

Amongst the American reviewers, it is noteworthy that four of the eight reviewers – Emil Lederer, Wassily Leontief, Hans Neisser and Joseph Schumpeter – in specialist academic journals were emigrés from continental Europe. In Britain, there was a preponderance of reviewers from Cambridge. This, however, largely reflects the position of Cambridge in the British academic system at the time. There were far fewer economists in provincial universities than is the case today, and Oxford was, in Economics, clearly in third place after Cambridge and the LSE. Lionel Robbins, or Friedrich Hayek, at LSE might have responded to Keynes, but chose not to do so. The task was left to Arnold Plant and to members of the younger generation, Hicks and Lerner, though they were not that much younger than Robbins and Plant. They absorbed the Keynesian message much more readily than did Robbins or Hayek.

Roger Backhouse
*University of Birmingham, 1999*

## ACKNOWLEDGEMENT
Don Moggridge was immensely helpful in assisting me with finding reviews in the Keynes archives at King's College.

# BIBLIOGRAPHY

Blaug, Mark (1990). *John Maynard Keynes: Life, Ideas, Legacy.*
Basingstoke and London: Macmillan.

Colander, David C, and Harry Landreth (eds.) (1996). *The Coming
of Keynesianism to America: Conversations with the Founders of
Keynesian Economics.* Cheltenham and Lyme, NH: Edward Elgar.
(Participants discuss the reception of Keynesian economics in the
country that was most important for the subject in the post-war
period.)

Dimand, Robert W. (1988). *The Origins of the Keynesian Revolution:
The Development of Keynes' Theory of Employment and Output.*
Cheltenham and Lyme, NH: Edward Elgar. (Chapter 3 contains a
review of the reviews of Keynes's *Treatise on Money.*)

Ellis, Howard S. (1948). *A Survey of Contemporary Economics,*
Volume I. Homewood, IL: Richard D. Irwin.

Galbraith, John Kenneth (1971). 'How Keynes came to America', in
*A Contemporary Guide to Economics Peace and Laughter.* London:
Andre Deutsch.

Harris, Seymour (ed.) (1948). *The New Economics.* (Chapter 3 contains sections on the reception of the book by 'early critics' and
'later Keynesians'.)

Hicks, John R. (1937). 'Mr. Keynes and the "classics": a suggested
interpretation', *Econometrica 5*, pp. 147–59.

Keynes, John Maynard (1919). *The Economic Consequences of the
Peace.* London: Macmillan. In *The Collected Works of John
Maynard Keynes*, edited by D. E. Moggridge, volume II. London:
Macmillan.

Keynes, John Maynard (1930). *A Treatise on Money.* Two volumes.
London: Macmillan. In *The Collected Works of John Maynard
Keynes*, edited by D. E. Moggridge, volumes V–VI. London: Mac-
millan.

Keynes, John Maynard (1936). *The General Theory of Employment,
Interest and Money.* London: Macmillan. In *The Collected Works
of John Maynard Keynes*, edited by D. E. Moggridge, volume VII.
London: Macmillan.

Keynes, John Maynard (1937). 'The General Theory: fundamental
concepts and ideas', *Quarterly Journal of Economics 51*,
pp. 209–23. In *The Collected Works of John Maynard Keynes*,
edited by D. E. Moggridge, volume XIV. London: Macmillan.

Klein, Lawrence A. (1952). *The Keynesian Revolution.* London: Macmillan. (Chapter 4 reviews some of the main academic reviews of *The General Theory*.)

Lekachman, R. (1964). *Keynes's General Theory: Reports of Three Decades*. London: Macmillan.

Moggridge, D. E. (1980). *Keynes*, 2nd ed. London: Macmillan.

Moggridge, D. E. (1992). *Maynard Keynes: An Economist's Biography*. London and New York: Routledge. (One of the two major biographies of Keynes. Chapter 23 discusses the reception of the *General Theory*, focusing on those economists with whom Keynes was in closest contact.)

Skidelsky, Robert (1983, 1992). *John Maynard Keynes. Volume I: Hopes Betrayed. Volume II: The Economist as Saviour, 1920–37*. London: Macmillan. (One of two major biographies of Keynes. Volume II, Chapter 16 reviews some reviews of *The General Theory*.)

Skidelsky, Robert (1996). *Keynes*. Oxford and New York: Oxford University Press.

Young, Warren (1994). *Interpreting Mr Keynes: The IS-LM Enigma*. (This tells the history of what, from 1937, rapidly became the standard interpretation of the *General Theory*.)

# Newspapers

# MR KEYNES ON INTEREST RATES: SOCIAL CONTROL OF INVESTMENT ESSENTIAL*
## Francis Williams

State control of investment, with as one of its main objectives the forcing down of the rate of interest to a level difficult or impossible to achieve under conditions of uncontrolled investment, is an essential condition of a permanent solution of the problem of unemployment.

That is the important conclusion – and though I have stated it baldly. I have not, I think, exaggerated it – reached by Mr. J. Maynard Keynes in his new book, 'The General Theory of Employment, Interest and Money' (Macmillan, 5s.).

I believe this may well prove the most important of all Mr. Keynes' publications. In it he sets out to examine the whole of the premises on which the theories of what are termed the classical economists have been based, and to argue that although the structure of classical economy has been erected with great logical consistency, it is at variance with the actual facts of the economic situation, and can offer the world no clear and intelligible guidance simply because the postulates upon which it is built are false.

### Control of Investment

Mr. Keynes' book has been written primarily for fellow economists. As such it is, almost inevitably, extremely difficult reading. And for that reason, despite the extremely reasonable price at which it has been published, is unlikely to have the wide sale of some of his former publications, though certain of the ideas expressed in it will, I believe, come to have a wide general circulation over a period of time.

But because it is not only a lengthy, but, in parts, highly technical piece of work, one cannot hope in the course of a comparatively brief article to deal at all adequately with all

* From *Daily Herald*, 4 February 1936.

the points raised and the arguments put forward – some of them highly controversial arguments – by Mr. Keynes.

Moreover, in this particular work Mr. Keynes, who has sometimes been suspect of his fellow economists for his concern in practical affairs, is more interested in theory than in the application of theory.

Nevertheless if his theoretical structure is sound the practical application of that theory must be of very substantial importance. It will be particularly so, I believe, in the reinforcement it provides for the belief which has for some time been developing, in some cases for reasons other than those of Mr. Keynes, that a national control of investment is an essential prelude to any permanent solution of unemployment, and may indeed prove to be the most important single factor in that solution.

### Rate of Interest

Mr. Keynes argues that the rate of interest on money plays a peculiar part in setting a limit to the level of employment, since it sets a standard to which the marginal efficiency of a capital asset must attain if it is to be newly produced.

He defines the rate of interest as the inverse proportion between a sum of money and what can be obtained for parting with control over the money in exchange for a debt for a stated period of time. It is, that is to say, a measure of the unwillingness of those who possess money to part with their liquid control over it and of the reward they demand for losing control.

And by the marginal efficiency of a capital asset is meant the relation between the prospective yield of a capital asset and its replacement cost, or, in any words, the relation between the prospective yield of one more unit of a particular type of capital, and the cost of producing that unit.

### Monetary Control Insufficient

And he suggests that the acuteness and peculiarity of our contemporary problem arise out of the fact that the average rate of interest which will allow an average reasonable level of employment is now one so unacceptable to wealth owners that it cannot be readily established merely by manipulating the quantity of money.

In other words the stimulation which can, for example,

be provided by a cheap money policy is not, under present conditions, sufficient to achieve an economic activity which will absorb the unemployed because the rate of interest compatible with full employment is, in an economy at the stage of development of our own, so low that it is insufficient to tempt the owner of wealth voluntarily to sacrifice his liquidity and to invest his money.

Consequently if the rate of interest is kept sufficiently high to tempt the wealth owner, it will not be of a nature to allow full employment, and if it is forced down by monetary means to a level sufficiently low to allow full employment, investment, if it remains a purely voluntary affair, will be withheld.

### Rentier Capitalism

That is, of course, a highly inadequate summary of only one phase of Mr. Keynes' complicated but logical argument, but its social importance can easily be perceived.

Mr. Keynes analyses the movements of the capital markets under existing conditions, and comes to the conclusion that in conditions of laissez faire the avoidance of wide fluctuations in employment is likely to prove impossible without a far-reaching change in the psychology of the investment market, such as there is no reason to expect, and concludes therefore that the duty of ordering the current volume of investment, cannot any longer safely be left in private hands.

He believes that what may be termed the rentier aspect of capitalism is a transitional phase which should disappear when it has done its work, and that the time for its disappearance has now arrived.

### Too Much Prudence

To take investment – in the economist's sense of that term – completely out of private hands would indeed be merely to speed up a trend which already exists, for, as he shows in his chapter on the propensity to consume, savings by institutions and through sinking funds are in existing conditions probably adequate for investment purposes.

Indeed, he argues with considerable force that the exercise of too much financial prudence in setting aside sinking funds may definitely prove an obstacle in the way of increasing employment.

He points out, for example, that sinking funds of Local

Authorities in this country now stand at an annual figure of more than half the amount which these Authorities are spending on the whole of their new developments, while in the United States by 1929, the rapid capital expansion of the previous five years had led accumulatively to the setting up of sinking funds and depreciation allowances in respect of plant which did not need replacement on so huge a scale that an enormous volume of entirely new investment was required, merely to absorb these financial provisions.

As a result it became almost hopeless to find still more new investment on a sufficient scale to provide for such new saving as a wealthy community in full employment would be disposed to set aside.

This factor alone was, he suggests, probably sufficient to cause a slump.

### Inequalities of Wealth

One very important conclusion socially is to be drawn from the recognition of the fact that saving by institutions through sinking funds may be adequate for capital needs. It is that so far from there being any social justification for the belief that wide inequalities of wealth are necessary because the growth of capital depends upon the strength of the motive towards individual saving and that for a large proportion of this growth we are dependent on the savings of the rich out of their superfluity, a redistribution of incomes is not only ethically but economically desirable.

Mr. Keynes urges, in fact, that under contemporary conditions the growth of wealth, so far from being dependent on the abstinence of the rich, is more likely to be impeded by it, and that one of the chief social justifications for the great inequality of wealth is thereby removed.

In another passage, he underlines what some economists, particularly of the Austrian school, have seemed to overlook, that consumption is the sole end and object of all economic activity.

Opportunities for employment are necessarily limited by the extent of aggregate demand, and aggregate demand can be derived only from present consumption or from present provision for future consumption, the latter being what is commonly termed Investment.

The consumption for which we can profitably provide in

advance cannot, moreover, be pushed indefinitely into the future.

### Increasing Consumption

Alongside of his examination of the rate of interest and of the measures necessary to provide adequate investment for full employment. Mr. Keynes urges therefore the necessity for measures to increase consumption.

'Whilst aiming at a socially controlled rate of investment with a view to a progressive decline in the marginal efficiency of capital' (the definition of marginal efficiency being as given above), 'I should support,' he writes, 'at the same time all sorts of policies for increasing the propensity to consume. For it is unlikely that full employment can be maintained, whatever we may do about investment, with the existing propensity to consume.

'There is room, therefore, for both policies to operate – to promote investment and at the same time to promote consumption, not merely to the level which, with the existing propensity to consume, would correspond to the increased investment but to a higher level still.'

### Socially Directed

Indeed, although he has, as any trained economist must have, various objections to the single under consumptionist theory, his only difference with the under-consumptionists, so far as practice is concerned, is in thinking that they lay too much emphasis on increased consumption at a time when there is so much social advantage to be obtained from increased investment.

That there is to-day need both for increased investment and increased consumption cannot, I think, be doubted. But the investment must be socially directed and not left to the vagaries of the individual striving for gain.

For, as Mr. Keynes says, in a fine passage, 'The social object of skilled investment should be to defeat the dark forces of time and ignorance which envelop our future, whereas, under existing conditions, the actual private object of the most skilled investment is "to beat the gun" – as the Americans express it, to outwit the crowd, and to pass the bad or depreciated half-crown to the other fellow.'

# WHAT *DOES* MR KEYNES WANT –
# POISON GAS?*
## Henry Douglas

Whether the book page or the news page is the better place to
note this book is a moot point. For not many are likely to read
a book designed for economists, yet Keynes is important and
what he says is important.

*Successful Man*
Keynes is in the Ricardo tradition: he is a successful business
man. The company, of which he is chairman, has earned 67
per cent free of tax on investment averaged over the last 15
years, better than any other investment institution. Last year
it made capital profits of £203,000 (Keynes, in fact, is no fool
when it comes to beating the gun outwitting the crowd and
passing the bad, or depreciating, half-crown to the other fellow
(p. 155), even if he is sometimes called rash (p. 157).

This practical acumen is one reason why he has seen that
'the characteristics of the special case assumed by the classical
theory happen not to be those of economic society in which
he actually lives' (p. 3).

Keynes, in tearing up the bases of the ordinary bourgeois
text-book 'economics', 'not so much in finding logical flaws in
its analysis as in pointing out that its tacit assumptions are
seldom or never satisfied, with the result that it cannot solve
the economic problems of the actual world' is actually in line,
if not in advance, of the modern economic statesman of the
monopolies.

'The considerable output of analytical work . . . has, in the
past decade, practically re-written the science', says Stamp,
Director of the Bank of England, L.M.S., Halifax, Building
Society, etc.

Bear this in mind in reading the book. Beware the Greeks . . .
For Keynes knows that planning is possible. He makes bitter

* From *Daily Worker*, 8 April 1936.

fun of the orthodox arguments against doing anything. If you don't want to build houses, he says, bury money in pits and dig it up again. He wants to 'euthanasia' the rentiers who are destroying the economy. He ridicules the theory that high wages cause unemployment.

He sees the destruction wrought by the modern disorganised speculator. 'When the capital development of a country becomes a by-product of the activities of a casino, the job is likely to be ill-done' (page 159). He reckons by units of labour, finding in practice none of the 'difficulties' put up by the anti Marxist pundits (pages 41 and 213). He argues and thinks about output and dismisses purely monetary manipulation.

He demands full employment of labour and resources in this power age. He has recognised the importance of effective demand which, ignored by neo-classical economists 'could only live on furtively, below the surface, in the underworlds of Karl Marx, Silvio Gesell or Major Douglas'. (p. 32.)

The underworld is taking its revenge. To defeat it a new, more intelligibly rooted theory is necessary.

This is the significance of this brilliantly written book, which, incidentally, published at 5s., 400 pages demy octavo, by the leading British publishers, makes a lot of our cheap-line political publishers look silly. It is in the 15s. class, format and all.

### Alternative

These recognitions by Keynes do not make him an ally. They do not mean (any more than his enunciation of the declining rate of profit means) that he is a Marxist, anything like.

His treatment of Marx is ludiciously inadequate. He is trying to provide an alternative to Marx: 'I believe that the future will learn more from the spirit of Gesell (a German business an he has dug up) than from that of Marx . . .' – (Page 355).

Keynes does not give the arguments against Marx because he hardly mentions him.

What he does is more dangerous. His theory is an adaptation to present needs. What are the present needs of British imperialism? Here Keynes meets his contradiction (apart from his theoretical contradictions). He produces hard suggestions in line with the necessities of British imperialism.

Thus he wants 'central controls' to control investment: apart from this 'there is no more reason to Socialise economic life than there was before', precisely the argument the new Big Man will use.

Thus, again, he advocates mercantilism, the old eighteenth century war preparation theory.

Not that Keynes wants war. He wants 'efficiency and freedom'. But he produces a modern variety of literal mysticism to cover the implications of his argument. Where to-day will he get 'efficiency and freedom'?

But Russia is not mentioned in the index!

### For Enemies

He has cleared a lot of ground – but for his enemies.

His theory is not a realistic one; except that it is the first bourgeois theory to recognise twentieth century economic methods. The actual twentieth century is in Marxism-Leninism and the U.S.S.R.

Keynes's theories not only in practice dovetail with those of monopoly capitalism. They also have a decided Fascist flavour.

### 'In Economics'

The 'Blackshirt' nearly three years ago claimed that 'in economics, at any rate, Mr. Keynes has come over bag and baggage to the Fascist ranks . . . how long will he continue to shrink from Fascist realities in action?'

What the 'Blackshirt' says is not evidence. But Keynes' nationalist economics and his attacks on usury and finance, his ignoring of Marx and of the U.S.S.R. (though it is rumoured that this book is designed as a reply to the great influence Strachey's 'Capitalist Crisis' had among the students) are all warnings.

Which 'reality' does Keynes want – Olympia and the poison-gas of Abyssinia, the end of Bloomsbury and all culture – or the flowering of new life (and full employment, his objective in this book) in the Soviet Union?

# MR J. M. KEYNES ON CHEAP MONEY*
Anonymous

## ESSENTIAL FOR FULL EMPLOYMENT

*Suggested Policy*
Mr. J. M. Keynes is publishing a new book to-day which contains much material that is likely to be of interest to our readers.

In the past his views on monetary policy, the tendency of interest rates, the broad trend in the market, &c., have always commanded much attention, especially since his forecasts have frequently been confirmed by events. The readers of his new book will be interested in particular in the parts which describe the author's present views regarding the prospects of interest rates.

*Further Decline in Rates?*
Mr. Keynes is more emphatic than ever that in the long run the trend of evolution will point towards a further considerable decline in interest rates. He maintains that the justification for a moderately high rate of interest in the past has been found in the necessity of providing a sufficient inducement to save. In his opinion, at present the rentier receives a bonus over and above the interest that would cover the allowance for risk and the cost of skill and supervision. This surplus is due to the scarcity value of capital.

> Interest to-day rewards no genuine sacrifice any more than does the rent of land. The owner of capital can obtain interest because capital is scarce, just as the owner of land can obtain rent because land is scarce. But while there may be intrinsic reasons for the scarcity of land, there are no intrinsic reasons for the scarcity of capital.

He considers it possible to increase and maintain the saving of

* From *Financial News*, 4 February 1936.

the community through the agency of the State, and to maintain it at a level which will allow the growth of capital up to the point where it ceases to be scarce.

### Transitional Phase

Mr. Keynes, therefore, sees the rentier aspect of capitalism as a transitional phase that will disappear when it has done its work. He has no doubt that interest rates will decline to a much lower level than has ruled hitherto. He regards as the aim of practical policy an increase in the volume of capital unless it ceases to be scarce so that its owner will no longer receive a bonus.

Mr. Keynes would like to see an increased degree of State intervention.

> The State will have to exercise a guiding influence on the propensity to consume, partly by its scheme of taxation, partly by fixing the rate of interest and partly, perhaps, in other ways. Furthermore, it seems unlikely that the influence of banking policy on the rate of interest will be sufficient by itself to determine an optimum rate of investment. I conceive, therefore, that a somewhat comprehensive socialisation of investment will prove the only means of securing an approximation to full employment, though this need not exclude all manner of compromises and devices by which authority will co-operate with private initiative.

Beyond this, Mr. Keynes is not in favour of State socialism. He regards his proposed compromise as 'the only practicable means of avoiding the destruction of existing economic forms in their entirety and as the condition of the successful functioning of individual initiative'.

### 'Increase Capital Volume'

He maintains that the world will not tolerate much longer the unemployment which, apart from brief intervals of boom, is inevitably associated with present-day capitalistic individualism. He hopes, however, to arrive at a solution without having to sacrifice freedom and efficiency by the adoption of an authoritarian State system.

The solution favoured by Mr. Keynes lies in the securing of full employment by means of increasing the volume of capital and lowering interest rates. In this connection he delivers an onslaught upon the pre-war system, through which fixed exchange parities were maintained with the aid of a high Bank rate.

For this meant that the objective of maintaining a domestic rate of interest consistent with full employment was wholly ruled out. Since in practice it is impossible to neglect the balance of payments, a means of controlling it evolved which, instead of protecting the domestic rate of interest, sacrificed it to the operation of blind forces. Recently, practical bankers in London have learnt much, and one can almost hope that in Great Britain the technique of Bank rate will never be used again to protect the foreign balance in conditions in which it is likely to cause unemployment at home.

### The Gold Standard

According to Mr. Keynes, under a system in which the quantity of credit and the domestic rate of interest are primarily determined by the balance of payments, as they were in Great Britain before the war, there is no orthodox means open to the authorities for countering unemployment at home except by struggling for an export surplus and an import of the monetary metal at the expense of their neighbours.

Never in history was there a method devised of such efficacy for setting each country's advantage at variance with its neighbour's as the international gold (or formerly, silver) standard. For it made domestic prosperity directly dependent on a competitive pursuit of markets and a competitive appetite for the precious metals.

Mr. Keynes declares that it is the policy of an autonomous rate of interest, unimpeded by international preoccupations, and of a national investment programme directed to an optimum level of domestic employment, which is calculated to help ourselves and our neighbours at the same time.

### Way to Economic Health

He regards the simultaneous pursuit of such independent policies by all countries together as a means of restoring economic health and strength internationally.

Mr. Keynes concludes:

If nations can learn to provide themselves with full employment by their domestic policy, there need be no important economic forces calculated to set the interest of one country against that of its neighbours. There would still be room for the international division of labour and for international lending in appropriate conditions, but there would no longer be a pressing motive why one country need force its wares on another or repulse the offerings of its neighbours, not because this was necessary to enable it to pay for what it wished to purchase, but with the expressed object of upsetting the equilibrium of payments so as to develop a balance of trade in its own favour.

International trade would cease to be what it is, namely, a desperate expedient to maintain employment at home by forcing sales on foreign markets and restricting purchases, which, if successful, will merely shift the problem of unemployment to the neighbour which is worsted in the struggle, but a willing and unimpeded exchange of goods and services in conditions of mutual advantage.

# MR KEYNES ATTACKS THE CITADEL*
## [T. S. Ashton]

### NEW THEORY OF EMPLOYMENT, INTEREST, AND MONEY

In a broadcast talk some time ago Mr. Keynes spoke of the economists strongly entrenched in their citadel of theory, but, he added darkly, 'I am outside.' The full meaning of that remark is in his new book, which is happily described on the dust cover as 'a general assault on the adequacy of the existing orthodox economic theory as a means for handling the problems of fluctuations in employment, trade cycles, and the like'. But let Mr. Keynes speak for himself:

> I have called this book the 'General Theory of Employment, Interest, and Money', placing the emphasis on the prefix 'general'. The object of such a title is to contrast the character of my arguments and conclusions with those of the classical theory of the subject, upon which I was brought up and which dominates the economic thought, both practical and theoretical, of the governing and academic classes of this generation, as it has for a hundred years past. I shall argue that the postulates of the classical theory are applicable to a special case only and not to the general case, the situation which it assumes being a limiting point of the possible positions of equilibrium. Moreover, the characteristics of the special case assumed by the classical theory happen not to be those of the economic society in which we actually live, with the result that its teaching is misleading and disastrous if we attempt to apply it to the facts of experience.

This extract constitutes at once the whole of Mr. Keynes's first chapter (and when a reviewer has the opportunity of quoting the whole of a chapter it is not to be lightly missed) and a complete statement of the position he takes up in this book. And this position is maintained with all his skill in argument

* From *Manchester Guardian Commercial*, 14 February 1936.

and in writing. Economists in our universities will be sitting down with pencil and paper even now to compose replies, interpretations, and denunciations; but there will be rejoicing among the heretics, for now Ben Adhem's name leads all the rest – and even Major Douglas gets a kind word.

### New Concepts

The theory that Mr. Keynes develops springs from the analytical use of several new concepts; effective demand, user cost, propensity to consume (particularly the marginal propensity), the investment multiplier. These things concern the method rather than the result, and they may be left to the professional economist. The theory itself rests on the solid ground of common sense and it is not perhaps unfair to describe it as an articulate statement in economic terms of the inarticulate economic ideas that have dominated trade union history and political statesmanship.

Mr. Keynes refers to Malthus and Mr. J. A. Hobson as imbued with the same fire that now animates him, but there were others who felt the flame. Walter Bagehot's essay on the postulates of English political economy, J. E. Cairnes to a lesser extent, and T. E. Cliffe Leslie from another angle put limits to the relevance of the classical theory. But Mr. Keynes has taken the matter further; from criticism by his own fire he has turned to incendiarism, setting alight the edifice of our theories of trade and employment.

The old theory based a self-adjusting propensity of the economic system on economic flexibility. This meant a liquidation of surplus productive capacity by way of competition plus a downward movement of wages. A reduction of wages would reduce costs and therefore prices, and hence stimulate demand. So, output would increase and with it employment up to the point where the process reversed once more. But, as many writers have pointed out, this theory ignores the vital relation of purchasing power as a whole to production. Mr. Keynes gets nearer still to the mark in putting the question at issue as

> whether the reduction in money-wages will or will not be accompanied by the same aggregate effective demand as before, as measured in money, or, at any rate, by an aggregate effective demand which is not reduced in full proportion to the reduction in money wages.

Mr. Keynes takes some 250 pages to develop his alternative theory, and it cannot be adequately dealt with in a few words. Roughly it is as follows: The volume of employment is determined by aggregate supply and aggregate demand, and the aggregate demand function relates employment to the proceeds which that level of employment is expected to realise. These proceeds are divided between consumption and investment, and the first half of Mr. Keynes's book is concerned with an examination of the factors governing this division.

*Employment and Investment*
Now employment can only increase as investment increases, and in given circumstances a definite ratio can be established between income and investment (this ratio is the investment multiplier). In turn this establishes a precise relation between aggregate employment and income and the rate of investment. An increase in the rate of investment will have to carry with it an increase in the rate of consumption, because people are only willing to widen the gap between their income and their consumption if their income is being increased. Thus full employment can only be reached by controlling the relation between propensity to consume and inducement to invest. To quote Mr. Keynes:

> The State will have to exercise a guiding influence on the propensity to consume partly through its scheme of taxation, partly by fixing the rate of interest, and partly, perhaps, in other ways. Furthermore, it seems unlikely that the influence of banking policy on the rate of interest will be sufficient by itself to determine an optimum rate of investment.
>
> I conceive, therefore, that a somewhat comprehensive Socialisation of investment will prove the only means of securing an approximation to full employment; though this need not exclude all manner of compromises and of devices by which public authority will co-operate with private initiative.
>
> But beyond this no obvious case is made out for a system of State Socialism which would embrace most of the economic life of the community. It is not the ownership of the instruments of production which it is important for the State to assume. If the State is able to determine the aggregate amount of resources devoted to augmenting the instruments

and the basic rate of reward to those who own them it will have accomplished all that is necessary.

One doubt occurs on a first reading of Mr. Keynes's book. That is, whether his theory provides adequately as it stands at present, for the important point (in relation to the future) that output per head per working day tends to increase – i.e., the fact of what is called technological unemployment. Must there not be some division of the State's supervisory function between augmenting the instruments and replacing instruments at the existing level? A balance between the two would have to be worked out to allow for changes in the rate of technical progress.

# MR KEYNES BOMBARDS A CITADEL*
## T. S. Ashton

This is a profoundly disturbing book. It is the work of an economist of the first rank whose ideas have influenced policy in more than one of the leading countries of the world. Yet its argument and conclusions are diametrically opposed to the whole trend of political economy from the time of Ricardo to the present day. If Mr. Keynes is right the economists of a century have been living in a looking-glass world; and, in so far as their teaching has been heeded, it has directed men backward. Mr. Keynes concedes, indeed, that classical theory may contribute to knowledge of production and distribution in conditions of full employment. But it is precisely because of its assumption that full employment is the normal condition to which economic forces tend that, in his opinion, it has been unable to make any significant contribution to the problems of the actual world.

Economists have generally accepted as self-evident that supply creates its own demand and that the whole of the costs of production must be spent, directly or indirectly, on the product. But according to Mr. Keynes aggregate demand price will equal aggregate supply price only at a particular level of output, and this is likely to be below that which affords full employment. When, for whatever reason, employment increases real income also increases. But we are reluctant to spend the whole of what we receive; and if the same number of people are to be kept at work there must be investment (which is another form of spending) sufficient to absorb the balance of output. The inducement to invest depends on the expected earnings of capital, on the one hand, and on the rate of interest (which is defined as the price paid for parting with liquid control over money) on the other. As capital increases the expected earnings of investment must fall. But psychological and other factors set a limit to a corresponding

* From *Manchester Guardian*, 24 February 1936.

fall in the rate of interest, and so a point is reached beyond which further investment becomes unprofitable. Hence (since total income depends on investment) the volume of employment and the standard of life are kept below the level which the technique of industry is capable of affording. Nor is this state of affairs a mere possibility: 'there has been a chronic tendency throughout human history for the propensity to save to be stronger than the inducement to invest.'

If, then, left to itself, the economic system cannot provide work for all who want it a deus ex machina must be invoked. The State must stimulate consumption by redistributing incomes through taxation (as urged by Mr. Hobson), by forcing down the rate of interest, even perhaps by periodically imposing a stamp duty on holdings of money. It must control investment; and, since the volume of foreign investment depends on the size of the favourable balance of trade, it must use tariffs and other expedients to ensure that this is adequate. Mr. Keynes leads us back, past Adam Smith, to the wisdom of the Mercantilists.

'The growth of wealth, so far from being dependent on the abstinence of the rich . . . is more likely to be impeded by it.' ' "To dig holes in the ground," paid for out of savings, will increase, not only employment, but the real national dividend of useful goods and services.' 'The remedy for the boom is not a higher rate of interest but a lower rate of interest.' Such are samples of the ammunition with which Mr. Keynes bombards not merely the outworks of orthodoxy but the very citadel itself. Perhaps the defence will be based on a denial of the validity of applying the apparatus of demand schedules and supply schedules to output and income in the aggregate: of insisting that logically, as well as chronologically, production precedes consumption, and that we are bound to derive expenditure from income and not income from expenditure. Or perhaps it will take the form of a counter-attack on Mr. Keynes's contention that interest is the price of liquid money and not of capital. In any case we ought to see a pretty fight.

The book is published at five shillings. Its size and form seem to justify a price three or four times that amount. What should be done with the balance 'saved'? Clearly economists who are convinced must not seek to hold it in liquid form. If they cannot find an investment perhaps they will pay labour to carry away their libraries of 'Principles' and make a bonfire.

For this would have the same beneficial effect as the pyramid-building and digging for hidden money commended by Mr. Keynes as alternatives to his own plan.

# A DANIEL COME TO JUDGEMENT: MR KEYNES ON CURRENCY*
## A. Wyatt Tilby

The latest contribution of Mr. Keynes to the economic controversies of the day is not in form addressed to the general public at all. They are only welcome as eavesdroppers at the debate; his real desire is to convince – that is, to convert – his fellow economists to the position he has found it necessary to adopt.

Unfortunately, economists are never converted by evidence. If facts tell against theories, so much the worse for the facts. Great is the formula, and it shall prevail: recalcitrant fact is mere filling for footnotes, to be described with a sigh or dismissed with a sneer as an insignificant exception or, what is worse, an impertinent intrusion of fallible human nature into the classical temple of orthodox economics.

The complacent rites and repetitions are occasionally disturbed, though seldom interrupted, by infidels and heretics, but Mr. Keynes is a different matter altogether. Less apostate than agnostic, he is the priest of the cult who has left the dim religious light and the frowst within, for the fresh air and the sun and the great gales and the jostling crowd of bankers and buyers and borrowers and lenders and gamblers and mere ordinary producers and consumers without. This disorderly world is as unlike the academic vision as the Atlantic Ocean is unlike the dark and placid pools inhabited by the blind cavefish of Kentucky. But it happens to be the world we live in, and if economics are to be taken seriously, the economists will have to live in it too.

Mr. Keynes's first complaint concerns the theory of supply and demand, which began life as a respectable approximation to the truth in the days when shortage was the normal condition of markets and currencies, but which has become more and more a conventional symbol and a shifty and evasive witness that breaks down and contradicts itself under cross-

* From *Observer*, 16 February 1936.

examination. Why, Mr. Keynes asks, have the classic authorities left the question of effective demand (under-consumption) to what he calls the economic under-world? One does not get at the truth by ignoring relevant factors: there comes a point when over-simplification of a problem by omitting a major possibility is simply distortion of the whole issue.

He might indeed have gone further in this particular section. Under-consumption manifestly exists. But it is a vague term, a shaded light that is better than darkness, but still not enough to see by, unless one has some quantitative idea of the actual amount by which the civilised world under-consumes its potential resources. True, that raises the whole question of the standard of living and the purpose of civilisation and the ultimate aims of society and the State. But why not?

The world's economy in future should logically be based on abundance of supplies, not on efficiency or deficiency of demand. This revolution in supplies will affect production, distribution, and consumption, but the right approach to that problem is the potential saturation point of consumption, not production.

At present we restrict production artificially because consumption is also artificially restricted: it is the obvious thing to do, and the easiest way to do it. But a moment's thought will show that, as a permanent policy, we have chosen the wrong horn of that particular dilemma.

If we are to get hold of the other end of the stick, however, we shall have to pray in aid of the sociologists and the statisticians, to say nothing of the medical men and the actuaries. But again, why not?

Mr. Keynes is so anxious to get to grips with the high problems of capital, currency, and interest that he hacks his way through these tangled woods of prices and production and population without ceremony and, what is more regrettable, he leaves rather a sketchy trail of public policy behind him. He stands broadly for more public works (details and direction unspecified) and for full employment of available labour, but he is silent as to methods of bridging the existing gap. As he objects to increased export trade on the ground that it is one of the causes of war, the problem of unemployment becomes to that extent more urgent.

On the other hand, he envisages a spending, not a saving community. His logic takes him to the point of distrusting if not actually denouncing thrift as anti-social; but in his dislike of the rentier, he hardly makes sufficient allowance for the haunting fear of old age on the part of the poor or near-poor, which accounts for most contemporary thrift and which is surely a stabilising factor. He stands for some measure of regulation of private investment by the State, and for a low rate of interest – the argument here is too long and complicated to be briefly summarised – but he wants more money rather than less money under our future managed currencies.

One would have thought that in a world of increased and more mechanised production, of prospectively stable if not actually diminishing populations, and therefore inferentially of falling prices, less money rather than more would have been needed. Is there any specific virtue in idle money?

It may be thought from this bald precis of Mr. Keynes's latest and brilliantly argued book that he has started more hares than he has caught. Probably, he has. But if one or two of them take refuge in the temple of orthodox economics and stir up the dust inside he will have achieved part of his purpose. He will not change the heart of the Old Believers, who are like paper money, inconvertible; but he will at least make them feel uncomfortable. For a time.

# An Economic Bombshell: Mr Keynes' Cure for Unemployment*
## F. A. L.

If Mr. Neville Chamberlain listens – or half-listens – to Mr. John Maynard Keynes, the economist, we may see:

*Treasury officials filling old bottles with banknotes;*
*Burying them in disused coalmines;*
*Filling up to the surface with town rubbish; and*
*Selling leases for digging the notes up again.*

And then, Mr. Keynes says:

There need be no more unemployment, and, with the help of the repercussions, the real income of the community, and its capital wealth also, would probably become a good deal greater than it actually is.

Mr. Keynes says that in a remarkable new book, published to-day.

*Lost Faith*
The book, like Mr. Keynes' famous 'Economic Consequences of the Peace', which riddled the Peace Treaties in 1919, is a bombshell. Particularly for Mr. Keynes' fellow economists and for all, including bankers, business men, politicians, and Whitehall officials, who hold fast by 'orthodox' economic ideas.

Mr. Keynes has lost faith in orthodox economic ideas. He may be said to have come to the rude conclusion that orthodox economics as handed down from the days of Ricardo, through Marshall, Edgeworth and Professor Pigou are perilously like orthodox bunk – or, should we say, obscurantism?

That might not matter so much if orthodox economics did not go further than the lecture halls and the learned societies where graphs are plotted, formulas are brewed and pleasant

* From *The Star*, 4 February 1936.

back-chat lisps in equations which look like something from the Zodiac.

But these things do not rest there. In one form or other, beginning with the great classic masters, they go out into the big, ordinary everyday world. And there they affect the lives of men.

### Into The World

They lead to men being in (or out of) work; to children being fed (or underfed); to slums breeding disease and to town mansions breeding baccarat scandals; to nations living and working in peace with one another, or to such things as happened between 1914 and 1918, and have gone on happening (on different fronts) ever since.

Whether we like it or no, Mr. Keynes contends, our daily lives and our earthly destinies are ruled by the ideas of economists and political philosophers. And the trouble is that, thanks to slavish subservience to 'classic' ideas, graphs, formulas and equations which only a few heretics have stopped to examine in the light of the facts, we are being ruled all wrong.

Mr. Keynes agrees that his book is a frontal attack upon ideas which he himself has taught and 'held with conviction for many years'.

> The composition of this book has been for the author a long struggle of escape, and so must the reading of it be for most readers if the author's assault upon them is to be successful – a struggle of escape from habitual modes of thought and expression . . . The difficulty lies not in the new ideas, but in escaping from the old ones, which ramify, for those brought up as most of us have been, into every corner of our minds.

Now the beauty of Mr. Keynes is that he knows all the formulas, graphs, equations and theories upside down and inside out. He can bandy these things about with the best of them. And in this book does so.

### Much To Say

He is not sparing in technical apparatus much of which will be quite unintelligible to the plain, bewildered layman. But he has much to say which all can see. For instance:

The outstanding faults of the economic society in which we live are its failure to provide for full employment and its arbitrary and inequitable distribution of wealth and incomes.

And, again,

It is certain that the world will not much longer tolerate the unemployment which, apart from brief intervals of excitement, is associated – and, in my opinion, inevitably associated – with present-day capitalistic individualism.

Talking of the unequal distribution of wealth, Mr. Keynes gives one instance of what, he contends, is (thanks to classic economics) general confusion of mind.

It is, he points out, a common belief that heavy death duties reduce the capital wealth of the country. (It is argued, on this belief, that if you tax the rich or remove the inequalities of wealth in some other way, you destroy wealth that is essential for investment to keep our economic machine working.) Mr. Keynes, however, contends

that in contemporary conditions the growth of wealth, so far from being dependent on the abstinence of the rich, as is commonly supposed, is more likely to be impeded by it.

*Consume More*

Put shortly, his view is not that we want to hoard more but that, if we are to prosper, we must consume more. By various measures – which in the end must involve State action – he would re-distribute wealth more evenly among the people.

He would see that more people have more money to spend: and that they spend it upon things which are consumed from day to day. Only by this means, his argument runs, shall we find useful work for idle hands and idle money and the way out of the mess labelled 'poverty amid plenty'.

His treasure hunt suggestion is incidental. It would, of course, he says, be more sensible to build houses and the like. But 'if there are political and practical difficulties in the way' – then the treasure hunt, fantastic as it sounds, would be better than nothing.

# THE BLUNDERS OF ECONOMISTS*
## Hartley Withers

### MR. KEYNES EXPLAINS

With that engaging candour which he has taught us to expect from him, Mr. Keynes devotes himself in this book to the task of exposing the mistaken assumptions on which many of the economic theories were based, of which he himself was once one of the most brilliant exponents. In his opening sentences he tells us that the postulates of the classical theory, as expounded by the 'classical economists' from Ricardo to Professor Pigou, are only applicable to a special case; that the characteristics of the special case assumed by the classical theory happen not to be those of the economic society in which we actually live; and that its teaching is consequently 'misleading and disastrous' if we attempt to apply it to the actual facts of life.

Most people who have tried to discover what economists mean out of the tangled mysteries in which they generally obscure their doctrines have felt that, in so far as they are comprehensible, they have little or no connection with the realities of business. Therefore Mr. Keynes's opening gives one, for a moment, a glorious hope that at last we are to get, from the horse's mouth, a clear exposition of the reasons for this divergence between economic theory and business fact, and its correction by the provision of a new theory which shall show us the way out of the wilderness.

### For Specialists

Unfortunately, Mr. Keynes disappoints this hope for all readers except a very select few who are sufficiently learned, and conversant with the jargon of the economists, to understand what he means. For his book, as he says frankly in his preface, is addressed to his fellow-economists. He hopes that it will be

---

* From *Sunday Times*, 23 February 1936.

intelligible to others, but he had better lay not that flattering unction to his soul.

This being so, it is evidently presumptuous for a mere financial journalist to attempt to criticise the banquet which has been prepared for the highly specialised palates of the economic *gourmets*. But in such passages as are more or less comprehensible, there occur certain statements which lead one to the suspicion that Mr. Keynes, in this new exposition of economic doctrine, is still telling us things which do not quite fit with actuality.

For instance, we learn that the employment of a given volume of labour by an entrepreneur involves him in certain kinds of expenses, including 'the sacrifice which he incurs by employing the equipment instead of leaving it idle.' This is really very puzzling, for most ordinary people would suppose that an employer who has got his equipment all ready would prefer to employ it; and that, far from making any sacrifice by doing so, he would incur much more real sacrifice, both personal and pecuniary, if he were obliged to leave it idle. An explanation of this 'user cost' is promised on a later page, but when it is provided it throws, for an ordinary reader, less than no light on this difficulty.

*Production and Labour*
Again, we find that it is preferable 'to regard labour, including, of course, the personal services of the entrepreneur and his assistants, as the sole factor of production, operating in a given environment of technique, natural resources, capital equipment, and effective demand'. But, surely, this given environment and the items included in it are as essential to production as labour, and so are factors of considerable importance. Or does Mr. Keynes suggest that the most skilful labour of workers and entrepreneur could produce anything without natural resources, equipment, etc., to work on?

And is it quite true, from a practical point of view, to say that gold-mining 'adds nothing whatever to the real wealth of the world'? It may be absurd that this process of 'digging holes in the ground' should make anyone better off. But there is the fact that the recent activity in gold mining, produced by the rise in the price of gold, has put increased purchasing power into the pockets of many countries, among which South Africa,

Russia, and Canada are conspicuous, and so has helped to stimulate trade and increase employment.

By the way, Pope's father did not retire, with his well-known chest of guineas, to 'his villa at Twickenham', which was actually acquired, according to Johnson's 'Lives', many years later by the poet himself. Which just shows that even great economists should verify their references.

But was it really necessary that Mr. Keynes should have tantalised his public by offering us, even at its very modest price, a book that we cannot be expected to understand? We all want our darkness on these matters lightened, and we look to him for light. Can he not be persuaded to get some student who knows what he means and can and will write in the vulgar tongue – which Mr. Keynes can do so well himself when he is in the mood – to produce a translation of this volume which might be so valuable if it could be understood?

# EMPLOYMENT AND MONEY: MR KEYNES'S VIEWS*
## Anonymous

Mr. Keynes here offers us, in 400 pages and for the remarkable price of 5s., the fruit of five years' reflection on the whole problem of money, unemployment and the trade cycle. In substance the book is inevitably difficult, and the semi-mathematical form of some parts of it may alarm the inexpert reader. But the book abounds as well in lucid argument, witty and illuminating digression, historical analogy, satire and pointed political judgment. All this the plain reader will both appreciate and enjoy. Indeed, if he reads these passages alone, he will obtain more for his 5s. than by reading the whole of a good many more expensive books. In particular, one brief but penetrating chapter on the Stock Exchange shows us Mr. Keynes at his most brilliant.

The main contention of the book as a whole, crudely and bluntly summarized, is that the criterion of monetary policy should be neither gold values nor exchange rates, nor even price levels, but the abolition of unemployment. Full employment, Mr. Keynes contends, can only be achieved by a correct monetary policy. For unless the level of effective demand – *i.e.*, the aggregate spending of the community – is maintained at a sufficiently high level, full employment is impossible. Unfortunately, however, as our income increases, we tend to save more, and effective demand tends to become insufficient. In these circumstances the only alternatives are either to expand investment by forcing down interest rates, or to stimulate consumption and restrain saving by redistributive taxation.

Mr. Keynes appears in this book, therefore, as a champion not merely of the cheap money policy that has always been associated with his name, but also of the expansion of social service expenditure as a necessary part of economic as well as social policy.

* From *The Times*, 10 March 1936.

# MR J. M. KEYNES JOINS THE HERETICS*
## H. A. Marquand

Five years ago Mr. J. M. Keynes, world famous for his accurate forecast of the economic effects of the Treaty of Versailles, advanced in his 'Treatise on Money' arguments concerning business fluctuations, which have been vigorously debated by economists ever since.

In the present volume he carries further the analysis then made, and launches an attack on the fundamentals of orthodox economic theory. It has long been clear that because of the regular oscillations between boom and slump which characterise the Western European economic system mankind was unable to make full use of its productive resource, and that waste of unemployed labour and capital was chronic. Recent research by American economists has proved that even in 1929 the United States, the most prosperous country in the world in that prosperous year, utilised little more than 80 per cent. of her productive resources Productive activity has again and again struggled up towards the point of maximum utilisation, only to fall back again into a period of depression. In the upward stages of this movement business men are optimistic, new capital issues are frequent, increased investment takes place, and the rate of interest tends to rise. In the downward stages business men are pessimistic, it is difficult to launch new enterprises, investors tend to purchase only gilt-edged securities, and the rate of interest falls.

*Major Problems*
One of the major problems of economics is to explain this cyclical movement, and to suggest remedies. The school of economists which has shaped the opinions of bankers and Governments in Western Europe (and usually in America), ascribes the chief blame for fluctuations partly to the undue optimism of the business man and his banker in times of boom,

* From *Western Mail*, 13 February 1936.

and partly to the rigidity of wage rates and of the prices charged by protected or monopolistic industries. The remedy advanced by this orthodox opinion has been the sharp raising of interest rates during boom, so as to discourage optimism and speculation, coupled with the breaking down of barriers to the freedom of international trade and an increase in the flexibility of wage rates.

Now Mr. Keynes comes forward to suggest that, on the contrary, rates of interest should be lowered during a boom, for 'a boom is a situation in which over-optimism triumphs over a rate of interest which, in a cooler light, would be seen to be excessive'. Spending and saving take place in the wrong proportions at different stages of economic development. In contemporary conditions, with a large unused productive capacity, increased saving actually impedes the growth of wealth. A greater proportion of the national income should be devoted to consumption, and 'measures for the redistribution of incomes in a way likely to raise the propensity to consume may prove positively favourable to the growth of capital'.

*His Claim*

Mr. Keynes is not concerned to work out the details of a policy, but rather to establish his theoretical case. But he claims that, if his arguments be correct, it is possible to achieve a state of society in which the passive receiver of interest will gradually disappear, but in which socialisation of the instruments of production will be unnecessary and a considerable measure of free competition can still prevail.

It is impossible here to summarise the arguments by which these remarkable conclusions are reached. Essentially, however, Mr. Keynes attacks orthodox economics for having made a fundamental error. Granted the assumption of full employment of resources, the logic of orthodox economics has been admirable, and its conclusions unassailable. But the assumption is unjustified, and the essential fact at the present time is that resources are not fully utilised. The counter-attack will be launched before long by the more orthodox theorists. The present reviewer will retire prudently from the firing line to await the outcome.

# General, Literary and Professional Journals

# MR KEYNES ON MONEY*
## Douglas Jay

Here is Mr Keynes' new book. It is a formidable book, in
many senses of the word. It assails a whole battalion of conventional ideas; it roots out fallacies ruthlessly and without pity;
it includes in its 400 pages sharp controversy, difficult semi-
mathematical analysis, fascinating sidelights on the history of
economic thought, delightfully written essays on a variety
of relevant topics, including the Stock Exchange, and a brilliant
sociological synthesis at the end. Intricate economic analysis
naturally preponderates: for Mr. Keynes' mind is unflagging.
Indeed, reading this book is rather like bathing in the Atlantic
surf. Before the exhausted reader has recovered his wits from
the shock of one exuberant paragraph, he is overwhelmed by
an even more staggering blow from the next. Now and then
there is a lull while Mr. Keynes pauses for an historical or
philosophical interlude. But, before long, the relentless surge
and thunder breaks over its victim once again.

Those, however, who are prepared to give Mr. Keynes' book
the time and concentration it deserves will obtain an altogether
new insight into the mechanism of the economic world at
whose mercy we are all trying to live. The book is in substance
an answer to the question: how is it that the classical or
orthodox economics, though in many respects true and
important, has failed to explain the glaring economic break-
down of the last 15 years? The classical conception of monetary
policy was that a banking system independent of politics should
maintain the gold value of the currency; and that if there was
unemployment, it must be cured by reductions in money wages.
This idea of economic policy, which has plainly failed in practice, is shown by Mr. Keynes to rest on faulty foundations of
theory. The belief that cuts in money wage could always cure
unemployment assumed that there was a certain level of real
wages at which all the available labour would be employed.

* From *The Banker*, April 1936, pp. 10–14.

This, however, neglects the fact that labour is often willing to go on working if the cost of living rises, but not if money wages are reduced by the same amount. Secondly, it forgets that reductions in money wages reduce effective demand and so intensify depression before the expected increase in profits ever has time to emerge.

The classical theory, in fact, misconceived the relation between wages and employment. It regarded them as merely related by the operation of wages as the price of labour and not also by their operation as the chief element in effective demand. Effective demand, i.e. the aggregate of money spent on consumers' and capital goods, is, together with 'full employment', the central conception in Mr. Keynes' book. The classical economists, in rightly pointing out that general over-production is impossible, have always maintained that the existence of general under-employment of resources is also impossible, on the ground that all goods produced constitute demand as well as supply – since trade is simply exchange. This is to forget, however, that the total of money spent on all the goods produced may conceivably fall short of the total of the costs incurred in producing them *plus* a normal profit. The maintenance of the highest possible output, therefore, and of full employment, depends on the maintenance of effective demand. If effective demand falls off, full employment cannot be restored unless effective demand is actually raised temporarily *above* the level of costs and normal profits.

There is, however, Mr. Keynes thinks, a persistent tendency for effective demand to become insufficient. For, as the community's income increases, it saves more; and unless this saving is covered by expenditure on capital goods, effective demand will become insufficient. In Mr. Keynes' 'Treatise on Money' divergences between saving and investment were treated as the origins of depressions and booms. An excess of saving caused a depression, and an excess of investment a boom. He now maintains, using this time a different definition of investment, that they must inevitably be equal. This – quite apart from his apparent indifference to the time problem involved – will certainly be very puzzling to the ordinary reader, particularly as Mr. Keynes continually seems to imply that when saving increases, investment may very well not do so.

The solution appears to be that Mr. Keynes defines 'investment' to include liquid and working capital as well as fixed capital. This means that if there is an increase in unsold stocks in warehouses and shops, owing to diminished spending and increased saving, there is an increased 'investment' in these stocks by their unfortunate owners. Such an argument seems to neglect a distinction which is vital from the point of view of the trade cycle and unemployment. An increase in the volume of fixed capital, due to a greater demand for finished products, means an increase in employment and effective demand. But an increase in stocks, due to a falling off in consumers' demand, leads to falling employment and effective demand. Would it not be possible so to define investment so as to include the first activity and not the second?

This difficulty, however, does not greatly embarrass Mr. Keynes' argument. For he proceeds to treat investment as in effect investment in fixed capital, to speak of investment in 'capital *equipment*', and to assume that only by a maintenance of such investment can effective demand be maintained. He accordingly asks what determines the rate of investment, and decides that it depends on the prospective money yield of capital equipment (the 'marginal efficiency of capital') on the one hand, and the rate of interest on the other. If the rate of interest is low enough to make it possible to borrow, invest in fixed capital, and obtain a reward after paying a risk premium, interest, management expenses, etc., investment will take place. The inference is, therefore, that if investment is insufficient, the rate of interest is too high and should be reduced.

How is the rate of interest determined? Mr. Keynes here elaborates two contentions which appear, at any rate at first sight, rather perverse. He denies that the rate of interest is in any sense, as economists have always maintained, a 'price of saving'. His first reason for this is that hoarders do not receive a rate of interest: which seems rather like arguing that a wage cannot be a payment for work because some men work for nothing. His second reason apparently is the fact that interest rates do not tend to bring saving and investment into equilibrium at that level which is compatible with full employment. But why should they? It would surely be better to say that though the rate of interest does bring saving and investment into some sort of equilibrium, it is not an equilibrium that has anything to recommend it.

Closely allied to his account of the nature of interest rates is Mr. Keynes' second contention that their level is determined, not by the supply and demand for saving, but by the quantity of money on the one hand and the willingness of the public to hold money on the other (their 'liquidity preference'). Illuminating as Mr. Keynes' analysis of 'liquidity preference' is, this contention will strike many readers as a confusion of the short with the long run. It is of course true that the movement of interest rates in the next few months in Great Britain depends on how many Government securities the Bank of England and the joint stock banks decide to buy and sell. At any moment, in fact, the banking system can determine the level of interest rates by varying the quantity of money. But this is surely true only because we assume, in the short run rightly, that the volume of the public's saving will not substantially alter. In any case, surely the volume of money can only determine *changes* in the rate of interest and not its absolute level.

Whether or not Mr. Keynes is right on these two points, however, there is no doubt that the banking system can normally force down the rate of interest by increasing the quantity of money and so expand investment and employment – as long as unemployment is genuinely 'cyclical' and 'monetary', and not merely due to maladjustments between different industries. The very important conclusion, therefore, emerges that when cyclical unemployment exists interest rates should be forced down, and held down until 'full' or 'normal' employment is reached. Only when a rise in prices beyond this point occurs, can we accurately speak of 'inflation'. The criterion, in fact, of monetary policy should not be gold parities nor fixed exchange rates but the maintenance of full employment. Full employment should be the test; and interest rates, the quantity of money, price levels, exchange rates and gold parities should be left to work themselves out accordingly. This may seem to some a revolutionary doctrine. But it is remarkable how monetary and banking policy in the sterling area has approximated to it in the last four years.

Mr. Keynes realises that such an ideal of monetary policy requires a new conception of our financial institutions: for they will have to take their part in the general scheme of national economic policy. He also realises that interest rates alone cannot always achieve everything, and that in some cases effective demand must be maintained by increased consumption and not increased investment. He explicitly states that he regards increased taxation on big incomes and estates, combined with increased social service expenditure, as necessary to maintain consumption and restrain excessive saving. It is impossible, however, to finish Mr. Keynes' book without the feeling that he overrates the importance of investment in comparison with consumption, and that in his future writings he may come to advocate direct measures to increase and maintain consumption. For, as Mr. Keynes himself says, the rate of investment very largely depends on the demand for consumers' goods. Why then, when effective demand falls off, should we stimulate investment and not consumption direct? Is it merely that we are so in the habit of thinking of monetary expansion in terms of producers' credits only? Mr. Keynes is not the man to be enslaved by intellectual prejudices or conventions. Will he not then take courage, like Socrates, and follow the argument where it leads?

# MR KEYNES ON THE CAUSES OF UNEMPLOYMENT*
## Austin Robinson

The appearance of Mr Keynes's new book has been eagerly awaited by all economists. Its publication is an event of major importance. For it makes available to all, with the opportunity of detailed criticism, material which had been known by oral teaching in Cambridge for some time past, and it will acquaint critics elsewhere with the latest, and not the discarded, theories of Cambridge.

The book is addressed primarily to the professional economist. To the layman it will prove difficult reading, not because the intrinsic ideas, or the method of their presentation, are beyond his grasp, but because the book is directed in large part to the clearing up of existing misconceptions, and a sufficient knowledge of the earlier literature is a desideratum. It is concerned in considerable measure therefore with refinements of analysis, and any attempt to expound its results to the layman must necessarily involve crudities of statement which to the professional economist will appear almost as misrepresentations.

This present book develops one stage further a line of analysis which had its origin in Cambridge, through the work of Mr D. H. Robertson, and which was carried on by Mr Keynes in his *Treatise on Money* in 1930. Up to that point both Mr Robertson and Mr Keynes himself had continued the traditional distinction between monetary theory and the theory of relative prices. Mr Keynes in his *Treatise* was concerned primarily with monetary theory, with the question why prices in general rose and fell. The traditional weapon of analysis here had been the quantity theory of money, relating price changes to changes in the quantity of money, in the number of times that each unit of money would change hands in the course of a year, and in the volume of transactions to be

* From *Cambridge Review*, 21 February 1936.

performed. Mr Robertson had seen that, when we reduce the number of times that a unit of currency changes hands, we are in fact saving, in the sense that we hold off the market rights to purchase that we might immediately employ. On the other hand, when we invest money in creating some new capital equipment, we are introducing into the market purchasing power unbalanced by a simultaneously added flow of consumable goods. Saving in excess of investment, it was held, would result in falling prices; investment in excess of saving in rising prices. Such, infinitely refined, was the point that the theory had reached in 1930.

Almost as soon as the *Treatise* had appeared two lines of development showed themselves. First, Mr Keynes's treatment, as he himself says in his preface to the present book, suffered from the fault that he failed to deal thoroughly with the effects of changes in the level of output. Second, he and others were led to inquire what happens to savings if they are not in fact used. These two lines have coalesced in the present treatment. But far more important, what started as a theory of prices has developed by insensible degrees into a theory of output and of cyclical fluctuations.

The greatest change in the present book as compared with the *Treatise* concerns the relations between saving and investment. Five years ago we had learned to think of them as fundamentally distinct processes, which in equilibrium were equal, but in disequilibrium were unequal. Mr Keynes now shows us that they must in all conditions be equal. But that does not imply that they are convertible synonyms, or even different aspects of the same phenomenon. Savings and investment must be equal in very much the same sense that any action and reaction must be equal. If an aeroplane is flying level at a constant speed thrust must equal resistance; if the throttle is opened the extra thrust must be absorbed, either by increased speed and increased resistance, or by lifting the aeroplane against gravity to a greater height. The aeroplane will continue to climb until it reaches the height at which the power-output of the engine is reduced to the point where thrust again equals resistance. In much the same way, if in a country with given employment saving is increased without any addition to investment, effective demand is reduced, output is reduced, income is reduced, and these reductions must continue progressively until the total income is reduced to that level at which the amount saved out of it equals the amount that can find investment.

Once one accepts this analysis, consequences follow that are fundamental to our whole approach to economics. Most of us have been taught to think of the rate of interest as being that price of loans that equates the supply of savings, as determined by the intentions of individuals, and the demand for savings, arising from opportunities for profitable investment. We had thought of it as a price determined like any other price. But in reality it would appear to be utterly different. For if at any give price the supply of savings exceeds the demand, what happens is not necessarily, or even probably, that the price falls. If the price is kept constant, the whole supply curve of savings is raised and the demand curve shifted until, at that given price, supply and demand of savings are equated. At any given rate of interest, that is, equilibrium will be reached between savings and investment through changes in the volume of output and income, and if savings tend to exceed investment, there is no automatically operating force which tends to lower the rate of interest. But there is one rate of interest, and one only, which will give full employment by permitting the investment of that quantity of savings which is freely made under conditions of full employment. Thus the economic system as a whole is not self-righting so far as concerns the re-establishment of full employment in times of unemployment, and intelligent management and control are necessary.

In developing this analysis Mr Keynes is led into many problems which, while fundamental to clear reasoning, need not concern us here. Accurate definition of saving and of investment is a necessary, but far from simple, first step. The inducements to consume, to save, and to invest require close scrutiny. But the central place in the whole study is taken by the rate of interest. This he regards as determined primarily by monetary considerations. If there were no rate of interest we should all prefer to keep resources in the most liquid form available, that is, in money. But the amount of money is limited. It is necessary, therefore, to induce people to dispense with the advantage of liquidity. The rate of interest must be such that people remain just, and only just, willing to hold the entire available stock of money. An increase in the stock of money will ordinarily lower the rate of interest, and *vice versa*.

This bald summary necessarily does scant justice to the many complexities of Mr Keynes's analysis. It is a great piece of work. Whether it is a final work we cannot know. But beyond question it has helped us to advance a long way towards the final goal. It is not an easy book to read. Partly this is the inevitable consequence of the difficulties of the subject; partly, I think, it is because it shows the signs of many patient revisions to meet the demands of critics who have worked through it during its growth. It is only in the more light-hearted chapters that Mr Keynes achieves that perfect tempo of exposition, in which mind and eye march happily in step, that we had learned to expect of him in his earlier writings. With the old it will not be a popular book. Mr Keynes's rapier is sharp, and few of us have learned to glory in our duelling scars. To the young it will be a testament, and they will be doubly indebted to a monopolist who has contented himself with a price that suits the pockets of youth.

# HALF WAY HOUSE*
## Virginius Coe

Keynes is the most unorthodox of orthodox economists. He here presents an exhaustive equilibrium analysis of employment, output, wages and interest, but also declares himself in favour of the usury laws of the Middle Ages, the economic views of the Church Fathers, the monetary and balance of trade ideas of the Mercantilists, the theory of Gesell (who has usually been regarded as a monetary crank) that the rate of interest is one of the chief evils of capitalism, the belief of Major Douglas that the habit of corporations of setting up large reserves for depreciation was an important cause of the slump in the U.S.A., – in favour of rigid wages and therefore rigid prices instead of flexible ones, and, finally, of state control of investment in order to reduce the interest rate to zero; this last proposal, he believes, would abolish poverty, unemployment and most of the inequality of wealth and income.

With some irony he extols pyramid buildings, the singing of dirges for the wealthy dead, gold mining and the modern millionaire's mansion as preferable to the only alternative under laissez-faire: depression and war. It is Keynes' view that a laissez-faire economy is by its fundamental nature such that, even if by a miracle everyone were employed and capital equipment was abundant, nevertheless the normal working of saving, investment and consumption in the system is such that losses would be made, men would be laid off, equipment allowed to rust, until the community was so poor that saving was zero. This conclusion is based on an argument so difficult and involved that few laymen can be expected to follow it, despite the many patches of brilliant and amusing writing. Classical economists are vigorously criticized, especially Marshall, Pigou and – Keynes. With the technical argument there is ample room for objections, but there are sections which will repay reading by everyone. Keynes points out the folly of

* From *Canadian Forum*, vol. 16 (May 1936), p.26.

expecting a market like Wall Street to allocate resources properly on the basis of future returns, since in fact the participants in Wall Street are engaged not in estimating future returns but in guessing the average speculator's estimate of the value of business in the near future. And what the average investor thinks about is short time values.

The last chapter dealing with the social philosophy behind the theory seems to have been over-looked by most socialists. It is true that Keynes now has less faith than before in the efficacy of monetary measures to make capitalism work, that he is, with qualifications, for a more equal distribution of income and wealth through taxation, and that he believes the state must assume the control of investments. But he believes that with this reform and possibly state control of monopolies, the free enterprise system ought to be left intact. He hopes his scheme would eliminate unemployment and he believes that driving the rate of interest down to almost zero would result in a tremendous multiplication of equipment within a generation, at the same time eliminating the rentier class.

Aside from the question as to whether a positive rate of interest is the main factor in keeping us poor, it is worth pointing out that Keynes' vagueness about state control of investment has saved him from showing that under it anything of laissez-faire is left. If the state were to control the purchases of a firm, it must supervise most of its functions too. This book, strangely enough, seems to overlook the ubiquity of monopoly, and the solution suffers at every turn from this neglect. Finally it is naive to assume that the rentier class will sit by peaceably while the euthanasia is accomplished.

# KEYNES COMMENTS ON MONEY*
## Henry C. Simons

The publication of a general treatise on money by the most famous economist of our time is, of course, an important event. Mr. G. D. H. Cole has announced – promptly and as injudiciously as did Sir Josiah Stamp in reviewing Mr. Keynes' earlier 'Treatise on Money' – that it marks a new era in the progress of economic thought; and the book has received serious and respectful attention in circles where its contents must be about as palatable as the communist manifesto. Mr. Keynes is popularly accepted as one of the authentic geniuses of his generation; and, in spite of his warning that he is writing for specialists, the book will enjoy a wide circulation outside, as well as within, academic circles. It is thus a choice item for laymen who cultivate reputations for serious reading and brilliant conversation.

The book is largely in the nature of a revision (if not a repudiation) of the first volume of the 'Treatise on Money' and, like that work, is full of brilliant insights and occasionally devastating criticism of other writers. As a general treatise on money, however, it lacks form and structure and represents simply a collection of interesting propositions, expounded awkwardly and presented with little or no indication of the special assumptions and postulates within which they might be valid or meaningful. Strange and novel terms of the analysis are seldom explicitly defined; and those necessary assumptions which the author does recognize (e.g., the assumption of fixity of wage-rates) are insinuated obscurely. Nowhere, moreover, can one discover, even from insinuation, the nature of the monetary system which the argument presupposes. Thus the author gives us a theory of unemployment, interest and money which attains generality by being about nothing at all.

Mr. Keynes' main point is that our economic system has been excessively exposed and subjected to deflationary pressures –

* From *Christian Century*, vol. 53 (22 July 1936), pp. 1016–17.

that individual savings are likely to get dammed up in hoards, instead of flowing on to finance the production of investment-assets. With this judgment, the reviewer is inclined definitely to agree. Indeed, if the whole book could be interpreted simply as a critical appraisal of the traditional gold standard, implemented through central-bank operations, one's judgment of its main ideas might be extremely favorable. The author, however, does not invite such interpretation. Moreover, if the book is good as criticism of monetary arrangements of the past, it certainly is not to be commended for its suggestions and implications regarding the desirable arrangements for the future.

Announcing a general theory, Mr. Keynes delivers merely a collection of generalizations and practical judgments which have substantial validity with reference to the particular conditions of post-war England, and of other countries since 1930. The nominal eschewing of practical proposals serves only to keep them in an obscure and ambiguous form. Clearly, however, his notions of solution run now in terms of a great and curious variety of expedients – in terms of a highly diffuse kind of political interference. The analytical passages indicate, often illuminatingly, how monetary disturbances are manifested in different aspects of economic behavior and in different phases of the economic process; and they seem intended to demonstrate that wise governmental policy must deal directly with many particular relationships. Thus, the state should use taxation to curtail private saving; it should supplement private consumption and investment with its own spending; and it should force down and keep down the rate of interest to promote new enterprise. At times the author seems to suggest outright fixing of the volume of investment and of the rate of interest by the government.

Mr. Keynes nowhere suggests the need for economy in the kinds of governmental interference; and he seems to disregard, or grossly to underestimate, the possibilities of controlling all the variables which his analysis emphasizes merely by controlling the quantity of money – i.e., by ordering fiscal practice (spending, taxing, borrowing and currency issue) in terms of deliberate monetary policy. He overlooks the need (clearly suggested by his own analysis) for the minimizing of monetary uncertainties and the achievement of a monetary system based on definite and stable rules. Thus, while expressing decided preference for an economic system of free enterprise, he does not seriously consider what monetary arrangements or what implementations of monetary policy are most and least compatible with that system.

Mr. Keynes submits his treatise as a frontal attack upon traditional economic theory. Orthodox economists are rather defenselessly exposed to the charge of making bad applications of their relative-price analysis – of applying carelessly an analysis which abstracts from monetary disturbances in the discussion of practical questions for which monetary problems are crucially important. (The usual academic lecture or textbook chapter on foreign trade and tariff policy is the striking case in point.) But the author attacks, not the bad applications of traditional theory, but the theory itself – with results which will impress only the incompetent.

If the attack upon orthodoxy is misdirected, it is also indiscreet. Not content to point out the shortcomings of traditional views, Mr. Keynes proceeds to espouse the cause of an army of cranks and heretics simply on the grounds that their schemes or ideas would incidentally have involved or suggested mitigation of the deflationary tendencies in the economy. The fondness for a labor theory of value may be pardoned as mere intellectual dilettantism; but the author might adequately have criticized economists for their neglect of monetary problems without endorsing mercantilism, *autarchie*, social credit, stamped money, fantastic governmental spending, the single tax, underconsumption theories and usury laws. The reviewer is not inclined to be more generous toward monetary orthodoxy than is Mr. Keynes. But the sophistical academic leg-pulling which he perpetrates in this volume, however delightful and entertaining in its proper place, should not be done publicly in times like these, least of all by persons of Mr. Keynes' repute.

Readers should be warned against the presumption that the author has eschewed advocacy of practical expedients in favor of objective analytical inquiry, and cautioned against hasty or credulous acceptance of analysis, arguments and critical judgments which are always highly sophisticated and often merely sophistical. Critical readers will find grounds for suspicion either that Mr. Keynes has become overly susceptible to his own clever persuadings or that, having few more laurels to win as an economist, he now aspires to be remembered also as a great wit. Attempting mischievous and salutary irritation of his peers, however, he may only succeed in becoming the academic idol of our worst cranks and charlatans – not to mention the possibilities of the book as the economic bible of a fascist movement.

Many economists, including the reviewer, will welcome opportunity to defend Mr. Keynes against all advocates of reactionary monetary policies, and against those who think they can talk sense about our urgent economic problems while abstracting them from monetary disturbances. But only a kind fate can spare him the approbation which he has invited from fools.

# [REVIEW OF] THE GENERAL THEORY OF EMPLOYMENT, INTEREST AND MONEY*
## Montgomery Butchart

Until the publication of this volume, classical economics concerned itself with a now non-existent, possibly never-existent, economic milieu in which full employment of the industrial and agricultural classes was the chief characteristic. Mr. Keynes so generalizes the classical theory that it describes the milieu in which economic activity must supposedly take place today, when some degree of unemployment is inevitable. The *general* theory of employment, etc., embraces the particular (classical) theory applicable only in conditions of full employment. 'Our criticism of the accepted classical theory of economics', Mr. Keynes says, 'has consisted not so much in finding logical flaws in its analysis as in pointing out that its tacit assumptions are seldom or never satisfied, with the result that it cannot solve the economic problems of the actual world'. (p. 378.)

What precisely are those problems?

Consumption – to repeat the obvious – is the sole end and object of all economic activity. Opportunities for employment are necessarily limited by the extent of aggregate demand. Aggregate demand can be derived only from present consumption or from present provision for future consumption . . . We cannot, as a community, provide for future consumption by financial expedients, but only by current physical output. In so far as our social and business organization separates financial provision for the future from physical provision for the future so that efforts to secure the former do not necessarily carry the latter with them, financial prudence will be liable to diminish aggregate demand and thus impair well-being, as there are many examples to testify. The greater, moreover, the consumption for which we have

* From *Criterion*, vol. 16 (October 1936), pp. 175–8.

provided in advance, the more difficult it is to find something further to provide for in advance, and the greater our dependence on present consumption as a source of demand. Yet the larger our income, the greater, unfortunately, is the margin between our incomes and our consumption. So, failing some novel expedient, there is . . . no answer to the riddle, except that there must be sufficient unemployment to keep us so poor that our consumption falls short of our income by no more than the equivalent of the physical provision for future consumption which it pays to produce today . . . Each time we secure today's equilibrium by increased investment we are aggravating the difficulty of securing equilibrium tomorrow. (III, 8, iv.)

If, then, the capitalist economy in which we live so operates that personal income is measured by the excess of new investment of capital over 'disinvestment', or use, and since such excess, continuously increasing the aggregate of capital, cannot be maintained indefinitely, what procedure seems most advisable?

Discover what determines at any time the national income of a given economic system and (which is almost the same thing) the amount of its employment; which means in a study so complex as economics, in which we cannot hope to make completely accurate generalizations, the factors whose changes *mainly* determine our *quaesitum*. Our final task might be to select those variables which can be deliberately controlled or managed by central authority in the kind of system in which we actually live. (IV, 18, i.)

The determination of national income under present conditions is described in the passage quoted above. The variables susceptible of central control are the 'propensity to consume' and the inducement to invest. The latter is determined largely by the rate of interest, which Mr. Keynes suggests should therefore be centrally controlled so that these two significant variables are so adjusted to one another that maximum employment results.

Mr. Keynes answers some of the questions regarding the general social implications of this proposal. 'Apart from the necessity of central controls to bring about an adjustment between the propensity to consume and the inducement to invest, there is no more reason to socialize economic life than there was before.

The central controls necessary to ensure full employment will, of course, involve a large extension of the traditional functions of government . . . Whilst . . . the enlargement of the functions of government, involved in the task of adjusting to one another the propensity to consume and the inducement to invest, would seem to a nineteenth-century publicist or to a contemporary American financier to be a terrific encroachment on individualism, I defend it, on the contrary, both as the only practicable means of avoiding the destruction of existing economic forms in their entirety and as the condition of the successful functioning of individual initiative.

For if effective demand is deficient, not only is the public scandal of wasted resources intolerable, but the individual enterpriser who seeks to bring these resources into action is operating with the odds loaded against him . . . But if effective demand is adequate, average skill and average good fortune will be enough.

The authoritarian state systems of today seem to solve the problem of unemployment at the expense of efficiency and freedom. It is certain that the world will not much longer tolerate the unemployment which, apart from brief intervals of excitement, is associated – and, in my opinion, inevitably associated – with present-day capitalistic individualism. But it may be possible by a right analysis of the problem to cure the disease whilst preserving efficiency and freedom. (IV, 24, iii.)

The high praise accorded this volume by the Press is deserved. If classical economic theory provided an at least crudely satisfactory working basis for finance, commerce and industry until, roughly, the European War, it has shown itself to be lamentably lacking in practicability since. Mr. Keynes has modernized that theory to make it applicable to the economic conditions obtaining from the conclusion of the War to the rise of economic nationalism about 1928.

Mr. Keynes's analysis of the cause of unemployment – an undirected national investment policy – is but half the story. It is not investment policy which stimulates agriculture, industry, commerce and the distributive trades to substitute mechanical and power devices for the labour of human hand and brain. Nor is it investment policy which retards that tendency, though it is true that the *fact* of capital having been invested in mechanical and power machinery often prevents its replacement by more efficient machinery as soon as such replacement is physically possible.

Yet the quantitatively most important cause of unemployment today is, not simply that machines are displacing men, but that machines are displacing men at a rate far in excess of the maximum possible rate of their reabsorption in new industries. When industries such as boot manufacture and coal mining, both notoriously resistant to mechanization, adopt machinery displacing human labour at rates often as high as ninety-six men out of one hundred, the limit of reabsorption must soon be reached over the whole of industry – a fact which appears especially clearly when it is realized that new industries upon their establishment proceed at once to increase their efficiency (decrease the man-hours required to produce the unit product), and within a few years or a few months are themselves adding to the lists of the technologically unemployed.

Mr. Keynes's revolution in economic theory has gone only half a turn. If unemployment is a sign of the collapse of economic theory, it is, nevertheless, a sign of the triumph of industry. The solution of the problem of unemployment is not re-employment (except so far as socially useful work remains to be done), but the provision of a minimum (at least) personal income paid irrespective of employment. (In his recent *Principles of Economic Planning* and *Fifty Propositions concerning Money* Mr. G. D. H. Cole suggests for this purpose a 'social dividend'.)

The modern world is divided into the employed and the increasingly numerous unemployed. What shall we do when half the population is presumably unemployed? Mr. Keynes has written the particular economic theory which describes the world in which the employed classes have their being. His task now is the *generalization* of that particular theory so that it may embrace as well, and give equal status to, the unemployed.

# MR KEYNES ON MONEY*
## E. A. G. R. [E. A. G. Robinson]

Mr Keynes' new book, like all that he writes or says, will provoke discussion and dispute. The methods of thought that he first developed in his 'Treatise on Money' he has now extended and modified. Where he was concerned before with the problem of prices, implicitly assuming a given level of output, he is now concerned chiefly with the factors that determine what that level of output will be.

At the outset Mr. Keynes claims that the classical and neo-classical economists have never developed any theory of output as a whole. Ricardo himself explicitly, and those who have followed in his footsteps sometimes less consciously, have been concerned with the problem of the pricing system, of the distribution of wealth and of productive resources between alternative uses, on the assumption always that resources devoted to one purpose were withdrawn from another. They assumed, that is, full employment. The explanations of unemployment were unnecessarily concerned with frictions and rigidities which prevented immediate absorption. The theory of output as a whole has been neglected, and it has been inferred with altogether too little consideration that it needed no independent system of thought or analysis to solve its problems.

Mr Keynes argues that this problem requires a technique of its own, and he has set out to give it to us. He starts with the concept of effective demand in the market for consumption goods. This depends first on the total volume of incomes, secondly on the propensity to consume those incomes. If employment is increased, incomes are increased; but ordinarily, since people will save some part of their additional income, effective demand is increased by something less than suffices to purchase this additional output. But if investment in the construction of new capital goods takes place, those who earn

* From *Economist*, vol. 122 (29 February 1936), pp. 471–2.

incomes from this source will add to the volume of effective demand without immediately adding to the volume of consumption goods.

Thus there is some given increase of investment which will make possible the continuance of this higher level of output, and apart from which the higher level cannot be permanently secured. For if, in a given state of employment, saving increases without any addition to the volume of investment, what will happen? Effective demand is reduced; prices will tend to fall; and the volume of output will be diminished by an amount that will depend upon the costs of producers. This reduction of output will in turn diminish incomes. If, out of these smaller incomes, individuals still save just as much as before (an amount, that is, in excess of the proceeds of current new investment), effective demand will still fall short of costs of production, and output and employment must fall still further. In such circumstances employment and industrial output will toboggan down an icy hill towards total inactivity. What then stops this ruinous process?

As output and incomes are reduced, the absolute amount of saving that individuals can afford will almost certainly be reduced. They may attempt to maintain savings. If they succeed, the glissade will be correspondingly prolonged; but ultimately reduction of incomes must reach a point at which savings will unavoidably be reduced. But meanwhile what of investment? As the result of the decline of output and of effective demand there will almost certainly be less industrial investment than before. On the other hand, certain other forms of borrowing may be increased; borrowings of the Treasury to finance the relief of the unemployed, borrowings of firms or merchants to carry unsold stocks of goods, may, temporarily at least, be greater than before. Moreover, negative saving (expenditure in excess of income both by firms and by individuals) will tend to some extent to offset actual saving. If the net decline of investment is considerable, the reduction of incomes and savings necessary to restore equilibrium will be correspondingly great.

In equilibrium, then, saving must equal investment. If these two tend to be unequal, the level of activity will be changed until they are restored to equality. But the restoration of equality does not depend upon any particular rate of interest. If the rate of interest is kept high, so that channels for profitable investment are few, the level to which savings, incomes and output will be forced to descend will be correspondingly lower. The fact that savings tend to exceed investment does not, in Mr Keynes' view, in itself reduce the rate of interest directly, though there may be repercussions on the rate of interest through reduced activity and reduced demand for money. But there will be one rate of interest and one only which will give full employment by permitting the investment of just that quantity of savings which individuals would make in conditions of full employment. It must be the task of the banking authorities to secure so far as possible that that rate shall be imposed.

If we accept Mr Keynes' analysis, our attitude to many of the problems of economic policy must be substantially modified. For in a fundamental sense, and not merely in detail, the economic system, if left to itself, is not inherently stable. There is no automatic tendency to re-establish full employment in conditions of unemployment. Governments and currency authorities have a responsibility far greater than that of merely making the rules and holding the ring.

The volume of employment at any moment will depend upon the propensity to consume, upon the marginal efficiency of capital and upon the rate of interest. The marginal efficiency of capital depends in its turn upon the expected returns over a series of future years to a given present investment. If, for example, future prices are expected to fall, if future capital equipment is expected to be more efficient, if estimates of the future are unreasonably pessimistic, the marginal efficiency of capital will be reduced. The rate of interest, on the other hand, is in Mr Keynes' view, determined mainly by monetary factors. It is the reward for abstention from *hoarding*. At any given moment there is a certain supply of money and of resources of a monetary character, in the sense that they can be converted into money immediately at a price known within very narrow limits. If there were no rate of interest everyone would prefer to hold resources in these liquid forms. But since the supply is limited, it is necessary to induce people to hold resources in less liquid forms by some sufficient reward. The rate of interest must be such that in aggregate people will decide to hold in the form of money a sum exactly equal to the available supply of money.

The inducement not to hoard is represented by the net

receipts which remain after deduction of taxation, and after deduction of an amount necessary to cover the risks and uncertainties involved in any loan. If the future course of security prices is highly uncertain, the net reward, necessary to induce individuals with definite commitments at definite dates in terms of money to part with the safeguards of liquidity, may be high. But the minimum rate at which loans can be made available to borrowers must include also some necessary payment for the organisation necessary to bring borrower and lender together. Thus, it is not inconceivable that it should be impossible to discover a rate of interest at the same time sufficiently high to induce lenders to part with liquidity and sufficiently low to induce borrowers to undertake the volume of investment necessary to secure full employment.

This may in particular happen during a depression, when pessimism leads to a low marginal efficiency of capital. Mr Keynes would not, therefore, hold that it is possible in all cases completely to avert cyclical unemployment by purely monetary action. He would wish to supplement in such cases private investment by public investment, or to increase the propensity to consume by social services or the redistribution of wealth. But this difficulty may ultimately prove more serious as a long period than as a short period problem.

It is in relation to the question of the efficacy of wage reduction in promoting industrial recovery that Mr Keynes' differences from his predecessors become most marked. If it be granted that any increase of real income will ordinarily result in increased saving, and that a transfer of wealth from wage-earners to employers will reinforce rather than diminish that tendency, a reduction of money wages can increase output and real income only if it increases investment, either by increasing the marginal efficiency of capital or by lowering the rate of interest. It is possible to conceive of cases where this will happen. But in a world free from the rigidities of the gold standard, in which uniform wage changes are difficult and to be achieved only through long and painful depression, the method of stimulating investment by wage cuts is, in Dr Keynes' view, both uncertain and unnecessary.

This bald summary of the more essential features does scant justice to the full complexities of Mr Keynes' argument. The important contribution of this book will lie not in the sometimes disputable conclusions that the author has himself drawn, but in the apparatus of thought that he has created. Mr Keynes from the beginning makes it clear that the book is addressed to the professional economist:

> Its main purpose (Mr Keynes says) is to deal with difficult questions of theory, and only in the second place with the applications of this theory to practice. For if orthodox economics is at fault, the error is to be found not in the superstructure, which has been erected with great care for logical consistency, but in a lack of clearness and of generality in the premises. Thus, I cannot achieve my object of persuading economists to re-examine critically certain of their basic assumptions except by a highly abstract argument and also by much controversy.

Even for the ordinary economist the argument, being largely in mathematical form, is difficult. Many will sigh for the earlier Keynes who possessed in unusual bounty the gift of translating theoretical ideas into realities and conveying them in words of one syllable. For most of the difficulties in economics can lie concealed in polysyllables and equations. But far more readers will be shocked or hurt by the tone of controversy. Like Horace's school-master, Mr Keynes whips his pupils into agreement, where modest reasonableness, many will feel, would better have achieved this end. But that is to misconceive the problem. What Mr Keynes is building is in total something wholly new. Some of the stones may have been drawn from earlier buildings and other uses. But old stones used by a new architect do not make an old house. His system of thought is a unity in itself. It may not be complete, but its essential shape is there. If, indeed, as some would say, much of this analysis is less new than Mr Keynes himself thinks, the difficulties of acceptance are *pro tanto* reduced.

# A CHALLENGE TO ORTHODOXY*
## Arnold Plant

What will impress the general reader most forcibly about Mr. Keynes's new treatise is the opening paragraph, in which this eminent economist, editor of the journal of the Royal Economic Society, solemnly condemns orthodox theory, 'which dominates the economic thought, both practical and theoretical, of the governing and academic classes of this generation, as it has for a hundred years past', as 'misleading and dangerous if we attempt to apply it to the facts of experience'. The book is issued at a price destined to give it a circulation far beyond the ranks of economists. True, 'the general public, though welcome at the debate, are only eavesdroppers', for Mr. Keynes writes primarily to convert his fellow economists to heresy, and the ordinary reader will follow little beyond the passages of rhetoric and ridicule. The atmosphere of the public meeting may be intended to provoke thought in unaccustomed places, 'for in the field of economic and political philosophy there are not many who are influenced by new theories after they are twenty-five or thirty years of age', but the move was a bold one, for Mr. Keynes's mind travels quickly, and if he should come to recant, a grave and lasting disservice may have been done to economic science.

Only early impressions from a first reading can yet be set down. General interest will probably centre on Mr. Keynes's practical conclusions. He believes firstly that those who wish to use direct taxation – income tax and surtax and death duties – in this country to reduce inequality of wealth and income need no longer fear repercussions upon the supply of savings. Secondly, he favours state action to lower the rate of interest. Thirdly, we might aim at an increase in the volume of capital until it ceases to be scarce, so that the functionless investor will no longer receive a bonus'. 'But beyond this no obvious case is made out for a system of State Socialism' . . . 'If our

* From *Fortnightly Review*, vol. 145 (1936), pp. 369–71.

central controls succeed in establishing an aggregate volume of output corresponding to full employment as near as practicable, the classical theory comes into its own again from this point onwards' . . . 'There will still remain a wide field for the exercise of private initiative and responsibility. Within this field the traditional advantages of individualism will still hold good . . . Individualism, if it can be purged of its defects and its abuses, is the best safeguard of personal liberty in the sense that, compared with any other system, it greatly widens the field for the exercise of personal choice'. Mr. Keynes's belief in orthodox economics remains so strong that it is the purpose of his political proposals to secure such alterations in the facts of experience as are in his opinion necessary to fit the theory.

Wherein lie the errors of the classical economists? Firstly, says Mr. Keynes, in that their theory assumes full employment. But if he will re-read (as I did recently at the suggestion of Professor Lionel Robbins) the essay on *The Influence of Consumption upon Production* written over a century ago by John Stuart Mill, he will find it argued that because of errors due to imperfect foresight it is normally the case that some producers ought to be contracting their operations while others expand, and that if all are extending their operations it is a certain proof that some general delusion is afloat. Again Mr. Keynes alleges that the orthodox theory concerning the relation between wages and employment is erroneous. (His own presentation suffers incidentally through an unnecessary preoccupation with the 'marginal disutility of labour', for the behaviour of workers can be adequately explained in terms of available alternatives.) The orthodox theory is *inter alia* at pains to exhibit the causes of rigidity of individual wage rates and its effect on mobility and earnings. But to Mr. Keynes, such analysis reveals the 'inexperienced person', for when practical policy is in question it is precisely changes in relative real wages which are resisted by Trade Unions. 'With the actual practices and institutions of the contemporary world it is more expedient to aim at a rigid money-wage policy than at a flexible policy'. A rise in prices secured by central action will, he argues, both reduce the burden of debt and diminish real wages without being resisted. These judgments of political expediency nevertheless in no way invalidate the classical analysis of the effects of monopoly restriction in preventing the poorer workers from improving their relative position, and in hindering the attainment of mobility and flexibility which would increase employment without necessarily lowering the average wage-rate at all.

If Mr. Keynes's colleagues are not all converted, he must attach part of the blame to his new terminology. Definitions introduced in his *Treatise on Money* are now largely superseded. In the discussions of employment, employment is reduced on Marxian lines to standard labour units, the money wage of which is called a wage-unit; and aggregate employment is taken as a measure of real income. Confusion inevitably arises when employment is measured in money wage-units which themselves are liable to fluctuation, and on occasion (e.g., p. 172) it is not certain that Mr. Keynes has remembered his own terminology. He makes too high a claim for his important definition of money Income, which is carefully built up on a business-accounting basis from sales, purchases, wear and tear, and opening and closing stock. Since both the stock figures are admittedly mere valuations based on expectations of future income-yield, the resulting income figure cannot be termed 'a completely unambiguous quantity'. Difficulties encountered in the handling of accruing sinking funds might have been lessened by consideration of Mr. R. F. Fowler's study of *The Depreciation of Capital*.

Mr. Keynes's new definitions are largely required for a central section, which I imagine will be least readily accepted by his fellow economists, in which he makes use of the concept of the Multiplier introduced by Mr. R. F. Kahn, of King's College, Cambridge. Briefly the argument runs as follows: Imagine a community in receipt of a given income, and suppose that income to be increased by a given increment. The part of the increment which will be consumed is determined by the Marginal Propensity to Consume; the balance will be invested. The increment of income can be expressed as a multiple of the amount invested. So far Mr. Kahn. Mr. Keynes now proceeds: 'It follows, therefore, that, if the consumption psychology of the community is such that they will choose to consume, e.g., nine-tenths of an increment of income, then the multiplier $k$ is 10; and the total employment caused by (e.g.) increased public works will be ten times the primary employment provided by the public works themselves, assuming no reduction of investment in other directions'. Because, *given* an increment of income, one-tenth would be invested, it is now asserted that a new investment will create ten times its amount of new income. I have still to discover in the book a demonstration of this proposition. If it were true, it might be supposed in the given case that since for the last previous increment of income the 'marginal propensity to consume' would also approximate to nine-tenths, a decision by the community to save and invest an additional one-tenth of this last increment and consume only eight-tenths would also produce a corresponding increment of total income. But not so: Mr. Keynes apparently will have none of it. He excludes throughout the possibility of changes in the propensity to consume, the importance of which his own emphasis on changing 'liquidity-preference' has well brought out. New investment by a government is even now apparently not excessive, despite his view that the supply of capital is already more than adequate. But, even at the margin, new investment arising from additional saving by individuals will in his view *diminish* employment and income, multiplier or no multiplier. It should be said that Mr. Keynes makes it clear that he entertains no such extravagant view of the magnitude of the multiplier applicable to public works in this country.

There is nevertheless much stimulus and instruction for economists in this book, and 'orthodox' students will find much that is parallel to their own recent thinking. Mr. Keynes develops very effectively under the name of the Marginal Efficiency of Capital the same concept as Professor Irving Fisher has enunciated in his *Theory of Interest*. He draws together and skilfully elaborates current ideas concerning 'liquidity preference', and educes a definition of the rate of interest as the price which those desiring liquidity have to pay to others who possess cash, in order to persuade them to part with it. Much remains to be done to link up this approach with that which stresses the function of saving in making liquid resources available to those who want them. 'Interest has been usually regarded as the reward of not spending, whereas in fact it is the reward of not hoarding'. Better still, it is the reward for not spending *and* not hoarding. On the more realistic side, his Chapter XII on Long Term Expectation is a brilliant discussion of the clash between speculative and investment interests on Stock Exchanges, revealing (in the criticisms and proposals it contains) the preoccupations of an insurance company chairman.

Mr. Keynes may prefer to regard himself as a heretic: certainly there is much in this volume with which his fellow economists will disagree and indeed some sections which they will deplore. But there is much also to suggest that the differences which exist arise more in the field of policy than of analysis. Economics is concerned far more with the scientific study of human behaviour than with giving opinions on matters of political expediency.

# THE CONVERSIONS OF KEYNES*
## Montague Fordham

Listening on a Sunday evening to our Editor's remarks on 'The spice of life', my mind turned to two incidents in my own life that gave it spice and pure pleasure. The first occurred when as a very small schoolboy I was presented with a tip of a golden half-sovereign by Mr Joseph Chamberlain; the second incident comes half a century later when Mr Maynard Keynes made a gracious and entirely unexpected gift to a young friend of mine. I have therefore an undying appreciation for both these distinguished persons.

Nevertheless I have never met Mr Maynard Keynes who stands on a pinnacle of fame far away from the likes of me. But we groundlings, viewing him from afar, tell stories of his conversions, and wonder whether he ever will be converted to our particular point of view – will he ever come down to earth.

Of these stories I venture to tell two: *Se nom è vero è ben trovato*. Some years ago Mr Maynard Keynes wrote a book: it was sent for review to a certain relatively humble person of my acquaintance. The reviewer pointed out that in the second half of the book Mr Keynes had destroyed the argument put out in the first. A mutual friend took, it is said, the review to Mr Keynes and asked him if he was going to reply. 'No', so the story runs, he replied, 'I changed my mind in the middle of the book.'

The second story refers to a series of articles that appeared in an important daily paper, at the time of the International Economic Conference. They were being discussed by the groundlings. Someone, it was suggested, ought to reply. The point was referred to what one might call a second-grade-celebrity – I mean the sort of man who neither pays nor is paid for being photographed but is photographed for nothing. He had read the first and last sentences of the articles and therefore was in a position to judge of the whole matter. 'I did

---

* From *G.K.'s Weekly*, 26 March 1936.

not trouble about the articles' he commented, 'I felt they could be left to a competent authority to reply – I mean, of course', he added, 'Mr Maynard Keynes – he will reply'. And sure enough a series of articles did come out by that writer in a weekly paper that seemed to meet the points at issue.

With this introduction we may now turn to Mr Maynard Keynes' last book.

Here again we have to deal with a conversion which Mr Keynes himself says arises from 'a natural evolution of thought that he has been pursuing for many years'. But the book now before me is not, as I hoped it might be from the reviews, a conversion from the school of thought that I venture to call 'abstractionism' to what some of us call 'realism', – it is, I judge a conversion from one abstract theory to another. To use a comely illustration, it is as if a Seventh Day Advent Baptist, having seen the fallacy of his particular teaching, hurries off to become a Plymouth Brother. The change of thought I suggest is not fundamental but a move over from one fallacy to another. One cannot test, far less prove, this interpretation of the conversion. One could indeed only do so if Mr Maynard Keynes were to adopt the Euclidian method and set out his axioms, and dogmas and ask for explanations. Why, for example, did he assume that social problems can be dealt with by mathematical equations? I should as an ex-mathematician like to know. Then again, why does he state that 'Money cannot be readily produced'? Why should it not be produced, even under our present system, for specific purposes according to the need? For example, as Branford, Trystan Edwards and other realistic writers have suggested, to my mind rightly, for the creation of material wealth such as houses, or as Douglas (an abstractionist I judge) suggests, to increase consumption? To take another point, I gather it to be axiomatic to Mr Maynard Keynes that there is a case for charging interest. I understand, though I do not accept the argument that if money is provided to sow a field with wheat, the increase in the amount and value of the crop justifies an increase in the money and so payment of interest; but I do not understand why if money be provided to build a house, which deteriorates as time passes and so decreases in value there ought to be increase in the money and so interest paid.

There are many other questions I should like to ask Mr Maynard Keynes: he may have a clear answer to them all.

'Whatever,' I should like to ask him, 'may be your theory of prices', why not direct our policy to reducing money to its position as 'a common measure of value' as Mr Penty tells us: what is the flaw in that idea? It involves no doubt accepting the theory of the standard price: but why not?

Those of us who are 'realists' want to know what is Mr Maynard Keynes' reply to the realist outlook.

We now come to the main issue: what lies behind this book and where does it go wrong. It is clearly not a mere intellectual fantasy like Adam Smith's powerful imaginative essay on 'The Wealth of Nations'. Neither is it a futile book like those on which I wrote recently in your paper.

I think that the flaw in this book is that it deals with the surface of economic life: it is superficial. That suggested explanation brings many thoughts to my mind: I think of a blind man trying to secure a right impression of a living organism, by passing his sensitive fingers over its surface: I think of a man trying the characteristics of a nut by a microscopic examination of the shells. Mr Maynard Keynes seems to fail to see below the surface of the nut. One has not only to open one's eyes but to employ x-ray methods of examination of social problems. This interpretation explains certain things. It explains why people sometimes say 'I look on Mr Maynard Keynes as a journalist', for the feature of journalism is that it deals with surface things. It explains Mr Keynes's changes of outlook, for the superficial things on which his views depend are always changing. It also explains why Mr Maynard Keynes has no contact with the school of thought sometimes called 'realist': indeed I do not find the name of even one realistic writer in the index. There is too deep a gulf between Mr Maynard Keynes' outlook and this school, and he deals with the surface of the nut and they with the kernel. So they never meet.

# PROFESSOR DURBIN QUARRELS WITH PROFESSOR KEYNES*
## [E. F. M. Durbin]

The outstanding faults of the economic society in which we live are its failure to provide full employment and its arbitrary and inequitable distribution of wealth and incomes. The bearing of the foregoing (book)[1] on the first of these is obvious. But there are also two important respects in which it is relevant to the second.

Thus concludes the foremost exponent of what was once a Liberal school of economic thought.

The main interest of Mr. Keynes' new book lies for Socialists in the implicit social philosophy that reaches explicit life at the end of the work. In the major part of *The General Theory of Employment, Interest and Money* Mr. Keynes sets forth his stimulating analysis of the causes of unemployment. In this part of the book he is in no danger of being accused of false modesty. He believes that he has set the wandering feet of economic theory, right after a century of sterile tramping in the deserts of classical *laissez faire* economics.

Yet at the end he returns to defend the fundamental economic institutions of capitalism, private enterprise and property. ' . . . no obvious case is made out for a system of State Socialism which would embrace most of the economic life of the community'.

To understand why Mr. Keynes rejects the rationale and retains the substance of capitalism it is necessary to follow the bare outline of his argument. According to Mr. Keynes, the cure of unemployment is fundamentally a simple matter. The amount of employment depends upon total effective demand.

---

* From *Labour*, April 1936.

[1] The following article is not a review of Mr. Keynes' new book *The General Theory of Employment, Interest and Money* (Macmillan, 5s.), but reflections suggested by the final chapter on the ' . . . Social Philosophy towards which the General Theory might lead', pp. 372–384.

Total effective demand varies with the amount of monetary investment and that is controlled by the Rate of Interest. In order to cure unemployment it is therefore only necessary to force the Rate of Interest sufficiently low and maintain it there. That, in barest outline, is Mr. Keynes' central argument. He does not explain, in my view, why such a policy differs in any way from the kind of recovery that has always led, in the past, to a new depression. The long-term Rate of Interest has fallen considerably in the last three years. A certain measure of recovery has taken place all over the world as a result. Apart from war that recovery will continue. But what will happen when the maintenance of a low interest rate has reduced cyclical unemployment to nothing? Beyond that point prices will rise. If you raise the Rate of Interest the usual cyclical depression will begin. What new policy does Mr. Keynes propose? What does he hope?

But, as I say, the main interest of Mr. Keynes' book lies for Socialists in the general social doctrines that emerge after Mr. Keynes has thus easily disposed of the unemployment problem. His full social and economic policy falls into two parts. In the first place he states that the Government will have to control the Banks and the investment market in order to determine the Rates of Interest and Investment. ' . . . I conceive, therefore, that a somewhat comprehensive socialisation of investment will prove the only means of securing an approximation to full employment; . . .' (p. 378). So far Socialists will agree with him. But beyond this point social ownership and control need not go – ' . . . It is not the ownership of the instruments of production which it is important for the State to assume . . .' And this for two curious reasons:

(1) Because private enterprise is a good thing in itself and also because it canalises the darker passions of men – impulses to tyranny and brutality – into harmless channels. 'It is better that a man should tyrannise over his bank balance than over his fellow-citizens, and whilst the former is sometimes denounced as being but a means to the latter, sometimes, at least, it is an alternative' (p. 374).

(2) Because Mr. Keynes believes that after the financially planned economy had cured unemployment society would get so rich that capital would be a free good.

The Rate of Interest would fall to nothing. The reward accruing to property would disappear – 'it would mean the (quiet and pleasant) euthanasia of the rentier' (p. 376).

Whatever the real cure for capitalism may be, Mr. Keynes has found the most bizarre and unconvincing reasons for retaining it. His solution of the problem of unearned income and unjust distribution is really too easy and simple. Ricardo wrote, over 100 years ago: 'The natural tendency of profits is to fall.' Since then the long-term Rate of Interest has moved up and down through whole decades, but the share of property has greatly increased and the inequality of distribution is not less marked. Mr. Keynes seems to have forgotten what Ricardo remembered – 'This tendency . . . is happily [*sic!*] checked at repeated intervals by improvements in machinery.' If we sit back with Mr. Keynes and await in comfort the disappearance of undeserved reward from the system of capitalist distribution we are likely to wait a long time.

Mr. Keynes' first reason for defending private enterprise is even more strange. Private enterprise is to be desired because it deflects impulses of domination and cruelty into the industrial sphere. 'It is better that a man should tyrannise over his bank balance than over his fellow-citizens.'

It is difficult to believe that Mr. Keynes is really serious about this, that he is unaware that private enterprise involves the domination of man over man in one of its most objectionable and uncontrollable forms. The necessary relation of employee to private employer may be, and too often is, oppressive to the one and degrading to the other. The historical trend of combinations among workers in democracies has been steadily to oppose and partially to limit the arbitrariness, the carelessness and the positive cruelty of irresponsible and uncontrolled private employers.

Moreover, Mr. Keynes' assumption that private enterprise means competition and that competition secures the right distribution of industrial resources is curiously arbitrary. Freedom of enterprise is freedom to combine, monopolise and exploit as much as it is freedom to compete. Why does Mr. Keynes assume that the one rather than the other will emerge? And if competition exists how can Mr. Keynes explain away the lack of foresight, the mistakes in investment, the uncontrollable psychological relationships of competitive employers?

Whether we accept Mr. Keynes' view that financial planning can cure unemployment without Socialism or not – and I certainly think most Socialists neglect this possibility far too easily – there seems no ground whatever for accepting Mr. Keynes' short and curious defence of capitalism. On this point at least he must either expand or retract his argument. It hangs, for the moment – rather like Mr. Lloyd George – distinguished, but in the air.

# MR KEYNES AS COPERNICUS*
## R. C. K. Ensor

Though this bulky and in parts highly technical volume is published at a democratic price, its author's preface almost warns off the ground any but the hierophants of his science. 'At this stage of the argument', he says,

> the general public, though welcome at the debate, are only eavesdroppers at an attempt by an economist to bring to an issue the deep divergences of opinion between fellow economists which have for the time being almost destroyed the practical influence of economic theory, and will, until they are resolved, continue to do so.

In brief, the backbone of the book – what it must stand or fall by – is an extremely intricate series of technical arguments, presented in a form (not infrequently mathematical), which few laymen will have the capacity or the desire to follow. Professional economists are expected to wrangle energetically about them for a long time to come; for indeed they purport to effect nothing less than a Copernican revolution in economic thought.

The character and consequences of this revolution will to the 'eavesdropper' become most easily apparent in the concluding chapters – particularly the last which gives him 'Notes on the social philosophy to which the general theory might lead.' The butt of the argument is thrift, as commonly conceived. Adam Smith wrote, 'What is prudence in the conduct of every private family, can scarce be folly in that of a great kingdom.' Mr. Keynes would persuade us that he was wrong; that the classical theories of employment and production from Ricardo downwards have erred in their postulates; that truth (though but part seen and imperfectly understood) has been with the theorists of under-consumption – Mr. J. A. Hobson, Silvio Gesell, and their earlier fore-runners, Mandeville and Malthus. Major

* From *London Mercury*, vol. 33 (April 1936), pp. 644–6.

Douglas can hardly, thinks Mr. Keynes, rank as the equal of these pioneers; his A + B theorem 'includes much mere mystification'; he is 'a private, perhaps, but not a major in the brave army of heretics'. Yet he 'is entitled to claim, as against some of his orthodox adversaries, that he at least has not been wholly oblivious of the outstanding problems of our economic system'.

The antithesis (passing over many 'ifs' and 'buts') is broadly this. According to the old theory, in which we have all been brought up, the less is spent, the more is saved; the more is saved, the more is invested; the more is invested, the more is produced; ergo, thrift means a rise in employment and production. According to Mr. Keynes's theory, it is not the amount saved but the amount spent in consumption, that determines the amount of investment; ergo, saving is bad and spending is good, from the standpoint of increasing employment and production. At least 'only in conditions of full employment is a low propensity to consume conducive to the growth of capital' – conditions which the classical economists postulated as normal but Mr. Keynes regards as quite otherwise. The argument favours the conclusion, among others, that 'in contemporary conditions the growth of wealth, so far from being dependent on the abstinence of the rich, as is commonly supposed, is more likely to be impeded by it'.

This removes one of the chief economic arguments for large inequalities of wealth – viz., that the community needs savings and must look to rich men to make them out of their superfluity. It also removes the defence for high interest as an incentive to saving. Mr. Keynes looks to a continuance and enhancement of the present low interest rates to a point at which rentier-interest, and with it 'the rentier aspect of capitalism', will disappear altogether. In his Utopia, which will not be Socialist, the entrepreneur will go on, though the rentier will have disappeared; a divorce that to anyone who does not live solely in a theoretic world may not easily commend itself as plausible. The State is to be the *deus ex machina* for all monetary purposes. It will control the supply of money, so as to ensure that there shall be enough to maintain full employment; it will also control the rates of interest, and will have the task of adjusting 'the propensity to consume and the inducement to invest'. That the former might sharply outrun the latter under the system which he visualizes, Mr. Keynes is free to admit; but in terms better designed to safeguard his prophetic reputation after the event than to blunt his propaganda effects before it.

On any showing he has written a remarkable book, teeming with ideas at all sorts of points in the economic argument, and relating to main economic theory certain factors (*e.g.*, 'liquidity preference'), which have seldom, if ever, been brought so fully into the analysis before. What the 'eavesdropper', however, will notice is that the practical policies, towards which the theory points, are all of the kind which Mr. Keynes has for many years past been advocating anyhow. It does not altogether inspire confidence when the effect of theoretic reasoning is to justify views held before it. The abstruse plunges into close and often mathematical argument, which form, as has been said, the real feature by which this treatise stands or falls, would have been more impressive, had they oftener demonstrated results unpalatable to the demonstrator. Mr. Keynes is undoubtedly right in what he says about the diminished esteem felt to-day for economic theory. But one reason is that it has come to seem too capable of proving anything that the economist favours.

# THE MAINSPRINGS OF CAPITALISM*
## Maxwell S. Stewart

In contrast to the general run of orthodox economists, Mr. Keynes has distinguished himself throughout the depression by proposing concrete measures for alleviating the crisis. While neither his own government nor that of the United States can be said to have given his suggestions a fair trial, his views have unquestionably influenced policy in both countries, though in a markedly different manner. His was one of the strongest voices in support of the easy-money and refunding policies of the British government, while his bold proposals for public-works expenditures, spurned in Britain, found favor with the Roosevelt Administration. Throughout this period Mr. Keynes has encountered vigorous opposition from his orthodox colleagues, who are patiently waiting for a reconstruction of economic life according to the copybook maxims of laissez faire theory.

It is these maxims, so firmly held by the majority of present-day economists, to which Mr. Keynes turns attention in the present book – his first important theoretical work since the 'Treatise on Money' published five years ago. While accepting many of the postulates of orthodox dogma, he finds it necessary to modify certain of its basic assumptions. He starts by challenging the view – widely held by economists as well as business men – that reduction of real wages is the only known road to full employment. As against the contention of the classical theorists, Mr. Keynes maintains that there is often no way by which labor as a whole can reduce its real wage by means of voluntarily accepted cuts in money wages, and any attempt to do so only aggravates the fundamental difficulties. A reduction in wages may aid a single establishment to curtail its costs, and thereby make it possible for it to expand production and employment, but a general wage cut can only reduce consumption and accentuate the deflationary process.

---

* From *Nation*, vol. 142 (15 April 1936), pp. 485–6.

Although this conclusion is fully in line with everyday experience during the depression, Mr. Keynes is compelled to reconstruct a considerable portion of the classical theory in order to show why the traditional economists are wrong. His argument is so technical and detailed that it is impossible to do justice to it in the scope of a brief review, but at the risk of oversimplification it may be said to run somewhat as follows:

The national income, measured in terms of real wealth, is obviously dependent primarily on the level of employment. An increase in the number of persons engaged in productive activity should normally yield a larger aggregate product to be divided among the population. The volume of employment in turn tends to be fixed at a point where business yields the maximum profits. In determining the level of business activity which they believe will give the highest return, entrepreneurs are guided by the status of three variable factors: (1) the propensity of the population to consume; (2) the prospective yield of new capital investment; and (3) the current rate of interest.

A number of influences play upon the 'propensity to consume', but the primary element is unquestionably the level of income. Most men will increase their expenditures for consumption as their income rises, though not to the full extent of their new income. Now a rise in employment and income can only come through an increase in investment. Any expansion in business activity requires capital. But investment cannot grow unless it is accompanied by a rise in consumption, for otherwise there would be no demand for the increased production. Nor can all of the new output be consumed, since there must be a margin of savings from which the capital can be drawn. It is possible to measure the effect of each new investment on the general level of employment, according to Mr. Keynes, by what he calls the 'marginal propensity to consume'. If the habits and psychology of a community are such that they consume, say, nine-tenths of each new unit of income, it follows that the total employment produced by increased public works, or any other new investment, will be ten times the amount of primary employment created by the new enterprise.

Business men will be inclined to invest in new capital equipment as long as the returns from such investment promise to be in excess of the current rate of interest. A rise in the interest rate discourages productive investment and reduces employment, while a lowering of the rate – within certain limits – tends to stimulate both. Thus while the orthodox economists assume that an increase in the interest rate would encourage savings and thereby promote investment, Mr. Keynes maintains that the only function of interest is to prevent people from hoarding; and if the public has confidence in the stability of economic conditions, 2 per cent may be fully as effective as 6 in accomplishing this result. He denies that the interest rate is affected under present conditions by fluctuations in either spending or investment, insisting that the rate is largely determined by tradition except where it is definitely controlled by the monetary authorities. Thus instead of being an automatic regulator of economic activity, as traditional theory has it, the rate of interest must be manipulated if it is to be helpful, and in the opposite direction from the change envisioned by orthodox theory. Thus a cut in real wages, instead of reducing the marginal demand for capital and thereby reducing the rate of interest and stimulating investment, would lower the 'propensity to consume' – by redistributing income in favour of the *rentier* class – and probably lead to a postponement of investment and increased tendency to hoard.

Stripped of the technicalities which might baffle the lay reader, there is much similarity between Keynes's analysis and that of Moulton in the 'Formation of Capital'. Both find the key to our present economic difficulties in the tendency toward oversavings, which is accentuated by the maldistribution of income; both show that the new investment which is necessary to revive employment is dependent on consumption rather than on savings; and both would agree – in opposition to the orthodox school – that a reduction in wages is self-defeating in that it inevitably curtails consumption. But between a price-lowering and a wage-raising policy, Keynes chooses the latter on the ground that it is more likely to maintain full employment. And for some reason he does not follow out the logical trend of his thought by considering, in any detail, the effect of a redistribution of income as a means of increasing the 'propensity to consume'. Despite a considerable amount of evidence to the contrary, he clings to the view that low money rates together with public expenditures will stimulate investment sufficiently to offset the deficit purchasing power of the underprivileged. While admitting that governmental expenditures must do more than replace private expenditures if they are to be effective, he does not foresee the danger – as exhibited in the WPA – that government investment may have the effect of depressing wages and thereby accentuating the underlying disequilibrium. It will be seen that the theoretical weakness of Mr. Keynes's position does not lie so much in the factors which he discusses as in those which he omits. He appears to assume, as do the orthodox economists whom he berates, a flexible or semi-flexible economic system which no longer exists, and he neglects the all-important phenomenon of an economy dominated by gigantic corporations and trade associations whose fundamental interests and policies are in conflict with the interests of society as a whole. Given the undeniable trend toward rigidity in our economic structure, the type of controls which he envisages are bound to become increasingly ineffective. This he tacitly admits in the final chapter when he suggests that it would be desirable ultimately to eliminate interest and advocates a more rigorous system of progressive taxation. Yet even these proposals, admirable though they are, seem to overlook the apparently irresistible counter-force exercised by monopolies and trusts, which utilize governmental power to strengthen their anti-social policies.

# MR KEYNES'S GENERAL THEORY*
## Horace Taylor

Unemployment, the most conspicuous and most painful symptom of unsoundness in the existing economic system, is the central problem to which Mr. Keynes addresses himself in this new book. His study is framed as an investigation of how it comes that there is not full employment, and of the means by which, in a system of free enterprise, full employment may be achieved and maintained. While his elaborate and highly technical analysis is presented in general terms, it is apparent that he is concerned primarily with British conditions and British policies.

Only an outline of the broader relationships treated by Mr. Keynes can be attempted here. Mr. Keynes assumes that a virtually full employment of labor can be attained. Assuming that there is less than full employment at a given time (which it is not difficult to do), the trend of actual employment will depend on whether the rate of investment of new capital is increasing or diminishing. This is because an increase (or decrease) in the rate of investment must carry with it an increase (or decrease) in the rate of consumption and of the effective demand for goods. The rate of investment of new capital, in its turn, depends on the prospective gain to be derived from the investment ('the marginal efficiency of capital') and also on the 'liquidity value' which money possesses over other valuable things. Whether there is a sufficient prospective gain to induce investment (and here we skip a number of steps in analysis) depends, taking industry as a whole, on the height of interest rates and of wages.

It follows, therefore, that the amount of prospective gain from investment (and thereby the employment of labor) can be enhanced, at any particular time, either by a reduction of money-wages or by a reduction of interest rates, *i.e.*, an increase in the supply of loanable funds. As between these

* From *New Republic*, vol. 86 (29 April 1936), p. 349.

(essentially British) alternatives, Mr. Keynes recommends the latter on grounds of justice, experience and expediency. He proceeds, therefore, to the conclusion that credit should be made easier as a means of obtaining a full employment of labor. The maintenance of such full employment would require, during a period of cyclical boom, the abandonment of the customary practice of raising interest rates to check credit expansion, and the substitution therefor of a policy of reducing interest rates and increasing credit expansion. Following this proposal, Mr. Keynes offers a number of qualifications and says: 'If we are precluded from making large changes in our present methods, I should agree that to raise the rate of interest during a boom may be, in conceivable circumstances, the lesser evil.'

I hope that this summary is not so inadequate as to be unfair to Mr. Keynes. His entire analysis is hedged about with technical exceptions and special considerations. Yet his central theme, while it runs in terms of pure theory, would scarcely serve as a central theme if it were so qualified as to have a significant meaning only in highly exceptional circumstances. One or two of the special considerations must be mentioned. Mr. Keynes recognizes and stresses the conventional and habitual addiction people have to high rates of interest – 'John Bull can stand many things, but he cannot stand two percent.' This consideration, added to certain administrative necessities, leads Mr. Keynes to 'conclude that the duty of ordering the current volume of investment cannot safely be left in private hands'. Such ordering of investment at low rates of interest clearly would require that the state do the investing. Again, when faced with the theoretical imperative of the under-consumption theorists that expenditures for consumption must be increased and savings for investment diminished, Mr. Keynes gives it as his practical judgment that both should be increased. Such a judgment would set the task of the monetary and credit authority.

Mr. Keynes's analysis adds substantially to our understanding of the process by which public investment and public ownership may – perhaps must – grow up within the system of private enterprise. Carried to its logical conclusion, such a program must mean that finally the prospectiveness of profit would cease to determine the rate of capital investment. I believe that Mr. Keynes has over-stressed the power of control vested in the interest rate, and that a great variety of disparities would arise within his scheme of economic adjustment, frustrating the efforts to maintain full employment. Mr. Keynes, while apparently conscious of these probabilities, appears also to forget them at times in his discussion of policy.

Mr. Keynes's critical views are invariably interesting. When he wrote 'The Economic Consequences of the Peace' he was interesting because he saw more clearly than most other people the errors made at Versailles. More recently he has been interesting for his forthright attacks on the errors which, in his own view, he himself has made. Three years ago, in a lecture on national self-sufficiency at University College, Dublin, he recognized that the grounds for his earlier support of liberal internationalism had shifted widely. Now in his latest book, while serving more positive ends than self-criticism, he courageously seeks to tidy up and to rectify certain theoretical positions he has tacitly or explicitly assumed in earlier works. He has made several changes – notably on the relation of saving and investment and in his cordiality to John A. Hobson's under-consumption theory. He no longer regards the influences of money as calling for study separate from the general theory of demand and supply. While he approached this theoretical position in his 'Treatise on Money', those who have followed his work will recognize, in the very title of the present book, an association of ideas somewhat incongruous to the Keynes they earlier have known.

Mr. Keynes undoubtedly will write other books as correctives to this one. In his present study he apparently has taken a step toward the positive position he will finally come to occupy in the history of economic theory. But since it is presented in a highly abstruse and mathematical fashion, 'The General Theory of Employment' probably will not add directly to his popular prestige.

# MR KEYNES BEATS THE BAND*
## G. D. H. Cole

Unemployment is, in the view of most people, the disease that is threatening our present capitalist societies with destruction. There are, indeed, some who protest that unemployment is not an evil, but will be a positive good as soon as we consent to convert it into leisure and to distribute it aright among the whole people. And there are others who maintain that unemployment is not a disease, but only a symptom of something far more deeply wrong with the economic systems under which we live. But against the apostles of leisure commonsense urges that, until most people are a good deal richer than today, most of them will prefer more goods to more leisure if they are given the choice. And against those who regard unemployment as no more than a symptom, it can fairly be argued that the distinction between symptom and disease is not so absolute as rhetoric can make it appear.

At all events, most statesmen and most economists profess to be in search of a cure for unemployment, and to regard this quest as at any rate one of the most important economic ends. The trouble is that they differ profoundly about the methods that are calculated to secure their object. Of late years quite a chorus of voices – from the City, from the business world, and from the academic groves of Cambridge and London – has been assuring us that the abnormally high unemployment of post-war years is the consequence chiefly of the 'rigidity' of wages – that is, of the folly of workmen, under Trade Union influences, in valuing their labour at higher rates than the market will bear. Let wages fall, till they coincide with the 'marginal productivity' of the last labourer, and all will be well. So we have been told with so much punditory self-assurance that it has been quite difficult for the plain man, confronted with a series of unintelligible equations, not to begin thinking that it may perhaps be true.

* From *New Statesman and Nation*, vol. 11 (15 February 1936), pp. 220–22.

There have been, of course, other voices – Mr. J. A. Hobson's for example – preaching a very different doctrine, and telling us that 'under-consumption' is at the root of all our difficulties. What is wanted, on this showing, is more consuming power; for ultimately the entire volume of economic activity is necessarily limited by consumption. Investment is useless, unless there is a market for the consumers' goods which it can be applied to making; for *all* demand is, in the last resort, a demand for goods and services to be consumed. But these voices, in respectable circles, have been drowned by the outraged clamour of the orthodox. 'Under-consumption' has remained a disreputable heresy; and of late, though Marx himself can be quoted on its side, Communist Marxists, such as Mr. John Strachey, have denounced it with hardly less gusto than they have directed against the more orthodox view – presumably because, when they are dealing with capitalist or other non-Marxist economists, they work on the principle of 'the horrider, the better'.

But now there comes, from one who is no Socialist and is indisputably one of the world's leading economists trained in the classical tradition, a book which with all the armoury of the classical method pushes at one blow off their pedestals all the classical deities from Ricardo to Wicksell, and all their attendant self-canonised sprites from Vienna and the London School, and puts in their vacant places not indeed Marx, but Mr. J. A. Hobson and the late Silvio Gesell. For Mr. J. M. Keynes, after many uneasy years of wandering amid the classical abstractions – years whose *stigmata* are still upon him – has discovered that after all, in the matters which practically matter most, Ricardo and Vienna and London and Cambridge have all this time been talking nonsense, whereas Gesell and Hobson (and Malthus in his most maligned moments) have had hold of the right end of the stick.

Mr. Keynes is evidently conscious of the supreme challenge which his new book offers to the entire economic practice of Capitalism, and to the relevance and conclusiveness of the fundamental economic theories put forward by most of his academic colleagues. Otherwise, he would hardly have published at five shillings a book of nearly four hundred pages which most trained economists will find stiff reading and most other people at some points wholly beyond their comprehension. By putting the book forward at such a price, Mr. Keynes is saying in effect: 'This is no ordinary book. It is a book that *has* to be understood because it really matters. It marks an epoch in economic thought.' And, in claiming this, Mr. Keynes is, without the smallest shadow of doubt, absolutely right. His new book is the most important theoretical economic writing since Marx's *Capital*, or, if only classical economics is to be considered as comparable, since Ricardo's *Principles*.

In the challenge which Mr. Keynes has thrown down to his orthodox colleagues, there are, of course, many elements that are not new. Indeed, Mr. Keynes's most signal service is that he has brought together, co-ordinated and rationalised many criticisms of orthodoxy which have hitherto been ineffective because they have been disjointed and unrelated to any clear body of fundamental theory. There are many points, at which Mr. Keynes's alternative construction is open to challenge. But it does give the critics of economic orthodoxy solid ground on which they can set their feet.

There is no space here for more than the briefest indication of Mr. Keynes's arguments. His book is in form chiefly an attempt to determine the underlying conditions which, in a capitalistically organised society determine the actual volume of unemployment. The classical economists, either explicitly or more often by implication, have been accustomed to set out from the assumption of 'full employment' as normal, and to prove their general theories without regard to the possibility of variations in total employment, treating the actual occurrence of unemployment as a deviation from the normal, due to some exceptional factor such as monetary mismanagement or the rigidity of wages. Mr. Keynes himself, in his earlier writings, had not got far from this method, though his explanation was different, for he formerly traced unemployment largely to divergences between the 'natural' and the market rates of interest. But he has now seen that, for the economic system as it is, 'full employment' cannot be treated as normal, and that the problem is to devise an economic order which will secure 'equilibrium' on a basis of 'full employment' and not by preventing booms at the cost of making semi-depression permanent.

Mr. Keynes now sees the factor which determines the total volume of employment under capitalism as the maintenance of investment at an adequate level. This seems, at first sight, to put him sharply in opposition to the 'under-consumptionists'; but actually it makes him their ally. For the will to invest depends, in Mr. Keynes's phrase, on the 'marginal efficiency of capital', which may be roughly translated as the marginal expectation of profit from investment over its entire life, as far as this is actually taken into account by the investor. This expectation, however, depends absolutely on the demand for consumers' goods; and accordingly the maintenance of investment at a satisfactory level depends on the maintenance of consumption.

In orthodox theories, consumption and investment stand in an antithetical relation. But Mr. Keynes is able to show the falsity of this view, except on the assumption that the available productive resources are being fully employed. More consumption, he shows, stimulates more investment, as well as more investment more consumption, up to the point at which full employment has been secured. In his earlier work, Mr. Keynes stressed the difference between 'saving', which is mere abstinence from consumption, and investment, which is the positive use of the 'saving' in the creation of capital. He now re-states his doctrine, so as to emphasise that, while from the collective standpoint 'saving' and 'investment' must be equal (for the only way of *really* saving is to invest), the processes of individual saving and individual investment' are wholly distinct. Accordingly, the attempts of individuals to save can, from the social point of view, be rendered wholly abortive by the failure of entrepreneurs to borrow these savings and apply them to real investment; and this failure, where it occurs, is bound to cause unemployment.

Mr. Keynes believes that failure of this sort is an inherent defect of the present economic system, and that it can be cured only by public action, taking at least three related forms. He wants the State to control the supply of money so as to secure its adequacy for maintaining full employment; and this involves a repudiation of the gold standard, or of any fixed international monetary standard, and also a decisive repudiation of all those economists who wish to stabilise the supply of money. Secondly, he wants the State to control the rates of interest (mainly by adjusting the supply of money) in order to keep these rates down to a point which will make investment worth while up to the level of 'full employment'. This involves a complete repudiation of the orthodox view that interest rates are self-adjusting to a 'natural' level. Thirdly, he wants the State largely to take over, or at any rate control, the amount and direction of investment, with the object of maintaining full employment on the basis of a balanced economic development.

These are Mr. Keynes's most fundamental points of advocacy. But perhaps most attention of all will be popularly focused on his views about wages. For he reduces to sheer absurdity the prevalent view that lower wages are a cure for unemployment. He begins by pointing out that this view rests on a fundamental confusion of thought between money wages and real wages. It assumes that, broadly, these can be spoken of together, and that if workmen could be persuaded to accept lower money wages, their real wages would fall. Actually, he points out, real wages have often risen when money wages have been reduced, and he offers reasons why this should be so. The reduction in money wages, unless it is expected to be soon reversed, sets up an expectation of falling costs and prices which positively discourages investment by reducing the 'marginal efficiency of capital'. Thus, instead of increasing employment, it reduces it, even if it raises the real wages of those who remain in work. Mr. Keynes considers that the tendency of Trade Unions to keep up money wages in times of depression is positively good for the capitalist system, and makes the depression less severe than it would be if the workmen yielded to the blandishments of Professor Robbins and his like.

There is in Mr. Keynes's challenge an enormous amount more than it has been possible even to mention in this necessarily brief summary of his central argument. But enough has been said to show that the book is one which must, sooner or later, cause every orthodox text-book to be fundamentally re-written. It is true that Mr. Keynes's conclusion is not that we should destroy the system of 'private enterprise', but only that we should drastically re-fashion it. Mr. Keynes rejects complete Socialism, and looks forward to a society in which private and collective enterprise will live together, but the *rentier* class will have practically disappeared – for the maintenance of full employment with the aid of investment kept up to the requisite point by State action will, he thinks, reduce the rate of interest almost to vanishing point. But this part of his argument is but briefly sketched in his closing chapter and is not a necessary deduction from his analysis. What he has done, triumphantly and conclusively, is to demonstrate the falsity, even from a capitalist standpoint, of the most cherished practical 'morals' of the orthodox economists and to construct an alternative theory of the working of capitalist enterprise so clearly nearer to the facts that it will be impossible for it to be ignored or set aside.

# MR KEYNES AND THE LABOUR MOVEMENT*
## A. L. Rowse

### I

The present moment is a very exciting and important one in economic thought. It is a time of considerable disarray in that powerful body of opinion which has exercised such a tremendous public influence for over a century (since the time of Adam Smith in fact), and has hitherto displayed an almost unbroken front, along with an unparalleled self-complacency. This disarray, this break-up of the former complacent and obtuse unity, is a sign which all who are concerned for the future of social and political thought in this country must welcome. Economics, as Mr. H. A. L. Fisher has recently reminded us, has something of the key-importance for politics to-day that theology had in the sixteenth century and earlier. We are all concerned in these issues, and it is important that the layman should understand their bearing, even if he does not appreciate all the technicalities of the subject or of the shorthand in which economists love to express themselves. Mr. Keynes recognises this, not least by publishing his new work, which should have cost 15s., at 5s. It is chiefly addressed, he tells us, to his fellow-economists; but he hopes that it will be intelligible to others.

The disputes that at present rage, the disagreement that exists, should have a most beneficial and fertilising influence upon economics itself. Mr. Keynes describes his book as 'an attempt by an economist to bring to an issue the deep divergences of opinion between fellow economists which have for the time being almost destroyed the practical influence of economic theory, and will, until they are resolved, continue to do so'. If this were all, if it were only a question of divergences of opinion, the prestige of economics would not have taken anything like such a knock as it has done in the past few years;

* From *Nineteenth Century*, vol. 120 (September 1936), pp. 320–32.

and, on the other hand, Mr. Keynes would be open to the reproach from his fellow-practitioners that he was only deepening the divergences, opening the ranks still further when they should be closed. But in fact he knows, no one better, that it is something more comprehensive than this which is responsible for the general lessening of respect in which the *ipse dixit* of the economist is held. There has been of late years a general trend among economists, led by what might be described as the London School, away from the real world of economic affairs. A certain scorn even that economists should concern themselves with 'realistic economics' breathes in the whole tone of the manifesto of this school, Professor Robbins's *Nature and Significance of Economic Science*. It is not to be wondered at that absurdities should have been perpetrated; like the translation, under their wing, of Ludwig Mises' *Die Gemeinwirtschaft*, which has a theoretical demonstration of the impossibility of any planned economy, in 500 pages, and no mention of the fact that in Soviet Russia a planned economy actually exists. How very German; how very foolish! Or there is Professor Gregory, who thinks that 'a planned society, as Professor Mises has abundantly shown, deprives itself of all those guides to rational conduct upon which the progress of economic life, in the last two centuries, has depended'. One does not need to multiply instances of this obtuseness; they are, alas, all too frequent. All one need do is to ask, if the economist's concern is not with the real world of economic matters, then what is it concerned with? – since we do not go to the economist for beauty, or grace, or æsthetic satisfaction, or love, or poetry.

Mr. Keynes is well aware of the root-cause of the loss of prestige that economic science has suffered: the unreality of mind of these (not all) economists, the persistent and even missionary doctrinairism entrenched in the academic teaching of the subject, the ostrich attitude towards men and affairs in the midst of most complex and critical issues. It needed an economist of Mr. Keynes's distinction, the most brilliant ornament of the science in this country, to say: 'It is astonishing what foolish things one can temporarily believe if one thinks too long alone, particularly in economics, where it is often impossible to bring one's ideas to a conclusive test either formal or experimental.' He notes in case after case the discrepancy between the results of entrenched theory and the facts of observation: 'a discrepancy which the ordinary man has not failed to observe, with the result of his growing unwillingness to accord to economists that measure of respect which he gives to other groups of scientists whose theoretical results are conirmed by observation when they are applied to the facts'. Of the cleavage, frequent enough, between the conclusions of economic theory and of common sense he says: 'The extraordinary achievement of the classical theory was to overcome the beliefs of the "natural man" and, at the same time, to be wrong.' He recalls 'Bonar Law's mingled rage and perplexity in face of the economists, because they were denying what was obvious. He was deeply troubled for an explanation. One recurs to the sway of the classical school of economic theory and that of certain religions. For it is a far greater exercise of the potency of an idea to exercise the obvious than to introduce into men's common notions the recondite and the remote.'

Mr. Keynes means by the *classical* school, the orthodox economic theory which 'dominates the economic thought, both practical and theoretical, of the governing and academic classes of this generation, as it has for a hundred years past'. Its practical importance it is impossible to exaggerate. Since the time when Pitt was converted by reading Adam Smith, it has had an enormous influence in forming economic policy, through the universities which train the personnel of the Civil Service, through the formation of its own professional opinion, upon politics generally and (to a lesser extent) the conduct of banking and trade. If there is any body of intellectuals (usually of such little practical importance) which has had a deep influence upon policy and action, it has been the economists. It may be judged how significant the case is when the foremost economist in this country deliberately challenges the whole tradition of economic orthodoxy, levels his attack against the postulates upon which the imposing structure has been built up, and rejects its conclusions upon the main issues of current policy:

> I shall argue that the postulates of the classical theory are applicable to a special case only and not to the general case, the situation which it assumes being a limiting point of the possible positions of equilibrium.

> Moreover, the characteristics of the special case assumed by the classical theory happen not to be those of the economic

society in which we actually live, with the result that its teaching is misleading and disastrous if we attempt to apply it to the facts of experience.

The conflict could not be more explicit, nor is it to be minimised.[1] Mr. Keynes has for some time been moving towards it, and now he has thrown over the orthodoxy in which he was brought up, which he knows at least as well as those exponents who remain in it, for he himself taught it for twenty years; and now no longer believes in it. In the appendix on 'Mercantilism' he makes recantations of former opinions based on the old cocksure orthodoxy – such as that Protection could never increase employment, or that the attitude of the mediæval Church towards usury was inherently absurd – pages which remind one of nothing so much as the pages at the end of Newman's *Essay on the Development of Christian Doctrine*, in which he retracts all that he had formerly said against the Catholic Church. History has been dawning upon Mr. Keynes – with results that might be expected; the process has to go a little, but not much, further. His book, it is evident, is an event of the first importance: I should say it marks a revolution in economic thought, but for the reluctance to use an overworked word. Since economics is the chief English contribution to the intellectual life of Europe in the past hundred years, it is to be hoped that the clash of ideas will prove a fertilising one: it is certainly in this country that the battle is at its most exciting. But should an overthrow of the old embattled orthodoxy result, and a new economics emerge, it will be a matter of still greater practical importance; for it may well guide us to new departures in our economic policy, on our way to a new epoch in the life of the nation.

Mr. Keynes, then, after long wandering, has arrived at a position entirely opposed to the hitherto prevailing orthodoxy. And not only as regards the theory of Employment, Interest and Money, to which the title of his book specifically refers; there is hardly any aspect of economic theory, whether on wages, prices, the trade cycle, or tariffs, where he does not traverse the orthodox position and put forward what may be described as the Opposition view. In more senses than one – since what constitutes the political importance of the book is

[1] As, for example, Mr. H. D. Henderson was at some pains to do in his review in the *Spectator*, February 14, 1936.

that at every point, without a single exception, it is in full agreement with Labour policy in this country, and, what is even more significant, expresses in proper economic form what has been implicit in the Labour Movement's attitude all along. Here at last is an economist of the first rank – indeed one of the foremost economists in the world – underwriting the whole Labour position in these post-war years and proving us to have been substantially right. No wonder Mr. Cole, in a vociferous welcome, has acclaimed the book as 'the most important theoretical economic writing since Marx's *Capital*, or, if only classical economics is to be considered as comparable, since Ricardo's *Principles*'. Mr. Cole is justified; it is impossible to over-estimate the influence that this book will almost certainly exert in the future. It may be described as, for the first time in this country, laying the foundations of a Socialist economics.

To illustrate its complete justification of Labour policy, let us take its attitude on wages, in practical politics one of the most controversial issues, one which has been responsible for much of our industrial troubles since the war. We have already noticed the beginning of his divergence from orthodox opinion on this subject. 'The Classical Theory', he says, 'has been accustomed to rest the supposedly self-adjusting character of the economic system on an assumed fluidity of money-wages; and when there is rigidity, to lay on this rigidity the blame of maladjustment'. How well we recognise, beneath the chaste academic language, the rough remedy of capitalists and capitalist economists alike for our prolonged industrial depression: Reduce wages – there is the cure for unemployment. Mr. Keynes recognises, as we all do, that there are certain circumstances in which a reduction in money-wages may afford a stimulus to output and consequently increase employment. But these circumstances are, in his view, exceptional ones, and to generalise from these that reducing wages will stimulate employment in all circumstances is quite unwarranted. For this view neglects to take into account the influence of the reduction upon demand; it assumes that demand will go on being what it was before. Whereas, in fact, the reduction sets up an expectation of falling costs and prices which positively discourages investment, and thus increases unemployment, instead of reducing it. He concludes that 'there is, therefore, no ground for the belief that a flexible wage policy is capable of maintaining a state of continuous full employment; any more than for the belief that an open market monetary policy is capable, unaided, of achieving this result. The economic system cannot be made self-adjusting along these lines.'

It happens, therefore, that the trade unions have been for the most part right in resisting wage-cuts, since wage-reductions do not necessarily or in general have the effect of increasing employment. In any case, as Mr. Keynes points out, 'since there is as a rule no means of securing a simultaneous and equal reduction of money-wages in all industries, it is to the interest of all workers to resist a reduction in their own particular cases'. The orthodox view maintains that the struggle over money-wages between the *entrepreneurs* and the workers determines the general level of real wages. In Mr. Keynes's view it does not:

> the struggle about money-wages primarily affects the *distribution* of the aggregate real wage between different labour-groups, and not its average amount per unit of employment, which depends, as we shall see, on a different set of forces. The effect of combination on the part of a group of workers is to protect their *relative* real wage. The *general* level of real wages depends on the other forces of the economic system. Thus it is fortunate that the workers, though unconsciously, are instinctively more reasonable economists than the classical school, inasmuch as they resist reductions of money-wages, which are seldom or never of an all-round character; ... whereas they do not resist reductions of real wages, which are associated with increases in aggregate employment and leave relative money-wages unchanged ... Every trade union will put up some resistance to a cut in money-wages, however small. But since no trade union would dream of striking on every occasion of a rise in the cost of living, they do not raise the obstacle to any increase in aggregate employment which is attributed to them by the classical school.

Mr. Keynes opts, therefore, as he always has done, for a flexible money policy rather than a flexible wage policy: the former being easy to put into practice and on its own merits desirable, while the latter is necessarily uneven in operation, unfair and so difficult as virtually to be impracticable. Actually, since 1932, the Treasury and the Bank of England have been carrying out a fairly flexible money policy on Mr. Keynes's lines and given up their attempts, persistent ever since the collapse of the post-war boom in 1920, to force wage-reductions upon the workers and deflation upon industry, in the interests of the *rentier* and of the City; though not before they had brought about the fall of the Labour Government of 1929, in itself no disadvantage to those who brought it about. Mr. Keynes now recommends our adhering to a policy of maintaining a stable general level of money-wages, certainly in the short period, and he gives reasons (pp. 270–271) for regarding it as the better long-term policy too. He suggests a most interesting consideration as regards the alternative, a flexible wage-policy:

> To suppose that a flexible wage-policy is a right and proper adjunct of a system which on the whole is one of *laissez-faire*, is the opposite of the truth. It is only in a highly authoritarian society, where sudden, substantial, all-round changes could be decreed, that a flexible wage-policy could function with success. One can imagine it in operation in Italy, Germany or Russia, but not in France, the United States or Great Britain.

At first sight, the reflection appears paradoxical, one is so accustomed to the received opinion that a flexible wage-system goes with *laissez-faire* and liberal institutions; but one has only to recall the brutal reductions in the general level of wages carried out by the Nazi *régime* in Germany for the sake of its enormous expenditure upon armaments (the real *raison d'être* of the *régime*) to realise that Mr. Keynes's observation is correct.

His treatment of wages expands into the general question of the importance of demand in relation to employment. Here, too, his position challenges the traditional theory. 'The idea that we can safely neglect the aggregate demand function is fundamental to the Ricardian economics, which underlie what we have been taught for more than a century'. He criticises the classical doctrine that 'supply creates its own demand', on the ground of its assumption that

> the aggregate demand price is equal to the aggregate supply price for all levels of output and employment . . . It is, then, the assumption of equality between the demand price of output as a whole and its supply price which is to be regarded as the classical theory's 'axiom of parallels'. Granted this, all

the rest follows – the social advantages of private and national thrift, the traditional attitude towards the rate of interest, the classical theory of unemployment, the quantity theory of money, the unqualified advantages of *laissez-faire* in respect of foreign trade and much else which we shall have to question.

All these things are in question; they come from assuming full employment[2] to be the normal condition of the economic system, that the system is self-adjusting at that level. Whereas, in fact, it adjusts itself to a condition far short of full employment, and settles down to a condition in which a large proportion of its resources is permanently unemployed. The problem is so to change the economic system as to secure equilibrium at full employment, bringing all its resources into use.

In building up his theory of employment, he makes use of 'only two fundamental units of quantity – namely, quantities of money-value and quantities of employment'. His definition of the latter, 'by taking an hour's employment of ordinary labour as our unit and weighting an hour's employment of special labour in proportion to its remuneration', reminds one of nothing so much as Marx's fundamental units of 'socially necessary labour', to which Mr. Keynes's conception seems to bear analogy. And indeed he says of the relation of labour to capital:

> I sympathise with the pre-classical doctrine, that everything is *produced* by *labour*, aided by what used to be called art and is now called technique, by natural resources which are free or cost a rent according to their scarcity or abundance, and by the results of past labour, embodied in assets, which also command a price according to their scarcity or abundance. It is preferable to regard labour, including of course the personal services of the *entrepreneur* and his assistants, as the sole factor of production, operating in a given environment of technique, natural resources, capital equipment and

[2] The concept of 'full employment' allows for a certain proportion due to 'frictional' or 'voluntary' unemployment, *i.e.*, does not include those who may be out of work owing to difficulties in transfer from one industry to another, unemployables, etc. 'Full employment' means all those employable over and above these particular categories – defined pp. 6–7 of *The General Theory*.

effective demand. This partly explains why we have been able to take the unit of labour as the sole physical unit which we require in our economic system, apart from units of money and of time.

It is natural, then, that wages should play the large part they do in his view of their relation to demand. 'For whilst the other factors are capable of varying . . . the aggregate income measured in terms of the wage-unit is, as a rule, the principal variable upon which the consumption-constituent of the aggregate demand function will depend.' (Is it too much to say that the crude political inference to draw is that it is the standard of living of the working class that chiefly matters in keeping up consumption?) Consumption, he reminds us, is 'the sole end and object of all economic activity. Opportunities for employment are necessarily limited by the extent of aggregate demand. Aggregate demand can only be derived from present consumption or from present provision for future consumption.' It is this consideration which refutes the advocates of wage-reductions, 'other things being equal', as a remedy for unemployment; for other things do not remain equal; the reductions themselves reduce effective demand. It would seem, then, that the complaints with which Labour platforms have resounded since 1931 as before (all too ineffectively, for there is no one so deaf as he that will not hear) were not only plain common sense, but good economics. What is the point of cutting wages if people can't buy the goods? we said roughly, and apparently were not wrong. It is comforting, years afterwards, to learn that we were on the side of the angels, that what we stood for, even if we were *gauche* and without a knowledge of the subtleties of orthodox economics, was in the better interests of the country. It is embittering to reflect, not as against Mr. Keynes, for he at least spoke out his mind in the gigantic fraud of 1931, but as against the unanimous orthodox opinion against us, that our case appears now to have been the better one. Orthodoxy is not what it was. For all that, the upper classes used it in 1931 to turn Labour out of power and to make themselves safe for ten years. They succeeded in putting it across large sections of the middle classes that Labour's economics meant financial ruin. (What they really objected to was that Labour policy was beginning to have a slight effect in redistributing wealth.) It will take years for the

Labour Movement to recover from the charge that was riveted upon it in the minds of the middle class. Only the other day the headmaster of one of our great public schools, an otherwise intelligent man, assured me solemnly that everybody recognised that the Labour Government of 1929 well-nigh ruined the country financially. It would have been of no use to recommend him to Mr. Keynes's economics; he, in common with millions of his fellow-countrymen, would simply not have understood them.

It is indeed impossible to give an adequate account of the central part of Mr. Keynes's book – the demand-consumption – employment relation – in brief space. Perhaps it may be shortly summarised in the words of *The Times* review, a suspiciously short review for so important a work:

> Unless the level of effective demand – *i.e.*, the aggregate spending of the community – is maintained at a sufficiently high level, full employment is impossible. Unfortunately, however, as our income increases we tend to save more, and effective demand tends to become insufficient. In these circumstances the only alternatives are either to expand investment by forcing down interest rates, or to stimulate consumption and restrain saving by redistributive taxation. Mr. Keynes appears in this book, therefore, as a champion not merely of the cheap money policy that has always been associated with his name, but also of the expansion of social service expenditure as a necessary part of economic as well as social policy.

That is to say, in less polite language, that the policy of adequate expenditure upon the social services, such as the Labour Party has always advocated, is not only socially desirable, but an economic necessity if we are to keep employment from decreasing still further. In plain words, there is a gap between the wealth the community could easily produce and the actual consumption which on the existing system of distribution, determined by private property, it is limited to satisfying. Moreover, as Mr. Keynes says,

> the richer the community, the wider will tend to be the gap between its actual and its potential production; and, therefore, the more obvious and outrageous the defects of the economic system. For a poor community will be prone

to consume by far the greater part of its output, so that a very modest measure of investment will be sufficient to provide full employment; whereas a wealthy community will have to discover much ampler opportunities for investment if the saving propensities of its wealthier members are to be compatible with the employment of its poorer members.

How paradoxical it all sounds to us in whose ears it has been dinned that there is no more important function to be fulfilled than that of the *rentier* class, in that it is upon their savings that the economic system revolves. Behold, it now appears that unless advantageous investment is deliberately planned to keep pace with positive saving, it is precisely upon the disproportionate saving of the *rentier* class that the system cranks and breaks down.[3] Blessed are they, in present circumstances, who spend, not they who save – 'the more virtuous we are, the more determinedly thrifty, the more obstinately orthodox in our national and personal finance, the more our incomes will have to fall when interest rises relatively to the marginal efficiency of capital. Obstinacy can bring only a penalty and no reward. For the result is inevitable.' How far we have moved from the self-complacency of the Victorians with regard to the *rentier* class and their vital function of providing capital from their savings! Indeed, Mr. Keynes thinks, as we shall see, that there is no longer any need for a *rentier* class to perform that function; and as for capital, it 'is not a self-subsistent entity existing apart from consumption'. These are certainly the economics of the age of relativity. Capital is not created, as we were taught and as the vast majority of our countrymen continue to suppose, out of past savings, but out of the decisions of the *entrepreneur* to produce on the basis of a certain expectation of profit. If this attitude becomes general it will do away with much of the case for the economic necessity of a wealth-owning class – regarding capital as a solid accumulation out of past savings. On Mr. Keynes's view, as in the eyes of Socialists, capital becomes merely the result of the claim that capitalists have upon the country's output, through their control of political power and expressed in the legal system.

Since, then, there is this disparity between our actual and

---

[3] *I.e.*, by causing losses to producers, and therefore dissaving and a decrease of incomes.

potential production, due to the insufficiency of effective demand – the explanation of the paradox of poverty in the midst of plenty – our attention should be directed to the necessity for increased consumption, the possibilities of further investment. Mr. Keynes does not appear to favour the direct subvention of consumption by consumers' subsidies, such as Mr. Durbin has proposed, but is in favour of tackling the position indirectly *via* social services and redistributive taxation. His own analysis of the trouble is mainly concerned with the inadequacy of investment in relation to actual savings. He suggests with bitterness, in view of all the lost opportunities for productive expenditure and for raising the standard of living in the years since the war, that even 'wasteful' loan expenditure may enrich the community on balance:

> Pyramid-building, earthquakes, even wars, may serve to increase wealth, if the education of our statesmen on the principles of the classical economics stands in the way of anything better. It is curious how common sense, wriggling for an escape from absurd conclusions, has been apt to reach a preference for *wholly* 'wasteful' forms of loan expenditure rather than for *partly* wasteful forms, which, because they are not wholly wasteful, tend to be judged on strict 'business' principles. For example, unemployment relief financed by loans is more readily accepted than the financing of improvements at a charge below the current rate of interest; whilst the form of digging holes in the ground known as gold-mining, which not only adds nothing whatever to the real wealth of the world, but involves the disutility of labour, is the most acceptable of all solutions. If the Treasury were to fill old bottles with bank-notes, bury them at suitable depths in disused coal-mines which are then filled up to the surface with town rubbish, and leave it to private enterprise on well-tried principles of *laissez-faire* to dig the notes up again (the right to do so being obtained, of course, by tendering for leases of the note-bearing territory), there need be no more unemployment, and with the help of repercussions, the real income of the community, and its capital wealth also, would probably become a good deal greater than it actually is. It would, indeed, be more sensible to build houses and the like; but if there are political and practical difficulties in the way of this, the above would be better than nothing.

Mr. Keynes goes on in a passage of Swift-like irony, bitter at the thought of so much stupidity in human affairs, to show how complete the analogy is between digging for his bottles filled with bank-notes and the function played by gold-mining in our economic system. History bears him out:

> At periods when gold is available at suitable depths experience shows that the real wealth of the world increases rapidly; and when but little of it is so available, our wealth suffers stagnation or decline. Thus gold-mines are of the greatest value and importance to civilisation. Just as wars have been the only form of large-scale loan expenditure which statesmen have thought justifiable, so gold-mining is the only pretext for digging holes in the ground which has recommended itself to bankers as sound finance; and each of these activities has played its part in progress – failing something better.

Moreover, gold-mining has several advantages to offer; 'if we are precluded from increasing employment by means which at the same time increase our stock of useful wealth'. Its value does not shrink with use like that of houses; no such disgusting utility disfigures the higher purpose which gold-mining serves:

> Since the value of a house depends on its utility, every house which is built serves to diminish the prospective rents obtainable from further house-building and therefore lessens the attraction of further similar investment unless the rate of interest is falling *pari passu*.

Mr. Keynes here fails to observe, or in deference to our intelligence omits what should be underlined, that the reason why gold-mining has the preference to housing is because it is more profitable to the capitalist. To imagine that you can persuade him to another course than his interest dictates, in other words, to suppose that you can change capitalist behaviour without changing the system, is merely silly – another example of the rationalist fallacy. But in fact Mr. Keynes does not draw the moral that it is the profit system which needs changing – though no doubt he would now largely agree. Instead he continues the irony in a superb passage which yields its own (if merely æsthetic) satisfaction:

> Ancient Egypt was doubly fortunate, and doubtless owed to

this its fabled wealth, in that it possessed *two* activities, namely, pyramid-building, as well as the search for the precious metals, the fruits of which, since they could not serve the needs of man by being consumed, did not stale with abundance. The Middle Ages built cathedrals and sang dirges. Two pyramids, two masses for the dead, are twice as good as one; but not so two railways from London to York. Thus we are so sensible, have schooled ourselves to so close a semblance of prudent financiers, taking careful thought before we add to the 'financial' burdens of posterity by building them houses to live in, that we have no such easy escape from the sufferings of unemployment. We have to accept them as an inevitable result of applying to the conduct of the State the maxims which are best calculated to 'enrich' an individual by enabling him to pile up claims to enjoyment which he does not intend to exercise at any definite time.

All this irony means that Mr. Keynes has been going through a dark night of the soul, in his sphere of knowledge and experience, no less than others of us who have been concerned chiefly with the hopes of international order and peace. The source of the bitterness is the same: the simple idiocy of human beings in managing their corporate affairs.

# KEYNES'S ECONOMICS*
## Fabian Franklin

To say that this book is extremely difficult reading is by no means to pronounce an adverse judgment upon it. The difficulty arises in the main from the qualities in the book which constitute its chief merit – inflexible adherence to the most exacting standards of accurate thinking, courageous admission of imperfections, honest acknowledgement and analysis of errors committed by the author himself in previous grapplings with the same economic problems. Whatever else may be said about the book, it is certainly one that demands most earnest attention and study on the part of all economists seriously concerned with the fundamental questions of their science.

That such a book can hardly be read with satisfaction by the general public goes almost without saying; and furthermore it is what Mr. Keynes himself says in his preface, at the same time stating very clearly the *raison d'être* of his work:

This book is chiefly addressed to my fellow economists. I hope that it will be intelligible to others. But its main purpose is to deal with difficult questions of theory, and only in the second place with the applications of this theory to practice. For if orthodox economics is at fault, the error is to be found not in the superstructure, which has been erected with great care for logical consistency, but in a lack of clearness and of generality in the premises. Thus I cannot achieve my object of persuading economists to re-examine critically certain of their basic assumptions except by a highly abstract argument and also by much controversy.

The matters at issue are of an importance which cannot be exaggerated. But, if my explanations are right, it is my fellow economists, not the general public, whom I must first convince. At this stage of the argument the general public, though welcome at the debate, are only eavesdroppers at an attempt by an economist to bring to an issue the deep

* From *Saturday Review of Literature*, vol. 13 (4 April 1936), pp. 32–3.

divergences of opinion between fellow economists which have for the time being almost destroyed the practical influence of economic theory, and will, until they are resolved, continue to do so.

The preface closes, however, with a statement which cannot be passed without challenge:

> The composition of this book has been for the author a long struggle of escape, and so must the reading of it be for most readers if the author's assault upon them is to be successful, – a struggle of escape from habitual modes of thought and expression. The ideas which are here expressed so laboriously are extremely simple and should be obvious. The difficulty lies, not in the new ideas, but in escaping from the old ones, which ramify, for those brought up as most of us have been, into every corner of our minds.

If, in point of fact, the ideas expounded by Keynes 'are extremely simple and should be obvious', the first duty of a reviewer must be to give, in simple language, the gist of Keynes's elaborate discussion. To the present writer, however, this seems an impossible task; and if it were an easy one he cannot help wondering why Keynes did not himself devote a few pages of his book to the performance of it.

Eminently just-minded as Mr. Keynes habitually is in his criticisms, his view of the source of the difficulty which readers will experience is unfair to the classical economists. That a prepossession in favor of the old ideas does obstruct the ingress of new ones is quite true; but a chief reason for the difficulty is that the old ideas were intrinsically far simpler. Indeed it was because of their intrinsic simplicity that the classical doctrines were enunciated in the first place, and that they acquired the sway which they so long enjoyed.

Even faintly to indicate the nature of the divergence between Keynes and the classical economists is beyond what can here be attempted. One or two points may, however, be mentioned. Whereas the classical economic theory was concerned almost exclusively with the way in which the proceeds of the aggregate production were divided among the various participants – landowners, capitalists, entrepreneurs, wage-workers – Keynes centers attention upon the conditions on which the maintenance of the aggregate itself at its fullest attainable volume depends. The doctrine that supply and demand are merely two aspects of the same objective fact is subjected to prolonged and minute examination, resulting in an invalidation of the traditional conclusion drawn from it that general overproduction is impossible. The invalidation turns largely on considerations, by no means obvious, relating to the psychological factors designated as 'propensity to consume' and 'propensity to save'. The maintenance of a proper balance between these two factors is seen to be essential to full employment of the nation's productive resources; and since such balance is never actually established, unemployment is a constant accompaniment of our economic order – a disease vastly aggravated in times of depression, but by no means confined to those times.

A striking contrast to the main body of the book is presented by the very brief chapter with which it closes. This is entitled 'Concluding Notes on the Social Philosophy towards which the General Theory might lead.' This chapter is perfectly easy to read and to understand and it is packed with judgments of momentous import upon vital issues of theory and of practice. A few of these judgments will suffice to show how deeply Keynes cuts into the very vitals of traditionally accepted economic opinion:

> The outstanding faults of the economic society in which we live are its failure to provide for full employment and its arbitrary and inequitable distribution of wealth and incomes.
>
> Up to the point where full employment prevails, the growth of capital depends not at all on a low propensity to consume but is, on the contrary, held back by it; and only in conditions of full employment is a low propensity to consume conducive to the growth of capital.
>
> Thus our argument leads towards the conclusion that in contemporary conditions the growth of wealth, so far from being dependent on the abstinence of the rich, as is commonly supposed, is more likely to be impeded by it. One of the chief social justifications of great inequality of wealth is, therefore, removed.
>
> The justification for a moderately high rate of interest has been found hitherto in the necessity of providing a sufficient inducement to save. But we have shown that the extent of effective saving is necessarily determined by the scale of

investment and that the scale of investment is promoted by a *low* rate of interest, provided that we do not attempt to stimulate it in this way beyond the point which corresponds to full employment.

Interest today rewards no genuine sacrifice, any more than does the rent of land. The owner of capital can obtain interest because capital is scarce, just as the owner of land can obtain rent because land is scarce. But whilst there may be intrinsic reasons for the scarcity of land, there are no intrinsic reasons for the scarcity of capital.

The bold and clear-cut way in which these conclusions are enunciated presents a striking contrast to the painfully accurate reasoning which has led up to them, and with which the body of the book is chiefly occupied. But it is to be observed that Keynes's attack upon classical economics is free from that character of arrogant contempt which is so frequently the dominant note of leaders of heterodox opinion. Indeed, his acknowledgment of merit in classical views, which are repudiated by many new-light economists, adds not a little to the weight of his criticism.

In view of the importance of his practical conclusions, as well as the searching character of his theoretical discussions, it is matter for keen regret that Mr. Keynes has not made his argument capable of being apprehended and assessed without the prodigious effort which an adequate study of his book demands. That its subtleties are necessary to an uncompromisingly thorough discussion of the subject may be quite true; but it is hardly possible that broad conclusions like those above cited, and others to which he attaches even greater importance, are so dependent upon those subtleties that they are incapable of being substantially established without them. To perform this task no one is better qualified – by knowledge, by intellectual ability, and by power of expression – than Mr. Keynes himself. It is to be hoped that he will feel called upon to follow up this book with another which shall take due account of the truth contained in old Hesiod's saying about the folly of those who know not how much more the half is than the whole.

# MR KEYNES'S ATTACK ON ECONOMISTS[*]
## H. D. Henderson

Mr. Keynes's new book presents the reviewer with an almost insoluble problem. It is avowedly a technical book, addressed, as Mr. Keynes tells us in the Preface, to his fellow-economists. Moreover, it is a very difficult technical book, involving much novel terminology, a considerable use of mathematical symbols, and above all an elaborate abstract argument which is sustained as a connected whole through more than 332 of the 384 pages. It is a book in short, for specialists, not for the general reader. None the less the general reader will wish to know much more *about* this book than he was content to know about, say, Mr. Keynes's own *Treatise on Probability*. For here is the most famous of living economists claiming to have demolished a large part of the classical theory of economics which he has himself taught for most of his life; and this classical theory, as he is careful to insist, is no esoteric affair but 'dominates the economic thought, both practical and theoretical, of the governing and academic classes of this generation, as it has for a hundred years past'. What, then, the general reader will ask, is the gist of Mr. Keynes's argument and is he right or is he wrong, or is it a matter on which opinions may legitimately differ? What is the issue and on what does it turn? To answer these questions, however crudely, in a review of tolerable length, is a difficult, and perhaps a hopeless, task.

Mr. Keynes accuses classical economic theory of proceeding on the assumption that the resources of production are, subject to certain qualifications, fully employed. It recognises, of course, that there may be a considerable amount of unemployment due to 'various inexactnesses of adjustment', *e.g.*, demand may shift from the products of one set of industries to those of another, and the shifting of labour required as a consequence may be a slow and painful process. Moreover, certain modern economists, notably Professor Pigou, have argued that there

* From *Spectator*, vol. 156 (14 February 1936), p. 263.

may be an additional element of unemployment, if the level of wages is maintained at an unduly high level. Subject to the foregoing, classical economic theory asserts that economic forces will work so as to bring the demand for labour into equilibrium with its supply. Mr. Keynes denies this, and maintains that unemployment may exist on a large scale, over and above 'frictional unemployment' and any 'voluntary unemployment', as the result of a general deficiency of 'effective demand'. Not only may unemployment occur for this reason; it is in fact likely to occur, remedial policy apart, as the normal rule; and its scale is likely to be larger the wealthier society becomes.

To elucidate the issue, we must turn to the mysteries of savings, investment, and the rate of interest. Mr. Keynes founds his argument on the 'fundamental psychological law' that the wealthier a man becomes the larger is the proportion of his income which he will seek to save. As society becomes more prosperous accordingly, the members of it will spend a diminishing proportion of their incomes on current consumption. If investment increases correspondingly, no harm is done; full employment may still be maintained. But, argues Mr. Keynes, there is no reason why investment should increase correspondingly; and, if it does not, unemployment will result, the productive powers of society will not be fully employed, and its aggregate income will be diminished.

What has the classical theory to say to this? It admits, of course, that this may happen for a period, as the phenomenon of a trade depression. But it asserts that such a state of affairs is not a 'position of equilibrium', and that there are corrective forces, which, however slowly and clumsily they may work, would prevent its indefinite continuance. It argues that, on the assumptions made, the supply of capital would exceed the demand for it in the capital market, that this would lead to a fall in the rate of interest, and that a lower rate of interest would check saving and stimulate investment until equilibrium were restored. Mr. Keynes does not dispute that a lower rate of interest would stimulate investment, and that it might check saving. On the contrary, he is emphatic that a reduction in the rate of interest is, in principle, the right and essential remedy. But he denies absolutely that natural economic forces would do anything whatever to bring about a fall in the rate of interest. He denies indeed that there would be any tendency for the supply of capital to exceed the demand. What would happen in the circumstances supposed is that employment would be deficient, so that aggregate incomes would decline, and the capacity to save would be diminished. It is anathema now to Mr. Keynes to suggest that savings may exceed investment. *That* he insists is impossible, if the terms are correctly employed; and the point seems to have for him a more than terminological importance. The rate of interest has become for him an 'independent variable'. It is not determined, as orthodox theory argues, by the relations between the demand for and the supply of capital, but by quite different influences, namely the quantity of money 'in conjunction with liquidity preference', *i.e.*, the extent to which people choose to keep their resources in cash or some other liquid form.

Mr. Keynes has much to say about the important part that may be played by variations in 'liquidity preference', as, for instance, by the spreading in an atmosphere of distrust of a disposition to hoard idle bank-balances; and his analysis of this matter forms in my opinion a valuable section of his book. But the possibility of such variations represents essentially a qualification of his main argument, the practical moral to which they point being the uncongenial one of the importance of maintaining 'confidence'. Subject to possible changes in this factor, it is Mr. Keynes's view that the rate of interest is determined by the quantity of money made available by the Central Bank, and not in the least by whether we are a thrifty or an extravagant people. If we are unduly thrifty we shall have heavy unemployment as a normal state of affairs; if we are sufficiently extravagant, we may maintain 'full employment'; but it will make no difference in either case to the rate of interest. This is the real crux of the controversy; and it is here, in my judgement, that Mr. Keynes fails to make out his case.

I should formulate as follows the answer of the classical school. They would agree that over a short-period monetary conditions exercise an important influence on the rate of interest and a dominating influence upon short-term rates. They would point out that depression and heavy unemployment will serve (subject to 'liquidity' complications) to bring about conditions of abundant bank-money, so that the natural corrective forces, though they may work far less smoothly than used to be supposed, are none the less really there. On the other hand, they would insist, the influence of changes in the quantity of money on the rate of interest is purely transitional. Other things (including the state of 'liquidity preference') being equal, an increase in the quantity of money, operating through the medium of lower interest-rates, will set in motion a tendency towards higher commodity prices, this will involve an increased use of money, and when prices have reached a level appropriate to the increased quantity of money, the complicating influence, so to speak, of money will be removed, and the more fundamental factors of the supply of capital, arising from the capacity and propensity to save, and the demand for capital, arising from the opportunities for investment, will resume their sway as the determinants of the rate of interest. There is nothing that Mr. Keynes has to say in his chapters on prices and wages which seems to me in any way destructive of this explanation; and though it may seem to the general reader in some respects remote from reality, this is due to the great short-term importance of those complications about changes in 'liquidity preference' which qualify Mr. Keynes's main assertions as much as those of the classical school.

Much of what Mr. Keynes has written in this book is a real and much-needed contribution to short-term economic analysis. But, as I have indicated, the practical implications of what he has to contribute in this field are of a conservative nature which is distasteful to him; and I suspect that it is largely a conflict between his desires and his intellectual apprehensions in the short-term sphere that has led him to undertake so fierce an offensive against classical long-term theory. It is true, in my judgement, that the long-term morals of the economic troubles of recent years are different (and decidedly less conservative) from the short-term ones. But it is unnecessary, in order to establish them, to discard the classical theory of economics for a brand-new system of thought.

# Employment and Money: Dilemmas of Saving and Spending*
Anonymous

Mr. Keynes issues his new book in a challenging fashion. It avowedly probes the foundations of the economic and monetary structure of contemporary society, and it claims to refute in certain important particulars the accepted, or 'classical', system of thought, on which so many of our institutions are based. It is published at the remarkably low price of 5s.; and though it is mainly addressed, as Mr. Keynes says, to his fellow economists, and is consequently in parts difficult and technical, there are large sections of the book, written in Mr. Keynes's lucid and brilliant style, which will delight the ordinary reader. And its conclusions are so important and so squarely based on the twin supports of analysis and experience, that it indisputably deserves the widest and most scrupulous consideration.

Five and a half years ago, in the first year of the great depression, Mr. Keynes published his two-volume 'Treatise on Money', arguing the case – which scarcely anybody would now deny – that the cyclical booms and depressions of modern times are mainly monetary in origin. His main contention was that an excess of saving over investment tends to cause falling prices and depression, and an excess of investment over saving to cause rising prices and a 'boom'; and that the aim of monetary policy should be to preserve that 'natural' rate of interest which would equate saving and investment. There was one important flaw in this argument. It was perfectly possible, on Mr. Keynes's definitions, for saving and investment to be equal and for huge unemployment to exist at the same time – and continue to exist indefinitely. The experience of the depression has made this so plain that Mr. Keynes has developed his analysis so as to place the main emphasis on full employment as the criterion of a successful monetary policy. It is the great and rare distinction of this book that it concentrates attention

* From *Times Literary Supplement*, no. 1780 (14 March 1936), p. 213.

on two conceptions: first the direct dependence of the volume of employment on monetary policy, and secondly the vital importance of 'effective demand' – *i.e.*, the total stream of money being spent on consumers' and capital goods. Mr. Keynes starts by examining the teaching of the 'classical economics' on these two points. He first considers the once accepted, though already discredited, view that if unemployment exists wages must be 'too high', and that the cure for unemployment is to reduce them. The basis for this view is of course the assumption that there must be a certain 'economic' level of real wages, at which alone full employment will be realized. This view, Mr. Keynes points out, has two fatal defects as an analysis of the contemporary world. First, it implies that any rise in the cost of living, which must reduce real wages, will inevitably lead to increased unemployment; and this we all know to be untrue. The moral of this is that labour often cares for money wages more than real wages, and that a disequilibrium between costs and prices can accordingly often be cured by a rise in prices and the cost of living, but not a fall in wages. Secondly, the advocates of wage reductions, who assume that 'other things are equal', forget that they are not equal because the reduction in wages itself reduces effective demand. The relation between money wages and employment, in fact, is much more complex than the accepted view has implied.

The link between them is effective demand. Mr. Keynes's analysis of the interaction of effective demand and employment is complicated; but it may perhaps be summarized without undue distortion as follows. The amount of labour which each business man is prepared to employ depends on the proceeds or 'profit' he hopes to earn. For each amount of labour employed, however, a certain total of costs will be incurred. If, therefore, full employment is to be attained, effective demand must be at that level which will enable business men to cover all the costs involved in employing all the available labour and also to earn such a profit as will induce them to employ it. There is, consequently, a certain level of effective – that is, money – demand below which full employment cannot possibly be attained. It must, of course, be realized that 'full employment' does not mean the absence of unemployment caused by 'frictional' factors – *i.e.*, the maladjustment of labour between different industries, the sudden loss of a country's export markets and so forth. What in turn determines the volume of effective demand? Mr. Keynes lays it down as a 'fundamental psychological law' that as a community's income increases it will spend more, but not as much more as the increase in its income. For it will also save more. But if it saves more and the extra saving is not spent on capital goods, effective demand will fall below the level compatible with full employment. If full employment is to be maintained, therefore, we must ensure that investment in capital must keep pace with the increase in savings. At this point a complexity is introduced into the argument which, it must be feared, will confuse many of Mr. Keynes's readers. In the 'Treatise on Money' divergences between saving (*i.e.*, refraining from consumption) and investment (*i.e.*, the purchase of capital goods) were the crux of the analysis. In the present book Mr. Keynes triumphantly demonstrates that such divergences cannot occur; and yet he appears to be assuming throughout most of the rest of the book that they can. The clue to this apparent inconsistency seems to be that Mr. Keynes now defines investment in such a way that an increase of unsold stocks in shops counts as an increase in investment. Now though this may be formally correct according to Mr. Keynes's definition, it is so far removed from the normal sense of the word investment that it will probably assist Mr. Keynes's less expert readers to assume that saving can diverge from investment.

It may thus be agreed that, when saving increases, effective demand can only be maintained by increasing either consumption or investment. Mr. Keynes is inclined to neglect consumption on the ground that, with our existing economic and financial institutions, consumers' subsidies financed by new money are impracticable. He consequently first analyses the factors determining investment, and decides that its volume depends on the rate of interest and the 'marginal efficiency of capital'. The 'marginal efficiency of capital' may be summarily interpreted to mean the prospective yield of the investment of a given sum of money in a unit of capital equipment over the whole period of its life. If the prospective yield is high enough to cover the rate at which money can be borrowed, and also provide for risk, expenses of management, &c., investment will go on. Since, therefore, the expected yield depends mainly on physical and technical facts, it is mainly through the rate of interest that the level of investment can most easily be influenced by public policy. What then determines the level of the rate of interest? Here Mr. Keynes introduces a peculiar argument which will probably be regarded by many critics as the weakest part of the book, though fortunately his main conclusions do not depend upon it. The 'classical view' of the rate of interest would be that it is determined by the supply and demand for saving; that it is the 'price' of saving or 'waiting' – *i.e.*, the postponement of consumption. Mr. Keynes summarily denies this, on the ground that hoarding involves postponement of consumption but is not rewarded by interest. Surely, however, the fact that some people postpone consumption without receiving interest does not show that the great majority of savers would continue to save in the absence of all interest whatever? Moreover, Mr. Keynes proceeds to maintain that the rate of interest depends not on the supply of saving, but mainly if not entirely on the volume of money created by the banks and on the willingness of the public to hold money in preference to interest-bearing assets (their 'liquidity preference'). Now it is only too true that *in the short run* the rate of interest mainly depends on the quantity of money rather than on the supply of savings. But to erect this important short-term maxim into an absolute long-term theory of interest rates, seems, to say the least, dubious.

For the purpose of practical policy, however, which Mr. Keynes has mainly in mind, it may be admitted that the rate of interest depends on the quantity of money created by the banking authorities, combined with the willingness of the public to hold that money. More important still, the influence of interest rates on investment and employment are greatly illuminated by Mr. Keynes's analysis. And that analysis is forcibly confirmed by the experience of the last four years throughout the sterling area.

Mr. Keynes's significant conclusion, therefore, is that where 'cyclical' unemployment exists, the rate of interest should be pushed down until only 'frictional' unemployment remains. The process of lowering interest rates should stop at the point where full employment has been reached and prices continue to rise. Mr. Keynes admits, however, that there is always the alternative of increasing not investment but consumption. He is doubtful of the practicability of this; but is strongly in favour of increasing social service expenditure financed out of taxation levied on big incomes and estates.

It may be that Mr. Keynes's main contentions are less revolutionary than he is inclined to indicate. For the most valuable contributions of the book seem to be its concentration on employment and effective demand: its contention that, where unemployment prevails, interest rates should be reduced: and its conclusion that in so far as this is ineffective, consumption should be expanded by redistributive taxation. For these reasons the book appears as essentially a development of the general economic analysis which Mr. R. G. Hawtrey and Mr. Keynes himself have been building up for many years past. Or, more accurately, perhaps, it might be regarded as a synthesis of their views with those of Mr. J. A. Hobson.

# Specialist Academic Journals

# [REVIEW OF] THE GENERAL THEORY OF EMPLOYMENT, INTEREST AND MONEY*
## Charles O. Hardy

This volume embodies a critical examination of the classical
theory of the relationships between the monetary and non-
monetary factors determining the flow of money income, the
volume of employment, the rate of interest and the levels of
consumption and investment, together with an elaborate
analysis of the inter-relations of these factors along lines which
differ sharply from the classical approach. In general the
Keynes doctrine as here outlined is an elaboration of concepts
that were envisaged by Malthus and Karl Marx; but the framework of the argument is largely new. The break with accepted
theory is sharp; for the new doctrine denies (a) that the demand
price of industrial output as a whole must be equal to its
supply price; (b) that the rate of interest is the price which
equilibrates the supply of savings with the rate of investment;
(c) that unemployment is due merely to frictional disturbances
plus unwillingness to work at the prevailing wage rate; (d) that
the lowering of money wages tends to increase the volume of
employment and of output; (e) the quantity theory of money.
It also involves a qualified acceptance of the mercantilist position with respect to the balance of foreign payments.

It is impossible in the compass of a brief review to summarize
the chain of argument by which Mr. Keynes supports his conclusions, much less to discuss their validity. The chief interest
in the book is in its purely theoretical sections, which in general
are fresh, coherent and consistent. There is no attempt at
statistical verification, and concrete data are used for illustra-
tive purposes only in very sketchy fashion. The criticism of
rival views is far from exhaustive, and is sometimes super-
cilious. The conclusions as to social policy are not satisfactorily
integrated with the theory. All these things, however, are of

* From *American Economic Review*, vol. 26 (September 1936), pp. 490–93.

secondary importance, if the book marks an advance in theoretical analysis, as I believe it does.

The theory may be outlined as follows, though I do not suppose Mr. Keynes would accept this as an adequate statement of his most important findings:

(1) The concept of the rate of interest as a price equilibrating the demand for and supply of savings breaks down, because savers have a choice between hoarding their savings in cash and putting them at the disposal of the investment market. The rate of interest therefore does not equilibrate the demand for liquid capital with the supply of saving, but rather with that of 'not-hoarding'. The amount saved is a function of income and of the propensity to consume, while the amount lent is a function of the supply of money and of the strength of 'liquidity preference'. The investors' demand for funds depends upon the marginal efficiency of capital, by which is meant not the actual, but the anticipated, marginal productivity of capital. An increase of income normally leads to an increased willingness and ability to save but also to an increased desire for liquid balances. With increasing income the absorption of savings through the attempt of savers to increase liquid balances leads to a decrease in the total flow of funds through investment and consumptive channels combined, and hence to decrease in income. Individuals endeavor to save more than they invest (otherwise than in cash balances) but total saving does not exceed total investment because the withdrawal of funds from circulation at one point forces either dissaving or decreased income and decreased saving at some other point.

(2) A decrease in the volume of funds flowing through the markets necessitates either a decline in the volume of employment or a fall in the wage rate. A fall in the wage rate, which would restore equilibrium in the labor market if income remained constant, fails to bring about equilibrium because it tends to cause a further decrease in income, and a further decrease in the amount of investment plus consumption. The price system cannot clear the market for labor.

(3) An increase in the quantity of money tends to remedy the situation in two ways: (a) because through lower interest rates it tends to bring about equilibrium between the marginal efficiency of capital and the rate of return necessary to induce savers not to hoard; and (b) because it supplies additional means of satisfying liquidity preference. But there is danger

that the very process of increasing the quantity of money may impair business confidence and enhance liquidity preference. There is more hope of a solution through the direct encouragement of investment, or of consumption, by state action.

The essential contribution of the book, as the reviewer reads it, is in the greatly increased emphasis which Keynes lays upon liquidity preference as a disturbing element in the equilibrium of the market. But liquidity preference needs much further analysis. It involves choices not merely between cash balances and loans, but also between forms of lending. Moreover, investment of borrowed funds involves loss of liquidity for the borrower as well as the lender, so that a general increase of liquidity preference means a decrease in the demand for, as well as the supply of, loanable funds. An increase in liquidity preference without a change in the money supply will actually lower the market rate on instruments (like short-term bills) which require the minimum sacrifice of liquidity for lenders and the maximum for borrowers, while it makes funds dear or unavailable for illiquid loans. A change in liquidity preference does not merely change *the* rate of interest, but tilts a whole scale of rates. The analysis on pages 180–181 breaks down because the assumption of an increase in investment without a change in liquidity preference is impossible. An increase in willingness to invest *is* a change in liquidity preference. Moreover, the money supply is affected directly by changes in the liquidity preferences of bankers and bank borrowers. Neglect of these factors has involved Keynes in difficulties comparable to those which, as he points out emphatically (p. 179), arise from the assumption that the demand curve for capital can shift without a change in total income.

Exception may be taken also to much of Keynes's argument to the effect that wage cuts tend to reduce total income and thus the volume of employment (pp. 262–64), though the conclusion may be correct. The transfer of income from wage earners to other factors is likely to diminish the propensity to consume, and hence to increase the volume of savings; but the essential point is not the amount of savings, but the amount used to satisfy liquidity preference. Do laborers hoard a larger or smaller proportion of their savings than do other savers? The point that if a reduction of wages leads to the expectation of further wage reduction it will have the short-run effect of discouraging investment is equally applicable to reductions of interest rates, which Keynes regards as wholly favorable. The point that the reduction in the wages bill will diminish the need for cash balances for income and business purposes is sound only on the assumption that total income will be reduced, which is precisely the point to be proved. Keynes's final point – namely, 'that the depressing influence on entrepreneurs of their greater burden of debt may partly offset any cheerful reactions from the reduction of wages' – is also circular. Price reductions do not increase the burden of debt if they are merely the reflection of cost reductions. Nor is the real burden of a national debt increased merely because prices and wages are lower, unless total income is lower. The argument thus assumes the conclusion.

# [FROM] MR KEYNES' THEORY OF EMPLOYMENT*
## J. R. Hicks

The reviewer of this book is beset by two contrary temptations. On the one hand, he can accept directly Mr. Keynes' elaborate disquisitions about his own theory, and its place in the development of economics; praising or blaming the alleged more than Jevonian revolution. Or, on the other hand, he can concentrate upon investigating these disquisitions, and tracing (perhaps) a pleasing degree of continuity and tradition, surviving the revolution from the *ancien régime*. But it seems better to avoid such questions, and to try to consider the new theory on its merits.

First of all then, what is the new theory about? It is presented to us, primarily, as a theory of employment; but before the book is ended, both author and reader are convinced that it is not only a theory of employment. It is sometimes presented as a theory of 'output in general'; sometimes as a theory of 'shifting equilibrium'. And the reader, at least, will take some time to get out of the habit of regarding it as a theory of money, for it is evidently a further development and superior re-formulation of those original ideas which tantalised and vexed us in the *Treatise*.

It may be suggested that the relation between these different aspects is as follows. The new theory is a theory of employment, in so far as the problem of employment and unemployment is the most urgent practical problem to which this sort of theoretical improvement is relevant. It is a theory of output in general *vis-à-vis* Marshall, who took into account many of the sort of complications which concern Mr. Keynes, but took them into account only with reference to a single industry. It is a theory of shifting equilibrium *vis-à-vis* the static or stationary theories of general equilibrium, such as those of Ricardo, Böhm-Bawerk or Pareto. It is a theory of money, in

* From *Economic Journal*, vol. 46 (June 1936), pp. 238–42, 253.

so far as it includes monetary theory, bringing money out of its isolated position as a separate subject into an integral relation with general economics.

Probably the most striking, to a casual reader, of the theoretical doctrines of this book is that which proclaims the necessary equality of Savings and Investment. This looks like a decided recantation of one of the most fundamental principles of the *Treatise on Money*, but inspection shows that it is nothing of the sort. It is merely a change in definition – but a change in definition which marks a very important change in point of view.

In the *Treatise*, Mr. Keynes was still to a considerable extent under the influence of the traditional approach to problems of the Trade Cycle. Ordinary (static) economic theory, so the old argument went, explains to us the working of the economic system in 'normal' conditions. Booms and slumps, however, are deviations from this norm, and are thus to be explained by some disturbing cause. Such theories therefore ran in terms of deviations: deviations between market and natural rates of interest, deviations between the actual money supply and some neutral money, forced saving, deviation between saving and investment.

The present theory breaks away from the whole of this range of ideas. It is no longer allowed that ordinary economic theory can give a correct analysis of even normal conditions; the things it leaves out of account are too important. But if there is no norm which we have understood, it is useless to discuss deviations from it. The changing, progressing, fluctuating economy has to be studied on its own, and cannot usefully be referred to the norm of a static state.

The new definitions of saving and investment reflect this new point of view. They are defined with reference to the changing economy itself, and have no element of normal profits hidden away in them.

They are equal because – and this takes us near the heart of Mr. Keynes' method – even in a changing economy, supplies and demands are equal. They are equal so long as we define supply as that amount of a commodity which sellers are willing to offer at a particular date in the market conditions of that date; unsold stocks being unsold because sellers prefer selling them later to selling them at a lower price now. These stocks being reckoned as part of future supply, not current supply, it follows that current supply and current demand must be equal – just because every transaction has two sides.

We can even reckon prices as being determined by current demand and supply, so long as we emphasise the word *current*, and exclude goods held over for the future. Current supply is then largely determined by people's willingness to hold goods over for the future, and that depends upon their expectations of the future.

There thus emerges a peculiar, but very significant, type of analysis. If we assume given, not only the tastes and resources ordinarily assumed given in static theory, but also people's anticipations of the future, it is possible to regard demands and supplies as determined by these tastes, resources and anticipations, and prices as determined by demands and supplies. Once the missing element – anticipations – is added, equilibrium analysis can be used, not only in the remote stationary conditions to which many economists have found themselves driven back, but even in the real world, even in the real world in 'disequilibrium'.

This is the general method of this book; it may be reckoned the first of Mr. Keynes' discoveries. It is, as a matter of fact, not altogether a new discovery, for several lines of inquiry have been pointing this way in recent years. One may refer, perhaps, to the writings of the econometrists,[1] who have enlarged the validity of their equations by explicitly introducing anticipations. And an even closer analogy to Mr. Keynes' work is to be found in the methods which have been common in Swedish economics for several years.[2] But this is only to say that he has had his forerunners, and that there are not a few centres of economic thought where this book will meet with a very sympathetic reception.

From the standpoint of pure theory, the use of the method of expectations is perhaps the most revolutionary thing about this book; but Mr. Keynes has other innovations to make, innovations directed towards making the method of anticipations more usable. That there was a great need for these

---

[1] *E.g.* C. F. Roos, *Dynamic Economics*.

[2] Lindahl, 'Prisbildningsproblemets uppläggning' (*Ekonomisk Tidskrift*, 1929), *Penningpolitikens medel* (1930); Myrdal, 'Der Gleichgewichtsbegriff als Instrument der Geldtheoretischen Analyse', in *Beiträge zur Geldtheorie* (1933). My own article, 'Wages and Interest' (ECONOMIC JOURNAL, September 1935), was written to some extent under Swedish influence.

latter innovations, no one will deny who has considered the great complexity of the factors determining output in general even under static assumptions – complexity which is likely to be increased when the assumptions are generalised. A great part of Mr. Keynes' work may be regarded as an endeavour to cut through this tangle, by grouping complex factors together into bundles. This process is one of drastic simplification, but it is necessary if the theory is to become an instrument of practical thought.

Before going on to these simplifications, we may, however, insert some remarks about the general method of expectations, remarks which apply not only to Mr. Keynes' work, but also to all other uses of the method, which have been made or may be made in the future.

The point of the method is that it reintroduces determinateness into a process of change. The output of goods and the employment of labour, together with the whole price-system, are determined over any short period,[3] once the stock of goods (goods of all kinds, including capital goods) existing at the beginning of the period, is given, and once people's expectations of future market conditions are given too. Further, we can deduce, by ordinary economic reasoning, what the outputs, employment and prices would be if expectations were different, capital equipment different, tastes different, and so on. But all that this reasoning gives us is hypothetical results; we can deduce what the system of prices and production would be *at this date*, if the fundamental determining factors were different. The method is thus an admirable one for analysing the impact effect of disturbing causes; but it is less reliable for analysing the further effects.

It is, indeed, not impossible to say something about further effects; for we can deduce what the stocks of goods will be at the end of the period if the decisions are carried out, and this gives us a basis for the analysis of a second period. But it is probable that the change in actual production during the first period will influence the expectations ruling at the end of that period; and there is no means of telling what that influence will be. The more we go into the future, the greater this source

---

[3] The period being taken short enough for us to be able to neglect changes in expectations within it. Its length will therefore depend upon the degree of precision we are aiming at.

of error, so that there is a danger, when it is applied to long periods, of the whole method petering out.

This source of trouble, it should be observed, comes in from the first. It is unrealistic to assume that an important change in data – say the introduction or extension of a public works policy – will leave expectations unchanged, even immediately. But this generally means only that there is a psychological unknown, affecting the magnitude of the impact effect. As more time is allowed, more and more scope is allowed for such variations, both in degree and kind. We must not expect the most elaborate economic analysis to enable us to see very far ahead.

Mr. Keynes is usually very careful in allowing for this sort of difficulty. But it has to be recognised that, for this reason, his analysis does not settle nearly as many questions as we might hope. Even if his theory is generally accepted, there will still be room for wide differences of opinion about the consequences of particular policies . . .

Thus, whatever we decide in the end to think about the Diminishing Marginal Efficiency of Capital, this population point is enough in itself to establish the high significance of Mr. Keynes' theory of long-period unemployment. Whether or not we are already engulfed in the dangers he diagnoses is a thing which can be disputed; but there is little doubt that we are heading for those dangers. They are, indeed, one aspect – perhaps the most important economic aspect – of that problem of adapting to less progressive conditions the institutions of a traditionally expansive civilisation, which already vexes us on many sides.

The technique of this work is, on the whole, conservative: more conservative than in the *Treatise*. It is the technique of Marshall, but it is applied to problems never tackled by Marshall and his contemporaries. In all this region they were content to take over the conclusions of the Ricardians, and never thoroughly tested these conclusions by means of their own technique. That testing has now been done, and the Ricardian conclusions found badly wanting. Thus we have to change, not so much our methods of analysis, as some important elements in the outlook which we have inherited from the classics. We have to realise that we can have too much, even of the economic virtues. It was indeed a happy age that could think the contrary; but the nineteenth century could only afford Ricardo because it sinned so luxuriantly against Malthus. To-day we must find a new sin; if it can give us a century before the day of reckoning it will have done well.

# [FROM] MR J. M. KEYNES' GENERAL THEORY OF EMPLOYMENT, INTEREST AND MONEY*
## A. C. Pigou

### I

When, in 1919, he wrote *The Economic Consequences of the Peace*, Mr. Keynes did a good day's work for the world, in helping it back towards sanity. But he did a bad day's work for himself as an economist. For he discovered then, and his sub-conscious mind has not been able to forget since, that the best way to win attention for one's own ideas is to present them in a matrix of sarcastic comment upon other people. This method has long been a routine one among political pamphleteers. It is less appropriate, and fortunately less common, in scientific discussion. Einstein actually did for Physics what Mr. Keynes believes himself to have done for Economics. He developed a far-reaching generalisation, under which Newton's results can be subsumed as a special case. But he did not, in announcing his discovery, insinuate, through carefully barbed sentences, that Newton and those who had hitherto followed his lead were a gang of incompetent bunglers. The example is illustrious: but Mr. Keynes has not followed it. The general tone *de haut en bas* and the patronage extended to his old master Marshall[1] are particularly to be regretted. It is not by this manner of writing that his desire to convince his fellow economists (p. vi) is best promoted.

### II

The group of persons whom, on this occasion, he parades as a foil, are the 'classical economists', with, as particular examples, 'Ricardo, Marshall, Edgeworth and Professor Pigou'. The device of lumping all these persons together is an ingenious

* From *Economica*, vol. 3 (May 1936), pp. 115–22, 131–2.

[1] Cf. the sarcasm – quite irrelevant to the argument – on p. 184.

one; for it enables the shortcomings of one to be attributed to all. For example, Professor Pigou, in a book on Unemployment, which is 'the only detailed account of the classical theory of employment which exists', (p. 7) has committed a variety of sins. Professor Pigou is a classical economist; therefore the classical economists have committed these sins! Moreover, when one of the arraigned persons has palpably not made a particular mistake, the method of lumping enables Mr. Keynes to say that he *ought* to have made it, and that, in not making it, he has been false to the 'logic' of his own school – has allowed his 'good common sense to overbear his bad theory', (p. 277). Finally, this device has, for anyone adopting it, the great advantage that it renders any complete reply impossible.[2] When a man goes on a sniping expedition in a large village, nobody will have the patience to track down the course of his every bullet. The best that can be done is to illustrate his methods by selected examples and to enquire in a broad way into his total accomplishment.

It is convenient to begin with a relatively small matter. On p. 20 Mr. Keynes quotes a sentence from *The Economics of Industry* written by Mr. and Mrs. Marshall in 1879. The sentence runs: – 'It is not good for trade to have dresses made of material that wears out quickly. For, if people did not spend their means on buying new dresses, they would spend them on giving employment to labour in some other way.' This sentence is cited by Mr. Keynes as a proof that Marshall at that time, though in later life he became 'very cautious and evasive' – the second epithet is characteristic – believed that 'an act of individual saving inevitably leads to a parallel act of investment' (p. 21). Now, it must be conceded that the sentence quoted is, as it stands, taken in isolation, inexact. But that Marshall was speaking in a limited context, and did *not* mean that a man *inevitably* expends on something the whole of his income, is apparent to anyone who will read the book to the end. For, in connection with general industrial fluctuations, which, after all, is the proper place for these considerations, it is explicitly stated: – 'Though men have the power to purchase,

---

[2] On pp. 138 and 148 Mr. Keynes goes one better and brings charges of ignoring, or not analyzing carefully, what the present writer had imagined to be familiar commonplaces, against 'most discussions' and against 'economists' without further specification!

they may not choose to use it.'[3] Mr. Keynes had himself quoted this sentence in another connection in a footnote on p. 19, but nevertheless has allowed the statement on p. 21, cited above, to stand. Here is a second charge against Marshall, this time much more important. The classical economists, speaking through him, discuss the money rate of interest on the basis of an analysis of distribution conducted exclusively in real terms. Now it is obvious that the money rate of interest cannot be determined by real factors alone. There is one equation short. The classical economists, again in the person of Marshall, failed to perceive this. Consequently their whole analysis breaks down. 'The perplexity which I find in Marshall's account of the matter [Interest Theory] is fundamentally due, I think, to the incursion of the concept "interest", which belongs to a monetary economy, into a treatise which takes no account of money. Interest has no business to turn up in Marshall's *Principles of Economics* – it belongs to another branch of the subject' (p. 189).[4] Now read Marshall: 'Throughout the present volume we are supposing, in the absence of any statement to the contrary, that all values are expressed in terms of money of fixed purchasing power, just as astronomers have taught us to determine the beginning or the ending of the day with reference, not to the actual sun, but to a *mean sun*, which is supposed to move uniformly throughout the heaven.'[5] Thus Marshall has deliberately and in express terms introduced a specific condition about money – i.e. provided the missing equation – the necessity for which Mr. Keynes accuses him of failing to perceive.

[3] *The Economics of Industry*, 2nd Edition (I have no copy of the 1st Edition), p. 154.

[4] In the course of this discussion of Marshall's Interest Theory there is a curious minor lapse. Marshall had written: 'An extensive increase in the demand for capital will, therefore, be met for a time, not so much by an increase of supply, as by a rise in the rate of interest.' Mr. Keynes comments: 'Why not by a rise in the supply price of capital goods? Suppose, for example, that the extensive increase in the demand for capital in general is due to a *fall* in the rate of interest' (p. 187). Is it not evident that this is just the thing which in the context must *not* be supposed? Marshall was speaking of a *rise of* the demand curve for capital. Mr. Keynes retorts by speaking of a movement *along* a stationary demand curve.

[5] *Principles of Economics*, p. 593. There are similar passages on pp. 69 and 150 of Mr. and Mrs. Marshall's *Economics of Industry* referred to above.

Misrepresentation of a like character is directed against the classical school in the person of Professor Pigou. In reading chapters by that writer in the *Theory of Unemployment* about the *elasticity of* the real demand schedule for labour, Mr. Keynes fails to find any reference to the consequences for unemployment of changes in the *position* of that schedule, and comments: 'It is, indeed, strange that Professor Pigou should have supposed that he could furnish a theory of unemployment which involves no reference' to such changes (p. 275). Had Professor Pigou really done this, 'strange' would have been much too weak a word. In fact in later parts of the book these matters *are* discussed (particularly in Part V, Chapter 9, and Part III, Chapter 15), and in the Preface it is explained that further discussion is dispensed with because it is already provided at length in the writer's *Industrial Fluctuations*.

There remains Mr. Keynes' fundamental charge against the classical school as a whole. This may be set out thus. According to that school the aggregate quantity of labour employed at any time is, subject to agreed qualifications, determined at such a level that the real wage rate offered by employers is equal to the real wage rate which workpeople ask for as a condition of that quantity of labour being supplied; broadly it is determined at the intersection of the real demand curve and the real supply curve of labour. Now 'involuntary employment', as defined by Mr. Keynes (p. 15), prevails if a rise in money prices relatively to money wages would bring about an increase in the volume of employment. 'So long as the classical postulates hold good, unemployment, which is in the above sense involuntary, cannot occur' (p. 16). For the classical school must hold that, the real supply schedule being given, a rise in money prices, unaccompanied by an equivalent rise in money wages, implying, as it does, a fall in the real wage-rate offered, will cause the amount of labour coming forward to decrease. 'This strange supposition apparently underlies Professor Pigou's *Theory of Unemployment*, and it is what all members of the orthodox school are tacitly assuming' (p. 13). Again: 'It is important to emphasise that the whole of Professor Pigou's book is written on the assumption (Mr. Keynes' italics) *that any rise in the cost of living, however modest, relatively to the money wage will cause the withdrawal from the labour market of a number of workers greater than that of all the existing unemployed*' (p. 277). The hiatus here is glaring. In order to demonstrate the futility of the classical economists, Mr. Keynes needs to father on them a *second* postulate; namely, that monetary happenings are incapable of *affecting* the real supply schedule of labour. For, of course, if they can affect it, they are competent to modify the volume of employment *in spite of* the real demand price and the real supply price of labour standing always in equilibrium. Mr. Keynes completely fails to see the need for fathering this postulate on them in order to validate his charge. If he had seen this need, he could not, of course, have met it. One 'classical economist' at least, in a book which he particularly criticises, has been at pains, not indeed to refute that postulate, for it never occurred to him that anyone would assert it, but to enquire *how* – in the short period – monetary happenings *do* alter the real supply[6] schedule of labour.

In my first draft a paragraph stood here characterizing in frank terms this macédoine of misrepresentations, from which I have extracted sample prints. The temptation to let that paragraph remain has been strong. But

> Why comes temptation but that man should mount,
> And master, and make crouch beneath his feet,
> And so stand pinnacled in triumph?

The reader has been given the facts. It is for him to pass judgment upon them.

### III

The positive parts of Mr. Keynes' discussion do not depend on the negative parts. Any bias that a reading of those parts may have generated in our minds must be firmly put aside, and the positive parts studied on their own merits. But here at once a serious obstacle is encountered. His argument is in places so obscure that the reader cannot be certain what precisely it is that he is intending to convey. That there should be this difficulty about Mr. Keynes' scientific writings about economics – it was present also in a less degree in the more theoretical parts of his *Treatise on Money* – is very curious. How is it that an author, whose powers of exposition enabled him to write on the philosophy of Probability in a way that amateurs could follow – not to say one whose vividness of phrase has made

---

[6] Cf. Pigou, *The Theory of Unemployment*, Part V, ch. 9.

him a valued contributor to the *Daily Mail*,[7] when he comes
to the subject to which he has devoted most attention, is barely
intelligible to many – for I am not alone in this – of his own
professional colleagues?
A part of the explanation is, beyond doubt, his loose and
inconsistent use of terms. Thus on page 5 (footnote) 'involuntary unemployment' is used in a different sense from that in
which it is defined on p. 15. On p. 5 'marginal product of
labour' is used for what, two lines lower down, becomes a
*value*, and on p. 6 is called 'value of the product attributable
to its marginal productivity'. On the same page we have 'the
utility of the marginal product', when what is meant is
the utility of the money wage. Again, on p. 5 the classical
economists are said to maintain that the utility of the wage is
equal to the disutility of the marginal employment, whereas
on pp. 14 and 15 it is the real wage itself, not its utility, that
is set over against the disutility of marginal employment.
Again, on p. 28 there suddenly appears 'the propensity to
consume', a new entity which is not defined till p. 90, while
no forward reference to the definition is given. But much more
serious examples of loose language occur in connection with
'liquidity preference' in Chapter XIII. At the beginning of that
chapter income means real income, and the demand for money
the real value that people choose to hold in money form; but,
later on, income means money income and the demand for
money some relation between the quantity of money and the
rate of money interest. Thus on p. 166 we read: 'An individual's
liquidity preference is given by a schedule of the amounts of
his resources, valued in terms of money or of wage units, which
he will wish to retain in the form of money in a given set of
conditions'; and on p. 167 the rate of interest is 'the "price"
which equilibrates the desire to hold wealth in the form of
cash with the available quantity of cash'. Here liquidity preference is, in effect, the Marshallian k, which, when real income
is given, depends, *ceteris paribus*, on the rate of interest. But
on p. 168 'liquidity preference is a potentiality or functional
tendency, which fixes the quantity of money [no longer the
real value held in the form of money], which the public will
hold when the rate of interest is given', and on p. 171 we have

[7] This poisoned dart is discharged – the skeleton must face the light – by one
who himself on one occasion yielded to the blandishments of the *Sunday
Express*!

'the schedule of liquidity preference relating the quantity of money to the rate of interest'.[8] When the Marshallian rabbit k has in this way become transmuted into a Keynsian fox, the hunter, faint but pursuing, suddenly sees it multiply itself by fission! On p. 119 he sees, flying before him over the greensward, *two* liquidity functions, one relating one portion of the quantity of money to quantity of income, the other relating a second portion to the rate of interest. What can any hunter feel but a wholly bewildered and half amused exasperation?

> As was the lot of the singer Apollo,
>   So hath the lot of his follower been,
> Beauty and youth through the valley to follow,
>   Winning no mead but a chaplet of green!

And even Apollo's nymph did not turn into *two* trees!

A second partial explanation of Mr. Keynes's obscurity is to be found, I think, in his desire to reach a stage of generality so high that everything must be discussed at the same time. For example, in his chapters on 'the propensity to consume' he wishes to consider what will happen in certain circumstances (i) if the money rate of wages is fixed, (ii) if it varies. The natural procedure would be to work out the problem first on the simpler hypothesis, and then to enquire how far the results reached need to be modified if the more complicated one is substituted for it. Mr. Keynes rolls the two enquiries together by asking, in effect, what will happen in the eventualities contemplated if *money income divided by money wage rate* is constant.[9] Since in fact different things will happen, or – not

[8] It is possible that 'quantity of money' is an extremely loose expression for 'proportion of money stock to money income'. If this is so, the confusion is merely verbal; for, of course, this proportion is identical with the proportion of real value held in money form to real income. But in a later passage Mr. Keynes writes: 'Men cannot be employed when the object of desire (i.e. money) is something which cannot be produced and the demand for which cannot be readily choked off' (p. 235). Here it seems clear that it is money itself, not merely a certain real value in the form of money, that, in Mr. Keynes' view, people desire to hold.

[9] It is, of course, obvious that to halve money wage-rates and to leave the sum spent on wages unchanged has the same effect on employment as to leave money wage-rates unchanged and to double this sum. But to double money income only implies doubling this sum in very special cases, i.e. if it has no effect on the quantity of employment or if the function describing labour's productivity (with the help of the given equipment) has one particular form.

to beg the question – since it is far from obvious that different things will *not* happen, when this quotient is constant because both money income and money wage rate are constant, and when it is constant because both are varying in the same proportion, the reader inevitably feels perplexed and insecure. There are many other examples of this method. Mr. Keynes' preference for attacking complex problems as wholes, instead of breaking them up and organising a methodical approach, makes the task of following his argument and disentangling his various assumptions exceedingly exacting.

A third partial explanation is the existence of a serious internal inconsistency among the premises with which he works. Thus on p. 114 he writes: 'The fluctuations in real income under consideration in this book are those which result from applying different quantities of employment (i.e. labour units) to a given capital equipment', and on p. 245 he says again that the quantity and quality of available equipment and existing technique are taken as given. But throughout the main part of his book he supposes that some new investment is being undertaken every year. It is evident that, if this is happening, capital equipment cannot be unchanged. He is assuming in fact a stationary state and at the same time a moving one. Moreover, on p. 335 he is found applying an analysis built up on the assumption of stable technique to a progressive state that is 'growing in wealth somewhat rapidly'. Nobody could make use of mutually inconsistent hypotheses in this way if he had achieved complete coherence among his ideas. The lack of clarity in Mr. Keynes' explanation is *mainly* due, I suggest, to a lack of clarity in his thought, a lack of clarity which he now himself recognises to have been present when he wrote the *Treatise on Money* but, naturally enough, now believes himself to have overcome.

In any event, whether this explanation is right or wrong, the fact of, and the difficulty resulting from, his obscurity remains. I am not confident of having fully grasped his meaning, and *may*, therefore, in attempting to evaluate his book, do injustice to it by neglecting or relegating to a subordinate place some element which he himself considers to be essential. I may even have missed, as has happened before now to critics of new work, some vital and path-breaking contribution to thought. None the less, the attempt must be made. Since, with a book of this character, a detailed running commentary would be both tedious and unilluminating, I shall not adopt that method, but shall build what I have to say round six dominant themes. These are the 'multiplier', the rate of interest, the problem of saving, the relation of money wages to real wages and employment, what I shall call Mr. Keynes' vision of the day of judgment, and his view that it is practicable by State and Bank action to abolish all unemployment other than what he conveniently calls frictional unemployment . . .

## IV

I am painfully conscious that this notice consists almost entirely of adverse criticism – adverse on the manner and matter of Mr. Keynes' comments upon other people, adverse on the form and content of his own major contributions. It is small atonement, I fear, to have confessed, as I have done on p. 122, a doubt whether I have fully grasped his meaning, or to add, as I do here, that on many secondary matters he has, as everybody acquainted with his writings would expect, made illuminating and suggestive observations. His discussion of the precise relationship between wages and prime costs (Chapter VI), his development of Mr. Hawtrey's point about the consequences of payments to depreciation account in excess of what is contemporaneously spent on renewals and repairs (Chapter VIII), his description of the precarious character of business forecasts and of the consequences of experts in these matters being chiefly interested in short-run developments (Chapter XII), are all admirable. 'The spectacle of modern investment markets has sometimes moved me towards the conclusion that to make the purchase of an investment permanent and indissoluble, like marriage, except by reason of death or other grave cause, might be a useful remedy for our contemporary evils' (p. 160). Admirable, too, is much of his 'Notes on the Trade Cycle'. Yet again, he has done good service to clarity by substituting new definitions of income and saving in place of those used in the *Treatise on Money*: while, by recognising (on p. 78) that Mr. Robertson's Hoarding, or excess of saving over investment, is equivalent to his own decrease of income, he has made it plain that in this field the matters still at issue have to do with verbal convenience rather than with fundamental principle. Finally, even those parts of his discussion which least command agreement are a strong stimulus to thought. We have watched an artist firing arrows at the moon. Whatever be thought of his marksmanship, we can all admire his virtuosity.

# [FROM REVIEW OF] THE GENERAL THEORY OF EMPLOYMENT, INTEREST AND MONEY*
## B. P. Adarkar

A reviewer's function is ordinarily threefold: to describe, to appreciate and to criticise. To describe Keynes's *General Theory* is perhaps the easiest task; to appreciate it fully in all its bearings, one must move on the same intellectual plane as Keynes; to criticise any part of it, one must indeed possess the boldness and the strength of an intellectual Hercules! For, indeed, this is one of the greatest of modern economic works, a fitting companion to Adam Smith's *Wealth of Nations*, Ricardo's *Principles of Political Economy*, Marshall's *Principles* and Pigou's *Economics of Welfare* – akin to these and yet dissimilar, inasmuch as its main theses, if they are finally accepted by economic logicians, bid fair to revolutionise the entire fabric of modern economic theory and practice and, withal, sweep away at one stroke much that is prosaic, artificial, vague and irrelevant in economic writing . . .

Keynes's principal grouses against the classical tenets are as follows: (*i*) He attacks, and I think, on the whole, most effectively attacks, the excessive preoccupation of the classical writers with the real economics of an economy which is essentially a monetary economy – a preoccupation which finds its fullest expression, *e.g.*, in Professor Pigou's *Theory of Unemployment*, which as Keynes rightly points out, gets 'out of the Classical Theory all that can be got out of it'. This preoccupation has given a wrong direction to the classical discussions of the relationship between wages (money and real) and employment, and of topics such as interest, saving and prices, – it has made the entire approach topsy-turvy and distorted. (Cf. pp. 8ff., 19–20, 175ff., and 292ff.) (*ii*) Next, the classical tendency of looking upon the economic world as possessing a

* From *Indian Economic Review*, vol. 7 (1936), pp. 229, 230–31.

rubber-like elasticity and as constantly moving towards a pre-
destined equilibrium, which would be realised only if we just
let well alone, and the celebrated optimism of the *laissez-faire*
doctrine that there is a natural tendency towards the optimum
employment, come in for a well-merited rebuke that to indulge
in these is to neglect 'to take account of the drag on prosperity
which can be exercised by an insufficiency of effective demand'
(p. 33). (*iii*) The failure of the classical writers to effect a
synthesis between the theory that prices are determined by
supply and demand and the theory that they are determined
by the quantity of money in circulation is the next grouse of
Keynes. (See pp. 292ff.) Wicksell was probably the first to
draw attention to this lack of synthesis. (Cf. Prof. Ohlin's
brilliant introduction to Mr. Kahn's Translation of Wicksell's
*Geldzins and Güterpreise*, under the title, *Interest and Prices*.)
Keynes has carried the discussion much further and utilised
what Prof. Ohlin calls 'Wicksell's most fruitful innovation in
bridging the gap between price theory and monetary theory',
by bringing total demand in relation to total supply and
deriving interesting conclusions regarding employment. This
further elaboration is indeed fundamental to Keynes's treatment of the subject. Keynes proceeds thus: Let Z be the
aggregate supply price of the output from employing N men,
the relationship between Z and N being written $Z = \phi$ (N),
which can be called the Aggregate Supply Function. Similarly,
let D be the proceeds which entrepreneurs expect to receive
from the employment of N men, the relationship between D
and N being written $D = f(N)$, which can be called the *Aggregate Demand Function*. The volume of employment is given
by the point of intersection between the aggregate demand
function and the aggregate supply function. The classical
theory, in assuming that the two functions always exactly
coincided (Cf. the dictum 'Supply creates its own Demand' or
the dictum that 'there cannot be any general over-production')
and that there could, therefore, be no obstacle to full employment, errs on the side of over-abstraction of a 'static' character.
'The classical theorists', says Keynes, 'resemble Euclidean
geometers in a non-Euclidean world, who, discovering that in
experience straight lines apparently parallel often meet, rebuke
the lines for not keeping straight – as the only remedy for the
unfortunate collisions that are occurring'. Yet, this 'axiom of
parallels', *viz.*, of aggregate supply and aggregate demand, is

itself a highly unreal abstraction. (*iv*) Accordingly, the classical propositions, (*a*) that the wage is equal to the marginal net product of labour, (*b*) that its utility is equal to the marginal disutility of the amount of employment, (*c*) that it is the 'real' rather than the money wage which is relevant to the wage-bargain, and (*d*) that it is the lack of plasticity in wages that is responsible for unemployment, – all these have been thrown overboard on the ground that they rest upon artificial assumptions regarding the manner in which wage-bargains are settled.

This indeed is the negative achievement of Keynes that he has demolished some of the jerry-building of classical economics: as regards his positive contribution, much might be written. However, for reasons of space I refrain from giving a detailed survey; all that I propose to do here is to summarise in the barest form what I think will be regarded as the most outstanding contributions of this book to economic science.

(1) Firstly, then, it has evolved a connected system of thought regarding the Theory of the Monetary Economy to be substituted for the partial, halting, one-sided, nibbling effort of classical economists.

(2) Secondly, it has developed a highly original and interesting apparatus for the understanding of the interactions of the supply function, the demand function, employment, prices and interest. (The most important parts of this apparatus are those relating to the 'employment multiplier', Chapter 10.)

(3) Thirdly, it has made a fuller investigation than has been possible in the *Treatise* of the properties of interest and money, of the nature of capital, and of the concept of 'marginal efficiency of capital'.

(4) Fourthly, it has thoroughly threshed out the 'economics of expectation' in relation both to the short term as well as the long term of investment. Keynes's views here are refreshingly original and represent a considerable advance on the work done in Sweden especially by Professors Myrdal and Lindahl, the neo-Wicksellians.

(5) And, fifthly, it has, consistently with the ideal of full employment (which here supplants the alternative ideals like stable employment, or maximum output, or stable value of money and so forth), developed a new trade-cycle thesis in favour of a 'permanent quasi-boom,' maintained by monetary expansion up to the point of a full-employment equilibrium. In Keynes's view, it is the cowardice of the banking system that

nips prosperity in the bud: 'The remedy for the boom is not a higher rate of interest but a lower rate of interest! For that may enable the so-called boom to last. The right remedy for the trade cycle is not to be found in abolishing booms and thus keeping us permanently in a semi-slump; but in abolishing slumps and thus keeping us permanently in a quasi-boom' (p. 322). He would encourage the 'propensity to consume' continually by stimulating the rate of investment. 'Thus it is to our best advantage to reduce the rate of interest to that point relatively to the schedule of the marginal efficiency of capital at which there is full employment' (p. 375).

# [FROM] MR KEYNES ON UNDEREMPLOYMENT EQUILIBRIUM* [1]
## Alvin H. Hansen

Mr. Keynes regards his new book as the fulfilment of the imperfect, though essentially correct, views of 'Mandeville, Malthus, Gesell and Hobson' – majors in the 'brave army of heretics . . . who, following their intuitions have preferred to see the truth obscurely and imperfectly rather than to maintain error reached, indeed, with clearness and consistency and by easy logic, but on hypotheses inappropriate to the facts'.[2]

Mr. Keynes announces in the first chapter of his book that it is his purpose to contrast his arguments and conclusions with those of the *classical* economists, by which he means Ricardo, Mill, Marshall, Edgeworth, and Pigou. He confesses in his Preface that the orthodox economist will probably fluctuate between the belief that his new book is quite wrong and the belief that it contains nothing new. For himself, however, the author feels that the composition of this book has been a long struggle of escape from habitual modes of thought and

---

* From *Journal of Political Economy*, vol. 44 (October 1936), pp. 667–73, 676–86.

[1] I wish to express appreciation of many stimulating discussions with Dr. Tord Palander of the University of Stockholm, and with Dr. Eugen Altschul and Mr. B. H. Higgins of the University of Minnesota.

[2] Keynes's new work is especially inspired by Malthus. In connection with his current appreciation of the work of John A. Hobson (only slightly in evidence in the *Treatise* of six years ago) it is not without interest to turn back to a review of Hobson's *Gold, Prices and Wages* (*Economic Journal*, September, 1913, pp. 393–98) written twenty-three years ago. In this review Mr. Keynes says: 'One comes to a new book by Mr. Hobson with mixed feelings, in hope of stimulating ideas and of some fruitful criticisms of orthodoxy from an independent and individual standpoint, but expectant also of much sophistry, misunderstanding, and perverse thought . . . The book is . . . made much worse than a really stupid book could be, by exactly those characteristics of cleverness and intermittent reasonableness which have borne good fruit in the past.' This characterization by Mr. Keynes himself is not altogether inapplicable, some will perhaps say, to his own book.

expression, and 'so must the reading of it be for most readers if the author's assault upon them is to be successful'. The difficulty, he says, lies not in the new ideas, which even though laboriously expressed are in reality extremely simple, but rather in the fact that the old ideas, on which we have all been brought up, ramify into every corner of our minds and keep us chained in fetters.

The reader who is familiar with the earlier work published six years ago, the *Treatise on Money*, is likely at first to be somewhat bewildered upon taking up this new book. Yet Mr. Keynes explains that what to others may appear as a confusing change of view seems to him to be a perfectly natural evolution in the line of thought which he has been pursuing for several years. With this interpretation the present reviewer finds himself quite sympathetic. For, while Mr. Keynes has now donned an entirely new suit of clothes, it is not difficult to see that it is, after all, the same man who wears them.

The imposing edifice erected in a *Treatise on Money* is, indeed, wholly abandoned. It had been shown that there was a serious error in his first fundamental equation.[3] The correctness of this criticism Keynes at once admitted,[4] and announced that in future editions of his book he would redefine the units in which the physical quantities were measured so as to correct this error. It was then pointed out that, were this done, his second fundamental equation would thereby equally be rendered of no practical significance.[5] Still more disconcerting was the conclusive demonstration by Hawtrey and Robertson that the disequilibrium between investment and saving as Keynes defined them was incapable of revealing the causal factors at work. It was shown that the inequality of saving and investment, as defined, merely reflected and registered the course of events; that this divergence could not be regarded as the 'cause of a windfall loss or gain, for it *is* the windfall loss or gain'.[6] These and other criticisms left his theoretical structure

[3] Alvin H. Hansen, 'A Fundamental Error in Keynes' *Treatise on Money*', *American Economic Review*, September, 1932.

[4] *American Economic Review*, December, 1932.

[5] Alvin H. Hansen and Herbert Tout, 'Investment and Saving in the Business Cycle', *Econometrica*, April, 1933.

[6] R. G. Hawtrey, *The Art of Central Banking* (1932), p. 349; and D. H. Robertson, *Economic Journal*, September, 1931.

without a foundation and compelled either an abandonment or a radical reconstruction.

The critics may well, however, be wary of assuming too much credit for the author's abandonment of the edifice so elaborately constructed only six years ago. For Mr. Keynes is one of those rare and delightful spirits who finds it quite impossible to live happily for long in contemplation of old ideas, even though those ideas are his own. He must forever be exploring new frontiers and evolving new insights and new solutions. It is this characteristic which makes Mr. Keynes one of those phenomena in our current age which helps to make life worth living. *The General Theory of Employment, Interest and Money* is no less stimulating than was the *Treatise on Money*.

The new book is not a treatise; it is a debate to which the public is invited, and the ticket is five shillings in England and two dollars in the United States. The publication of a book with so difficult and complicated an analysis at a best-seller price is itself indicative of the power and prestige of Mr. Keynes as a social prophet in the current distracted world. The shafts are directed, as the author himself announces, at the classical school from Ricardo to Pigou, but in the midst of this major contest Mr. Keynes finds ample strength for many a dart at the neo-Viennese and London school.

And what is the debate about? Very briefly it may be stated as follows: Ricardo had built up quite logically and consistently a theory of prices and distribution based on the assumption of an equilibrium position at which the factors of production were fully employed. It is Keynes's purpose, however, to develop – what he thinks the classicals had neglected – the general theory of employment. He criticizes the classical school, not for their analysis of the manner in which the factors of production are combined or of how the value of the final product is distributed between them, but because they neglected to consider the determinants of the volume of employment and output as a whole. They assumed that there was but one equilibrium position – that of full employment. Keynes argues that this position is but a limiting point of a whole range of possible positions of equilibrium. It is the essential function, indeed, of his new book to show that in the actual conditions of the current economic order equilibrium is reached at a point far below full employment, and to elucidate the factors which determine at what level any one equilibrium position is reached. What is criticized, therefore, is not the theory of prices and distribution of the classical school, but the assumption that there is only one equilibrium point, and in particular the disastrous and misleading attempt to apply the characteristics of the special case of equilibrium at full employment to the quite different facts of experience in the economic society in which we actually live.

What is correct policy in the case of equilibrium at full-employment may turn out to be quite a wrong policy in an equilibrium position at underemployment. At full employment equilibrium one is concerned only with the proper allocation of the factors in the production of consumption goods and of investment goods. One is not concerned with the problem of full employment of these factors, since that is assumed. Under these conditions consumption and investment stand in a competitive relation to each other. If investment is increased, consumption must perforce be reduced, and vice versa. In such a society the question of how much to save and how much to consume involves exclusively the problem of future satisfaction of wants as against present satisfaction of wants. Increased investment may, under these circumstances, be justified as a means of increasing future production. Neither investment nor consumption has any relation to the problem of employment as such, since full employment is assumed regardless of the ratio of consumption to income. But if the society is at equilibrium at a point of underemployment the matter is quite different. Under these circumstances consumption and investment stand not in a competitive relation but in a complementary relation to each other. With under-employment, an increase of investment, far from requiring a restriction of consumption, will, because of the resulting increase in employment and income, tend to increase consumption. Likewise an increase in consumption (i.e., an increase in the percentage of the income consumed) will raise the prospective profitableness of investment. Thus both consumption and investment are simultaneously increased and thereby also, employment, output, and income. While a puritanical policy of thrift and saving may be quite appropriate in a society in equilibrium at full employment, prodigality may be the appropriate social virtue in a society in equilibrium at under-employment.

It is evident that the great problem for a society in equilibrium at underemployment is to bring under social control the determinants of equilibrium. Only in this manner can the position of equilibrium at full employment be achieved. What now are these determinants? They are: (1) the propensity to consume, (2) the schedule of marginal efficiency of capital,[7] and (3) the complex of rates of interest on loans. These are the determinants of the volume of consumption and of investment, which in turn fix the volume of output, income, and employment for society as a whole.

The ultimate causal forces are therefore found outside of the price system, in the mores, customs, habits, and behavior patterns of the people. The fundamental psychological factors are the psychological propensity to consume, the psychological expectation of future yield from capital assets, and the psychological attitude to liquidity. Psychological propensities, mores, and behavior patterns are thus the root forces which lie back of and control consumption and investment and thereby determine what the point of equilibrium shall be.

In this connection let it be noted that when modern capitalism was in process of developing, and when it was in full bloom, it did not rely solely on the automatic functioning of the price system to supply an adequate volume of saving. It preached the doctrine of thrift and sought to establish a propensity to save.

On the classical assumption of full employment one need have no concern about the propensity to consume, for what was not consumed was saved. And saving merely meant a diversion of production toward the creation of investment goods. The rate of interest was the regulator which controlled the ratio of consumption to income. If the rate of interest fell, less was saved and a larger percentage of the income was consumed. If the rate of interest rose, more was saved and less was consumed. Thus in the earlier view the supply curve for savings assumed the familiar, normal shape. Later to be sure,

---

[7] Keynes alleges that current business-cycle theory fails to see that the marginal efficiency of capital depends on the prospective yield of capital (pp. 141, 145–46). In this he is, however, definitely in error. See, for example, chaps. iv and vi (esp. pp. 82–86 and 134–35) in my *Business-Cycle Theory* (1927), where a survey is given of writers who analyze the cycle phenomenon in terms of 'fluctuations of the marginal efficiency of capital relatively to the rate of interest'.

this definite inverse correlation between the rate of interest and saving was subjected to criticism. In neo-classical thinking doubt had been raised with respect to the precise relationship between the rate of interest and saving. Within certain limits, indeed, a lower rate of interest might induce a larger volume of saving. All this is familiar ground, and needs no elaboration here. It was held, nevertheless, that while a fall in the rate of interest up to a certain point might indeed stimulate saving, below a certain minimum level any further decline would reduce the volume of saving and stimulate consumption. Cassel in his *Nature and Necessity of Interest* had argued that, because of the shortness of human life, capital depletion would set in, once interest fell below a certain point. Below this minimum rate consumption would be stimulated at the expense of saving.

Thus, while neo-classical thought refused to accept the doctrine of an invariant relation between interest and saving, it did not go so far as to break completely the dependence of saving upon the rate of interest offered in the market. While under modern high standards of living it had come to be believed that the growth of population had little relation to the rate of wages, it was only within certain limits that the same position was taken with respect to the supply of capital as a variable independent of price. The view of Hobson – that saving had no relation to the interest rate, that it was determined wholly by the mores, customs, and behaviour patterns of the population, by the propensity to consume and its inverse, the propensity to save – remained the unorthodox view.

With Keynes (as with Cassel, but for quite different reasons) there is a minimum rate of interest below which – unless, indeed, determined action is taken by society – the rate of interest cannot fall. He suggests that this minimum rate is 2 or 2½ per cent. But with Keynes, despite this minimum rate, society (because of a fixed propensity to consume only a limited proportion of its income) continues to pour out a steady flow of savings. Thus the marginal efficiency of capital may well fall to a point below the minimum rate of interest. Here, then, is to be found the mechanism which drives the economic system to an equilibrium level below the point of full employment. According to Keynes, at this minimum rate of interest saving is not deflected toward consumption, as Cassel had it; instead, it is at this point that hoarding begins. If saving continues willy-nilly by reason of a fixed psychological propensity without regard to price factors, and if the marginal efficiency of capital in a wealthy community falls below the minimum interest rate, then of necessity a part of the planned individual savings cannot find an outlet in realized investment.

At this point it becomes necessary to inject a brief consideration of terminological difficulties. In the new book Keynes formally abandons his former highly artificial definitions of income and savings.[8] But his new terminology is by no means wholly satisfactory. In the reviewer's opinion his entire exposition would have been very greatly facilitated had he adopted outright Robertson's definitions of income, saving, and investment.[9] This would have made it far easier for him to make clear the factors of disequilibrium. For Robertson's terminology enables one to see very clearly the disequilibrating effects of hoarding and dishoarding and of credit creation and debt cancellation . . .

Returning to the main argument, why, according to Keynes, does not the continued pressure of savings force the rate of interest[10] down below the marginal efficiency of capital? The answer is that the loan rate is not merely a pure interest rate; it includes also the cost and risk of lending. Thus, if one assumes that the pure rate were driven to zero, and that the cost and risk of lending were 2 per cent, it is clear that the minimum rate could never fall – so long as there is the alternative of hoarding – below this 2 per cent. In addition there is the special risk (a risk which becomes greater the lower

---

[8] According to these definitions, income included the 'normal' return of entrepreneurs. In calculating the income of entrepreneurs no account was taken of windfall profits or windfall losses. Thus in a depression, despite windfall losses, the income of entrepreneurs, as defined, remained unaffected. And, since saving was defined as that part of income which was not spent on liquid consumer's goods, it followed that a large part of the saving in a depression consisted of business losses!

[9] D. H. Robertson, 'Saving and Hoarding', *Economic Journal*, September and December, 1933.

[10] With respect to Keynes's criticism (chap. xiv) of the neo-classical treatment of the theory of interest, it should be noted that circular reasoning (such as he here attacks) can be found in all partial analyses of isolated factors in which it is necessarily assumed that 'other things remain equal'. One can get out of the circle only by the method of the general equilibrium analysis. Moreover, his own interest theory is wholly inadequate, since it leaves out of account the most important variable, the marginal efficiency of capital.

the rate received) that any slight rise in the rate of interest in the future will drive the capitalized value of the investment down to a point at which the entire interest earnings have been wiped out. At the present moment, with the very low yield on long-term government bonds, a slight rise in the rate of interest would cause an appreciable loss on the principal. This is the danger which banks now run in holding long-term government bonds and which causes them, in large part, to prefer complete liquidity. Thus, below a certain interest rate, complete liquidity is deemed preferable to investment. The rate of interest, therefore, fails to fall to the point to which it would have to be driven in order that the whole flow of planned savings might find a ready outlet in investment. Taking, therefore, the propensity to hoard (liquidity preference) in conjunction with the relatively constant propensity to save, it is discovered that the rate of interest does not equilibrate the volume of planned individual saving and realized investment. In consequence, a part of the available purchasing power in the community finds no outlet in the market. Unemployment, reduced output, and declining income ensue until a level of impoverishment is reached at which the propensity to consume is increased sufficiently so that the flow of planned individual saving equates with the volume of realized investment. For, with a higher ratio of consumption to income, the marginal efficiency of capital now rises to the level of the rate of interest. At this point an equilibrium is reached. The rate of interest now equates with the marginal efficiency of capital, and planned individual saving with realized investment. But this point of equilibrium is one at which there is underemployment of the factors of production. Until there is a change: (1) in the propensity to consume, (2) in the marginal efficiency of capital, or (3) in the rate of interest, this equilibrium position remains fixed.

By what policies might the industrial system be shoved off this dead center of underemployment equilibrium? Keynes considers, in this connection, the rôle of wages, the rôle of money, the rôle of income distribution, and the rôle of socially controlled investment.

Keynes does not deny (as doubtless many superficial readers will conclude) the possible efficacy of reduction in wage rates as a means of lifting the economic system to a higher equilibrium position at fuller employment. He admits that a reduction in wage rates would release a proportion of the money supply and tend to lower the rate of interest. But he holds that there are other ways in which this same end could be accomplished without the social cost of wage reduction, and that it is therefore folly to resort to this method. Keynes admits, moreover, that a general systematic scheme of wage reduction, carried out by a highly integrated or authoritarian society, might prove effective in raising the marginal efficiency of capital. But in Western democracies this method is not applicable – wage reductions, in fact, come piecemeal, now in this industry and now in that. The effect of such wage reductions upon political confidence and popular discontent might be to raise materially the schedule of liquidity preference. Moreover, if the reduction in wage rates leads to the expectation of a further wage reduction in the future the effect on current investment is likely to be unfavorable. In addition the transfer of income from wage-earners to other factors is likely to diminish the propensity to consume. For these reasons, piecemeal reductions, which leave the future uncertain, are not likely to prove an effective method of increasing employment. Wage reduction, moreover, tends to load the whole weight of any existing maladjustment upon the single factor, labor, and this is surely inequitable. Finally, the wasteful and disastrous struggles, to which this method almost certainly gives rise, threaten the whole social fabric and make it an impracticable device in the modern world. If the wage level is too high, other methods must be found of increasing the marginal efficiency of capital to a point at which equilibrium at full employment may be reached.

With respect to Pigou's theory of unemployment Keynes does not disagree with the static relationship which Pigou finds between the rate of real wages and the volume of employment. What he does charge (surely without justification) is the failure of Pigou to analyze the dynamic factors which control the rate of real wages, especially the factors – the marginal efficiency of capital and the rate of interest – which control the volume of investment.

Everything considered, a flexible wage policy as an instrument of control is ruled out as dangerous – and, indeed, it is argued that, under the institutional arrangements of Western democracies, genuine stability can better be achieved by an inflexible wage policy. Other methods of control must be discovered to secure full employment.

To this end, money plays for Keynes an important rôle,

although less important in this book than in the *Treatise*. A controlled rate of interest, relentlessly held at a point below the marginal efficiency of capital and driven still lower as marginal efficiency falls with fuller investment, might eventually achieve – possibly even within a generation – the condition of completely 'full investment'. This means that the supply of capital would have been increased to a point at which it would yield no net return over its replacement cost. At this point, the *rentier* class would be eliminated, and capital as a factor in production would have made its full contribution to maximum output.

A difficulty with this method – and one which Keynes sees – is that if full employment were reached prior to the point of full investment inflation would set in. To prevent inflation the rate of interest would have to be raised to the level of the marginal efficiency of capital. But if equilibrium at full employment were reached short of full investment, and if the society really wished to achieve a condition of full investment, resort would have to be made to other methods, such as direct social control of the volume of investment.

If a controlled rate of interest should prove quickly effective in achieving full employment, and if this policy were joined with a policy of taxation designed to bring about more equal income distribution, it might turn out that the rate of accumulation would be even lower than in the existing society. This would place us even farther than now from the condition of full investment. Should it therefore turn out to be an easy matter to achieve full employment by means of a controlled interest rate it might not be desirable, Keynes thinks, to increase the propensity to consume. For, at full-employment equilibrium, consumption becomes competitive with investment, and this would prevent the society from moving toward that level of productivity which full investment would make possible.

The relentless maintenance of a sufficiently low rate of interest to maintain full employment, Keynes points out, is unattainable in an international gold-standard system. For if you must defend your balance of payments against gold drains by raising the rate of interest you thereby sacrifice the goal of full employment. Thus the rigorous maintenance of an adequately low interest rate involves the adoption of a policy of flexible exchange rates.

In Keynes's view the condition of underemployment equilibrium will inevitably persist indefinitely in modern societies unless drastic measures are taken to control the determinants of employment – namely, the propensity to consume, the marginal efficiency of capital, and the rate of interest. Is this position tenable? Is it true that the condition of underemployment equilibrium (without action such as that indicated above) is stable? I do not think it is, unless one introduces certain definite assumptions which Keynes does not do.

There is one necessary condition, in my view, without which stable underemployment equilibrium is not possible. It is the condition of cost rigidity (including wage rates) and monopolistic control of supplies. And this situation is made much worse should it turn out that we are approaching a society in which the outlets for investment are likely to prove more limited than in the past century.

The current orthodox theory – represented, for example, by Pigou – has so fully elaborated the theory of underemployment equilibrium, under conditions of cost rigidity and monopolistic control of supply, that it is only necessary here to make reference thereto. We can be reasonably certain that these restrictive institutional factors and rigidities will continue to prevail to a sufficient degree in the decades ahead to produce a very considerable amount of unemployment apart from the normal cyclical fluctuations. It will, therefore, be quite impossible from a mere observation of the course of future events to determine whether or not Keynes's analysis is valid.

With respect to economic progress, the rapid development of new products, new processes of production, new ways of utilizing natural resources, and new combinations of the productive factors have the effect of raising the marginal efficiency of capital and thereby stimulating investment. Thus economic progress constantly tends toward equilibrium at full employment. Should it turn out, however, that the next decades will witness a relative stagnation in innovations in the utilization of the resources of nature, the marginal efficiency of capital may (in view of existing and prospective cost rigidities) fall to a point so low as to produce a stagnation in investment.[11] In the past enormous investments have been made in large capital-

---

[11] Unemployment and stagnation, moreover, foment psychological conditions which intensify the international strain and threaten world-chaos.

consuming developments, such as railroads, roads, and other public utilities. It is not impossible that the technological innovations of the future will be of a character that will require less capital than many of the developments of the last century. Moreover, certain types of technological innovations are definitely capital economizing rather than capital using.

The frontier for the entire world is largely gone and population is approaching stabilization – if not, indeed, decline.[12] This affects the outlet for the investment in durable goods both at home and abroad. Rural electrification schemes, housing projects, and the like, carried out under the stimulation of low interest rates, may, however, turn out to be really important investment outlets.

In view of the prevailing (and probably increasing) cost rigidities, and in view of the possibility of a slowing down in capital-consuming technological innovations, the problem of structural, or secular, unemployment (altogether apart from the cyclical unemployment of ordinary industrial fluctuations) is almost certain to present itself for solution in the decades before us. The all-important question therefore (whether or not Keynes's theoretical analysis of underemployment equilibrium is correct) is how to remedy this situation. Keynes's proposals are designed to offer a substitute for a completely planned socialistic or communistic economy. His solutions are, as we have seen: (1) the rigid maintenance of the rate of interest below the marginal efficiency of capital until full employment is reached, (2) the forced redistribution of income through

---

[12] 'And if some approach to an even rate of growth was attained in the nineteenth century, when both population and the area of effective economic intercourse were rapidly increasing, it may turn out (paradoxically enough) to be harder to attain in a planet which, thanks to the activities of the prospector and the pioneer and to the success of the propagandists of birth control, is rapidly ceasing to be a worthy member of an expanding universe.'

'[Thus] it seems evident that the ship of economic life may be set a problem in re-orientation which transcends the capacities alike of its navigators and of its monetary steering-gear. Under such conditions the popular instinct which finds the root cause of dislocation in undigested plenty may be a surer guide than the laborious but one-eyed analysis which finds it in flouted scarcities and unjustified rigidities ... But again, if private enterprise remains sovereign, can it, at its most successful, find any way of countering slumps save by the perpetual stimulation of increasingly meretricious wants and increasingly hectic habits of life? Can it, consistently with its own nature, succeed in the more subtle task of transmuting into diffused leisure the concentrated unemployment of today?' (D. H. Robertson, *Stand der Konjunkturforschung* [Festschrift für Arthur Spiethoff, 1933], pp. 240–41.)

taxation designed to increase the propensity to consume, and (3) socially controlled investment.

The first proposal is in line with current monetary theory. But efforts at general monetary control have already revealed the weakness of this method. Indirect control – open-market operations and discount policy – is in process of being supplemented by direct monetary intervention (witness current measures to control the volume of funds placed at the disposal of the stock market) which borders on regimentation and rationing – a kind of monetary NRA. The third proposal goes far in the direction of a planned economy and might, indeed, lead straight into thorough-going socialism. How far taxation of incomes and wealth (the second proposal) may be carried without breaking down is problematical. Whether or not a drastic program of taxation carried far enough to effect a genuine redistribution of income is compatible with a system of private enterprise and private initiative; whether or not such a program would only serve to make a 'flat situation still flatter', thereby leaving no alternative except complete socialization, may perhaps finally be decided at the bar of history.

It will be noted that all of these methods seek to establish full employment either: (1) by a curtailment of the volume of individual savings through a redistribution of income, or (2) by forcing these savings into investment at low interest rates through a program of socially controlled investment. But there is a vast difference between a spontaneous expansion of investment and employment, such as we witnessed in the nineteenth century, and a forced investment such as Keynes seeks to bring about by artificially contrived measures. When spectacular fields for profitable investment are opened up through the development of new resources, the introduction of technological innovations, the expansion of population, and the growth of new industries, then savings are sucked up, labor is scarce, and industry booms through the drawing power of an expanding demand. When, however, savings must be forced, the outflow of funds into real investment becomes difficult and sluggish, and business is likely to stagnate – unless, indeed, the state goes the whole way and assumes full entrepreneurial responsibility.

In brief, it is not improbable that the continued workability of the system of private enterprise will be made possible, not by changes in prevailing economic institutions (such as those advocated by Keynes), but rather by the work of the inventor and the engineer. Just as technological progress has been mainly responsible for the great advance in real wages and in standards of living during the last century, so also it may well turn out that in the future we shall have to look to new outlets for profitable investment – new discoveries in technique, new ways of utilizing nature's resources, new products, and new industries – if we expect the prevailing economic system to survive.

Whether or not Keynes's proposals will in fact prove effective, it is clear that they are currently popular and are likely to be tried on an expanding scale. Modern communities appear to be in process of reverting to the behavior patterns of the precapitalistic period. Leisure and luxurious consumption were leading characteristics of that era. Numerous holidays, magnificent entertainments, prodigality in consumption (*vide* cathedrals, castles, art products requiring infinite detail and leisurely, time-consuming workmanship) – these distinguish the precapitalistic period from the nervous speed and the emphasis on thrift and saving which characterized the nineteenth century. Keynes's economic system is, as he himself admits, a reversion to the economic doctrines of mercantilism. Modern societies are, in his view, being driven by the logic of events into pursuit of the same ideals which the mercantilists cherished. They were right, he thinks, in the enforcement of usury laws designed to maintain a low rate of interest. They were too close to the experience of an exuberant prosperity and rising prices, which the inpouring of precious metals from the new world had generated, to overlook the importance of an abundance of precious metals. They were right, he thinks, in their preoccupation with the balance of payments and their fear that a drain on the precious metals would, by affecting the terms of lending, check the growth of investment and employment. They were right in their 'deep rooted belief in the utility of luxury and the evil of thrift'. These are the corner stones of Keynes's economic philosophy, and it is not difficult to see that, whatever may be true of the correctness of his theoretical analysis or the workability of his proposals, the enigma of unemployment and business depression has already impelled modern capitalistic economies far toward the reconstruction of a mercantilistic world.

In conclusion, a word should be said about Keynes's view of the trade cycle. Let it be noted that *The General Theory of*

*Employment, Interest and Money* is only incidentally concerned with the trade cycle. Cyclical fluctuations may occur in either a full-employment equilibrium system or in an under-employment equilibrium system. The theory of the trade cycle is, therefore, something substantially apart from the theory of long-run underemployment or full-employment equilibrium. In his 'Notes on the Trade Cycle' (chap. xxii) – a brilliant performance, even though, as Keynes admits, it contains essentially nothing new – Keynes finds that the cycle is mainly due to fluctuations in the marginal efficiency of capital. The movement is cyclical in the sense that the forces propelling the system upward at first gather force cumulatively but gradually lose their strength until a point is reached at which they tend to be replaced by opposite forces, which in turn gather force cumulatively until they, too, wane. The movement is cyclical, also, in the sense that these upward and downward movements occur with a recognizable degree of regularity in time-sequence and duration. A complete explanation of the cycle must, moreover, involve an analysis of the crisis – the sudden and violent turning point from boom to depression.

Let us consider these points briefly and in their inverse order. The phenomenon of the crisis may be explained by the precarious character of expectations of future yield on new investment – expectations based on highly shifting and unreliable evidence. The boom progresses on overoptimistic expectations. Disillusionment brings a sudden and drastic collapse in the prospective rate of profit – the marginal efficiency of capital.

Periodicity of the cycle rests upon two bases: (1) the length of life of durable assets in relation to the normal rate of growth, and (2) the carrying costs of surplus stocks.

The increase in the marginal efficiency of capital awaits the depreciation and obsolescence of the capital stock accumulated during the boom. This, of course, is nothing new. Karl Marx, Aftalion, Robertson, and others have stressed the relation of average durability of capital to the length of the depression.

The carrying costs of surplus stocks is the second important factor, in Keynes's view, which determines the duration of depression. The carrying charges tend to force the absorption of surplus stocks within a certain period, usually within three to five years. While the process of stock absorption is going on there is negative investment and, therefore, deflation and unemployment.

Keynes's emphasis on fluctuations in the marginal efficiency of capital as the moving cause of the trade cycle is in line with Spiethoff's analysis, though there are many points of difference. Moreover, the conclusion that the collapse in the marginal efficiency of capital may be so complete that the most favorable monetary condition is quite inadequate to produce a revival, is also in line with Spiethoff's view. With Spiethoff, however, the increase in the marginal efficiency of capital (without which revival would be impossible) is caused by inventions, discoveries, the development of new resources, new products, and new industries. With Keynes the absorption of stocks, the depreciation and obsolescence of fixed capital, and the effects of these upon the prospective yield of new investment, are the points stressed.

Keynes supports, as one remedial measure for the trade cycle, the program of redistribution of income designed to increase the propensity to consume. However, according to his own analysis, the cause of the trade cycle is fundamentally to be found in *fluctuations* in the marginal efficiency of capital, and it is difficult to see how a permanent change in the distribution of income could affect these fluctuations. In other words, at this point Keynes is clearly confusing the problem of long-term equilibrium with the problem of short-term cyclical fluctuations.

Keynes's new book, as with everything which comes from his pen, will stimulate thinking on fresh lines in the field of economic dynamics. There are too many obscure corners in our science to permit of comfortable dogmatism. The economic order is clearly in a state of transition to no one knows what. The system is half rigid, half flexible. A theoretical apparatus applicable to a flexible system is not always adequate for an analysis of current economic life. The problem of wage rigidity, for example, is not as simple today as formerly. A system which stands somewhere between a laissez faire economy and a regimented economy presents exceptionally difficult problems for public policy. We are living in a time when economics stands in danger of a sterile orthodoxy. The book under review is not a landmark in the sense that it lays a foundation for a 'new economics'. It warns once again, in a provocative manner, of the danger of reasoning based on assumptions which no longer fit the facts of economic life. Out of discussion and research will come bit by bit an improved theoretical apparatus (Keynes's interest theory contains promising suggestions) and a more accurate appreciation of social psychology (the brilliant chapter on long-term expectation) and of the precise character of the economic environment in which humans act as individuals and in groups. The book is more a symptom of economic trends than a foundation stone upon which a science can be built.

# [FROM] REVIEW OF KEYNES'S GENERAL THEORY*
## J. A. Schumpeter

A book by Mr. Keynes on fundamental questions which are right at the heart of the practical discussions of the day is no doubt an event. Those who had the opportunity to witness the expectations of the best of our students, the impatience they displayed at the delay in getting hold of their copies, the eagerness with which they devoured them, and the interest manifested by all sectors of Anglo-American communities that are up to this kind of reading (and some that are not) must first of all congratulate the author on a signal personal success, a success not in the least smaller in the cases of negative reaction than in those in which the book elicited fervent admiration. The unfavorable reviews in a sense but testify to the reality of that success, and I for one, being about to write another of those unfavorable reviews, heartily rejoice in this implication and wish it to be understood that what I am going to say is, in its own unconventional way, a tribute to one of the most brilliant men who ever bent their energies to economic problems. Expression of a teacher's gratitude should be added for the gift of what is, in its vigorous exposition and extreme simplicity, an invaluable starter of discussions. Speaking to us from the vantage ground of Cambridge and from its author's unique personal position, defended by a group of ardent and able disciples, the book will undoubtedly dominate talk and thought for some time.

In his preface Mr. Keynes underlines the significance of the words 'General Theory' in his title. He professes to address it primarily to his fellow economists and seems to invite purely theoretical discussion. But it is not quite easy to accept that invitation, for everywhere he really pleads for a definite policy, and on every page the ghost of that policy looks over the

* From *Journal of the American Statistical Association*, vol. 31 (December 1936), pp. 791–5.

shoulder of the analyst, frame his assumptions, guides his pen. In this sense, as in another, it is Ricardo all over again. The advice offered implicitly and the social vision unfolded explicitly, do not concern us here. That advice (everybody knows what it is Mr. Keynes advises) may be good. For the England of today it possibly is. That vision may be entitled to the compliment that it expresses forcefully the attitude of a decaying civilization. In these respects, this book invites sociological interpretation in the Marxian sense, and nothing is more certain than that such interpretation will be administered to it before long.

It is, however, vital to renounce communion with any attempt to revive the Ricardian practice of offering, in the garb of general scientific truth, advice which – whether good or bad – carries meaning only with references to the practical exigencies of the unique historical situation of a given time and country. This sublimates practical issues into scientific ones, divides economists – as in fact we can see already from any discussion about this book – according to lines of political preference, produces popular successes at the moment, and reactions after – witness the fate of Ricardian economics – neither of which have anything to do with science. Economics will never have nor merit any authority until that unholy alliance is dissolved. There is happily some tendency towards such dissolution. But this book throws us back again. Once more, socialists as well as institutionalists are right in judging economic theory as they do.

Ricardian as the book is in spirit and intent, so it is in workmanship. There is the same technique of skirting problems by artificial[1] definitions which, tied up with highly specialized assumptions, produce paradoxical-looking tautologies, and of constructing special cases which in the author's own mind and in his exposition are invested with a treacherous generality. In one fundamental point it actually falls short of the line already reached by those writers who in the sixties of the past century

---

[1] The definition of involuntary unemployment, page 15, may serve as an example. Taken literally (which of course it would be unfair to do) it would mean that there is no practically conceivable case in which workmen are not partially unemployed by definition. For if prices of wage goods rise a little, other things being equal, it is clear that both the demand for, and the supply of, labor will increase under competitive conditions, the latter at least as long as the flexibility of the marginal utility of income to the workmen is what present statistics lead us to believe.

criticized some of the tenets of what *to them* was 'classical' doctrine,[2] notably Longe and Thornton. These knew perfectly that the old supply and demand apparatus renders its very limited service only if applied to individual commodities, strictly speaking to individual commodities of relatively small importance, and that it either loses or changes its meaning if applied to comprehensive social aggregates. This was in fact their foremost objection to the wage fund theory. Mr. Keynes' fundamental construction (which is all we can consider here) rests on a contraposition of expected[3] net 'proceeds', equal to expected profits plus expected current payments to factors (for definition see page 24), and *those* proceeds the expectation of which would be sufficient and not more than sufficient to induce entrepreneurs to decide on producing the corresponding output. Two schedules or functions are imagined in order to describe the behavior and the relation to one another of these two fundamental variables. The analogy of the first with the ordinary Marshallian demand curve and the analogy of the second with the ordinary Marshallian supply curve are obvious. In fact, Mr. Keynes speaks of Aggregate Demand in

[2] Mr. Keynes' definition of the word 'classical', which is made to include Professor Pigou, who cannot be counted among classics by virtue of any criterion except the one of outstanding achievement, reminds me of a little experience I had in a group of students. I observed that one of the members kept on referring to a highly unconventional proposition as 'orthodox'. I asked him why he did so, seeing that the proposition was no part of received doctrine. His answer was, 'I simply call orthodox everything I don't like'. Protest should be filed in passing against Mr. Keynes' methods of criticism. But beyond that it is regrettable that so brilliant a leader should set so bad an example of utter absence of *verecundia*. I am no Marxian. Yet I sufficiently recognise the greatness of Marx to be offended at seeing him classed with Silvio Gesell and Major Douglas. Mr. Keynes is unjust even to Major Douglas for there is no warrant whatever for thinking little of that writer once one has accepted the views of this book. Certainly Marx and the classics (in the proper sense of the word) were grievously at fault in very many points as it is natural that pioneers should be. Yet they are right as against Mr. Keynes. His attitude toward Marshall's teaching is for Marshallians to judge.

[3] The emphasis on *expected* as against *actual* values is in line with modern tendencies. But expectations are not linked by Mr. Keynes to the cyclical situations that give rise to them and hence become independent variables and ultimate determinants of economic action. Such analysis can at best yield purely formal results and never go below the surface. An expectation acquires explanatory value only if we are made to understand *why* people expect *what* they expect. Otherwise expectation is a mere *deux ex machina* that conceals problems instead of solving them.

the one case and Aggregate Supply in the other and makes them yield a unique 'point of intersection'. There is as little justification for this extension of the 'Marshallian cross' as there is for its application to the case of money, which has remained a besetting sin of the Cambridge group to this day. Transition to the central theme of the book is effected by relating those two fundamental variables not to output but to employment, and not to employment of resources in general but to employment of labor. Mr. Keynes is as careful to point out that number of workmen employed is not proportional to output as Ricardo was to point out that value cannot be proportional to quantity of labor. But exactly as Ricardo reasoned as if it were, so Mr. Keynes assumes that employment of labor is an 'adequate' index of the output resulting from it. The arguments offered by both authors, in support of what is a procedure obviously inadmissible in anything that pretends to be a 'general' theory, are curiously alike. In particular both display a desire to banish the variations of output – or, in Ricardo's case, of 'riches' – from the realm of theory.

It should be clearly realized what that means. Readers of this *Journal* will shrug their shoulders at a theory which deserts the statistician in his struggle with the momentous problems surrounding the Index of Production. But disregarding this, reasoning on the assumption that variations in output are uniquely related to variations in employment imposes the further assumption that all production functions remain invariant. Now the outstanding feature of capitalism is that they do not but that, on the contrary, they are being incessantly revolutionized. The capitalist process is essentially a process of change of the type which is being assumed away in this book, and all its characteristic phenomena and problems arise from the fact that it is such a process. A theory that postulates invariance of production functions may, if correct in itself, be still of some use to the theorist. But it is the theory of another world and out of all contact with modern industrial fact, unemployment included. No interpretation of modern vicissitudes, 'poverty in plenty' and the rest, can be derived from it.

The central thesis that under-employment can exist in a state of stable equilibrium and that saving is responsible for it is then made to follow from two additional hypotheses. The one – embodied in the concept of Propensity to Consume – is that 'when aggregate real income is increased aggregate consumption is increased, but not by so much as income' (page 27). This Mr. Keynes dignifies, in the worst style of a bygone age, into a 'Psychological Law'. The question of fact apart – statistics of installment selling and other forms of consumers' credit obviously suggest the possibility of doubt – such a 'propensity' is again nothing but a *deus ex machina*, valueless if we do not understand the mechanism of the changing situations, in which consumer's expenditure alternatively increases and contracts, and redundant if we do. Postulating, however, an independent and systematic tendency to that effect, Mr. Keynes finds a 'gap' in expenditure resulting from it which may or may not be filled by investment and tends to widen as communities grow more wealthy. This amounts to introducing another hypothesis: the hypothesis of failing 'Inducement to Invest'.

Since Mr. Keynes eliminates the most powerful propeller of investment, the financing of changes in production functions, the investment process in his theoretical world has hardly anything to do with the investment process in the actual world, and any proof, even if successful, that (absolutely or relatively) falling 'Inducement to Invest' will produce under-employment would have no greater practical importance than a proof that motor cars cannot run in the absence of fuel. But that proof, even under its own assumptions and granting that in Mr. Keynes' world there would be a systematic tendency for Inducement to Invest to grow weaker,[4] meets the obvious objection that Propensity to Consume and Inducement to Invest are not independent of each other. In some passages (for example, page 30) Mr. Keynes seems indeed to hold that they are. We can absolve him, however, from the grave error this would spell, because each time (for example, page 31) he in fact admits the existence of an equilibrating mechanism. But then the whole *theoretical* case, that is, the case in terms of fundamental features of the economic process, collapses, and we are *practically* left with friction, or 'stickiness,' institutional inhibitions, and the like, which in particular may prevent the

---

[4] To many people statement of such a tendency will sound 'realistic'. This is however entirely due to recent experience and would have equally been the case after, say, 1720 or 1825 or 1873. No support of the theory in question can be derived from this, since it rests exclusively on observation of the surface mechanism of a deep depression *already in progress*, the explanation of which must be worked out independently of it.

rate of interest from reacting promptly or, in general, prevent the whole of that equilibrating mechanism from functioning adequately.

Space forbids our entering into a discussion of the Multiplier, its relation to the Propensity to Consume, the system of Wage Units, and other tools by means of which Mr. Keynes works out his basic ideas. I wish however to welcome his purely monetary theory of interest which is, as far as I can see, the first to follow upon my own. Unfortunately, I must add that the similarity stops there and that I do not think my argument open to the objections which this one is sure to meet. Some differences would vanish, if the concepts of a demand for money stocks and of 'liquidity preference' – which is another *deus ex machina*; there is a whole Olympus of them – were replaced by concepts drawn from the economic processes that lie behind the surface phenomena denoted by those two. But then many of the striking inferences would also vanish. The whole vision of the capitalist process would change. Interest would lose the pivotal position which it holds in Mr. Keynes' analysis by virtue of the same technique which made it possible for Ricardo to hold that profits depend upon the price of wheat. And a completely different diagnosis of modern difficulties would follow.

The less said about the last book the better. Let him who accepts the message there expounded rewrite the history of the French *ancien régime* in some such terms as these: Louis XV was a most enlightened monarch. Feeling the necessity of stimulating expenditure he secured the services of such expert spenders as Madame de Pompadour and Madame du Barry. They went to work with unsurpassable efficiency. Full employment, a maximum of resulting output, and general well-being ought to have been the consequence. It is true that instead we find misery, shame and, at the end of it all, a stream of blood. But that was a chance coincidence.

# [REVIEW OF] THE GENERAL THEORY OF EMPLOYMENT, INTEREST AND MONEY*
## R. F. Harrod

Economic theory, as developed by the great English classical school of Adam Smith and his successors and further refined more recently by English speaking and continental writers, has been thought to justify, and in a considerable degree does justify, the system of free competition. It shows that within that system efficiency may be expected to be advanced, and that through the agency of markets and the 'pricing process' consumers may be expected to secure the goods which they most desire, having regard to the cost of producing them. The system is open to criticism because it has produced and of its nature tends to produce a very unequal distribution of wealth and income. Reform has been directed to mitigating these results; socialists have argued that no reform, that is practicable within the limits of the system, can reduce the inequalities sufficiently to render them tolerable, and that the system itself must be swept away.

Another kind of criticism has also been made by socialists and others, attacking the system on the ground of its inefficiency and claiming that the processes of private enterprise and free exchange have some inherent flaws in them, productive of crisis and unemployment and ultimately of disruption. Some of these critics have concerned themselves with the general theory of value, others, the monetary cranks, have confined themselves to ferreting out some defect in the monetary mechanism. The argumentations of both alike have on the whole been so deplorably muddle-headed and have contrasted so lamentably with the brilliant lucidity of the orthodox school, that those who put implicit faith in clear and honest thinking and instinctively distrust the easily recognizable croak of the charlatan, have been content to believe, even if reluctantly, that the defence has had right on its side. Concessions

* From *Political Quarterly*, vol. 7 (April/June 1936), pp. 293–8.

might be made to the pleas of sentiment and to the political arguments of the egalitarian school; but their economics has, on the whole with justice, not been taken too seriously. Mr. Keynes claims to have discovered a radical defect in the free system. His diagnosis, like those of the monetary enthusiasts, points to the possibility of remedy within the limits of the system, albeit probably involving far-reaching changes; but his analysis, unlike theirs, is concerned with the fundamental theory of value and exchange.

Mr. Keynes brings to his task an endowment very different from that of the critics already mentioned. His analytic and constructive powers are probably as distinguished as those of any writer who has ever devoted himself to the study of economics. His knowledge of the development of economic doctrine is far-reaching; he is well acquainted with the ground occupied by his adversaries, not merely with the form which their agreements usually take, but with the foundations on which they rest. And he is capable of matchless lucidity. The present work is a difficult one and its arguments cannot be mastered without considerable effort. But the effort is worth while. The reader may fear at first that all attempts to extricate himself from the maze of argumentation, in which he finds himself set, will be unavailing. He may take courage and rest assured that if he takes sufficient trouble, in the end he will see the reasoning as a unity. The underlying structure of thought has a beautiful simplicity; the apparent complexity is due to the fact that at every turn existing doctrines have to be dealt with, not always demolished, often merely re-sorted and allotted to their proper place in the general structure of theory.

This is not the place to undertake an examination of Mr. Keynes' substantive doctrines. As he himself claims, the matter must be argued out by the body of professional economists using their own weapons. The most essential point may, however, be set forth. It has usually been held that supply creates its own demand, that a particular commodity may be produced in excess, but that, since every increment of production entails an increment of demand on the part of those responsible for this extra production, there cannot be an excessive supply of commodities in general. Mr. Keynes seeks to make a breach in this doctrine by reference to saving. Here it is usually pointed out that income saved also gives rise to a demand for goods, namely, for capital goods. The people who actually do the saving, however, are not the same as those who give orders for capital goods. The latter are concerned with the prospect of demand for the products of capital goods in the coming time.

Suppose that we ask the question whether in the event of the current output of consumable goods being increased to the extent of £100 worth, a sufficient demand for them may be expected. If £100 of extra income is distributed to the various parties responsible for the production of the extra goods, the demand for consumable goods will be directly increased by the amount that those parties spend on consumable goods, say, by £80. £20 is saved. If at the same time future prospects are such that business men feel encouraged to add to their holding of capital goods to the extent of £20 worth, the income of those set to work to make the capital goods, being £20, will if expended and added to the £80 of expenditure on consumption aforementioned, make up a total extra demand for consumable goods of £100 and so justify the increase of output of consumable goods. But if prospects do not justify the extra capital construction, the demand for consumable goods will be £20 short, and those responsible for the production of consumable goods will restrict output at the next round. So long as people tend to save any part of their income the producers of consumable goods will only find sufficient purchasing power to justify them in their act of production, if those responsible for looking after the future feel disposed to make capital goods equal in value to the amount of saving which the community is choosing at the moment to make. If the demand for consumable goods proves deficient, those responsible for making them will restrict output on the next round, there will be less activity and less earning of income, and this restriction will proceed, until the amount of saving that people do is, by reason of their diminished income, reduced, so that it is no greater than the value of the capital goods currently being produced; for only so can the gap between the demand deemed sufficient to justify the production of consumable goods and the actual demand for them be eliminated. Thus the production of the community may be held far below its potential capacity simply because its members tend, in regard for their own personal requirements, to save more than industry deems it wise to use in the production of capital goods.

The orthodox view of the matter is that such a deficiency of demand will tend to be righted not by a slump of income and activity and consequent unemployment, but by a fall in the rate of interest which stimulates the production of capital goods. Mr. Keynes denies that this will necessarily or even probably happen. The rate of interest depends on how people value capital assets of which the yield is expected to be so and so much. Unfortunately the future yield is never exactly known. If a man chooses to hold any given capital asset he is involving himself in a measure of uncertainty; this is true even of assets on which there is a fixed contracted rate of interest. For the market value even of these assets may vary in future, as the rate of interest varies, and the holder of them may find himself involved in a loss if he wants to realise the assets and obtain cash. The rate of interest must be such as to make it worth while for a sufficient number of people to involve themselves in uncertainty of this nature. Such a rate of interest may be higher than that rate of interest which would so stimulate the production of capital goods that there would be a vent for all the saving people tend to make when the community is making money as fast as possible. If it is, there will be a deficiency of purchasing power, activity will run down, the community will not be allowed to make money as fast as possible and there will be unemployment. The productive system will not be used at its full capacity. The greater that capacity and the higher the national income would be if only it were fully used, the greater the danger that it will not be fully used; for people tend to save a large amount out of a large income. The menace of unemployment is a growing one.

Severe slump and crisis and widespread unemployment give point to socialist criticism of the existing system. Its defenders are filled with fear and alarm, and, in the absence of an adequate diagnosis, are at their wits end to know what to do. They attempt piece-meal remedies, tinkering with this industry and that, quite in vain so far as the general situation is concerned, and seek refuge in protectionism or autarky. The atmosphere of extreme depression is thundery; there is severe suffering, and fierce indignation; drastic action is demanded. The last slump produced revolution everywhere; who can predict the outcome of another severe recession in this country?

Some socialists welcome an atmosphere of tension, desiring a quick and drastic change of system. The greater part would prefer to avoid a sharp head-on conflict of interests, and to secure change by the gradual process of conciliation and conversion. In the head-on conflict other precious things might be lost – liberty and democracy. And in the present state of the world few would view with equanimity the weakening of this country which serious civil dissension must entail. The recurrence of a great slump, coming perhaps when the amount of unemployment was still large at the outset, would tend to strengthen the extremists. And even if a socialist party led by extremists were quickly routed and suppressed, this would be a grave political loss not only from the point of view of the socialists, but from that of all who cherish our free constitution.

Mr. Keynes' book is of supreme political interest because it offers an exact and intelligible diagnosis of the evil of unemployment. If the diagnosis is accepted, the quest for immediate remedies may be begun. Mr. Keynes provides a precise criterion by which proposed remedies may be tested. The present volume is concerned with the main structure of theory and not with the details of its application. This much may be said now, however, that the remedies would certainly be concerned with the operation of the banking and financial system, the volume of investment and public finance. They would entail collaboration between the government and the institutions concerned with these economic processes. How much government control or 'socialization' would be necessitated, would depend on the degree to which loyal co-operation could be secured.

If Mr. Keynes' diagnosis is right and if it is possible to obtain general agreement about it, the prospect is opened before us of keeping the existing system running without any drastic upheaval. Thus we should be afforded a breathing space, within which large social changes could be encompassed with mutual goodwill. If effective remedies could be applied along his lines, an atmosphere of comparative calm could be maintained, in which alone progress is possible in a free constitution. His proposals are hardly likely to resolve the fundamental conflict of interests between rich and poor. They would merely set the scene, in which that conflict might be resolved in a peaceful way without violent passion and disruption.

One point may be mentioned, however, which does bear upon the fundamental conflict. If his views are correct, our system ought so to be managed that the rate of interest falls to a very low level. This suggests that the present position of the rentier class might be gradually and peacefully liquidated – great profits might still be made but they could no longer form the basis for the maintenance of permanent economic predominance. And existing vested interests would in a community of growing income become of diminishing relative importance even if they were maintained, and in any case would be subject to the process of ordinary wear and tear, so that a more equitable distribution would eventuate without the nasty conflicts involved in expropriation.

It is to be hoped that Mr. Keynes, having got thus far in his work of construction, will apply his unique powers to giving a more popular exposition of these views, that are of such vital concern to the democracy.

# [REVIEW OF] THE GENERAL THEORY OF EMPLOYMENT, INTEREST AND MONEY*
## Benjamin Haggott Beckhart

In his new volume Mr. Keynes attempts to formulate a 'general' theory of employment, interest and money in contradistinction to the 'classical' approach, which is applicable only to a special case (p. 3). According to his analysis, classical theory has failed to integrate the theory of value and the theory of money and prices (p. 293). The traditional view is that the monetary system simply creates frictional disturbances (pp. 19–20). Mr. Keynes sets out to consider the dynamic factors involved in determining the volume of employment (p. 89) and in this attempt is interested not so much in the factors that govern the *distribution* of the national dividend as in those that promote a *full utilization* of available resources.

For some reason the members of the 'classical school' are Mr. Keynes's favorite *bête noire*. They are lumped together in a common brotherhood, and the theories of one are imputed to all. Other schools of economic thought are summarily dismissed or are not considered. Böhm-Bawerk is disposed of in a footnote which simply refers to Marshall's famous footnote. An appeal to a 'classicist' to trounce an Austrian! No reference is made to Wicksell's effort to synthesize value and monetary theory some forty years ago or to numerous other such attempts. Exceptions to the short shrift accorded economists in general occur in the case of the mercantilists, of Gesell, and of the underconsumption school of trade cycle theory.

A summarization of Mr. Keynes's argument is very difficult. So many are the sunbeams he pursues, so obscure the argument, so loose the use of terms, that the reader is left bewildered by the roadside. Somehow a beginning must be made, and perhaps we can start the circuitous route best with Mr. Keynes's concept of the propensity to consume. According to his analysis, this is a 'fairly stable function' (p. 95), so

* From *Political Science Quarterly*, vol. 51 (December 1936), pp. 600–603.

that on the basis of the psychological postulates set forth, the conclusion is reached that employment 'can only increase *pari passu* with investment' (p. 113). Hence to increase employment, investment must be furthered, and this can be stimulated only if the money rate of interest is below the marginal efficiency of capital (pp. 136–7). The increment of employment induced by the increased investment is determined by the investment multiplier (pp. 115–7), which Mr. Keynes declares to be somewhat greater than unity (p. 251).

Would it not be equally possible, however, for employment to be increased by a reduction in wages? No, replies Mr. Keynes, for a certain volume of unemployment would exist irrespective of the willingness of labor to work for reduced money wages (pp. 9, 262 *et seq.*). This is termed involuntary unemployment, which is so defined (p. 15) that its existence apparently can be determined only after the event by a kind of post-mortem examination.

To condense the argument greatly, the sequence in economic processes is from investment to income to savings. Capital accumulation is a derivative of the propensity to consume and is stimulated by bank lending rates which are under the marginal efficiency on capital. Consumer thrift impedes capital accumulation and hence is something to be discouraged. As defined, savings are always equal to investment. Everything is in balance, and the economic system is brought into a happy accounting equilibrium.

In the space alotted to this review it is not possible to follow the intricacies of each of Mr. Keynes's thought processes along its particular tortuous path. Of necessity one must concentrate on certain aspects of his theoretical formulations. It is for this reason that in what follows, his theories of the rate of interest, occupying a central position in his whole scheme, have been singled out for special consideration.

Mr. Keynes fails to develop any consistent theory respecting the rate of interest, and it is precisely in his failure to do so that his entire edifice reveals alarming cracks. To list a few of the statements relative to interest which appear at different stages in the volume:

As an approximation, the rate of interest can be identified with the rate of time discounting (p. 93).

Interest is a 'reward for parting with liquidity for a specified period' (p. 167).

The rate of interest is highly conventional (p. 203).

The current rate of interest depends on the strength of the desires to hold wealth in liquid and illiquid forms (p. 213).

The money rate of interest is 'nothing more than a percentage excess of a sum of money contracted for forward delivery' (p. 222).

The author is apparently in agreement with Gesell that the rate of interest is a purely monetary phenomenon (p. 355).

Interest is paid 'because capital is scarce'; it 'rewards no genuine sacrifice, any more than does the rent of land' (p. 376).

From the above statement one is puzzled to know whether Mr. Keynes thinks of interest entirely as a monetary function (in agreement with Gesell) or as determined in part by 'real conditions'. At one point he speaks of the 'pure rate of interest' (p. 208) as if it were something distinct from the money rate. From the point of view of his own argument this is a vital matter. If interest is not a purely monetary phenomenon, then it cannot be controlled wholly by the banking system, and hence investment cannot be stimulated continuously or solely by monetary means.

Mr. Keynes seems troubled by the inconsistency of his own interest doctrines. This shows itself in a growing skepticism of the efficacy of monetary policy directed towards influencing the rate of interest (p. 164). The illogical nature of his own position forces him finally to discard the central thesis that control of the money rate of interest is sufficient in the main to eliminate unemployment, and to conclude that 'a somewhat comprehensive socialisation of investment' is required to secure an approximation to full employment (p. 378).

Passing to the dynamics of interest theory, Mr. Keynes asserts that the trade cycle is due to fluctuations in the marginal efficiency of capital and that the crisis results from a collapse in the marginal efficiency of capital, which precipitates a rise in the rate of interest (pp. 313–16). The remedy for the boom, he declares, is not a higher but a lower rate of interest (p. 322). In this way slumps can be abolished and the economic system kept in a state of semi-boom.

How then does Mr. Keynes, in his trade cycle theory, meet

the contention that manipulations of the monetary rate of interest and their accompaniment of forced savings through a boom will bring about distortions in the structure of production of such a character that a crisis will be induced irrespective of monetary policy at the moment? Apparently he fails to see the importance of this aspect of the Böhm-Bawerk-Wicksell-Mises-Hayek theory of capital in relation to his own doctrines and contents himself with a categorical denial that credit expansion will allow investment to take place to which no genuine savings correspond (p. 82). The concept of forced savings, he declares, has no validity except in conditions of 'full employment' (pp. 79–81).

A study of developments through the German inflation indicates that forced saving as an economic force was more operative in the period preceding hyperinflation, i.e., preceding 'full employment', than it was during the period of hyperinflation itself. (See articles by Professor C. Bresciani-Turroni in recent issues of *Economica*.) It was in the period prior to hyperinflation that the productive forces were diverted so largely to investment goods and that large sums were invested or 'mis-invested' in new plant equipment. The increasing capital equipment at a time of great shortage in consumption goods resulted in a production structure so distorted in character that it could not long endure. Here again Mr. Keynes fails to distinguish between monetary and real conditions and fails in his objective to unify the theory of value on the one hand with the theory of money and prices on the other.

However much we may admire Mr. Keynes's crusading zeal, his latest work is likely to remain for the academician but an interesting exhibit in the museum of depression curiosities. To the inflationist, who will be able to bolster his specious arguments by appeal to authority, it will serve as a *vade mecum*.

# [FROM] MR KEYNES ON THE CAUSES OF UNEMPLOYMENT*
## Jacob Viner

The indebtedness of economists to Mr. Keynes has been greatly increased by this latest addition to his series of brilliant, original, and provocative books, whose contribution to our enlightenment will prove, I am sure, to have been even greater in the long than in the short run. This book deals with almost everything, but the causes of and the future prospects of unemployment, cyclical and secular, are its central theme. It brings much new light, but its display of dialectical skill is so overwhelming that it will have probably more persuasive power than it deserves, and a concentration on the points where I think I can detect defects in the argument, tho it would be unfair if presented as an appraisal of the merits of the book as a whole, may be more useful than would a catalogue – which would have to be long to be complete – of its points of outstanding intellectual achievement.

Written tho it is by a stylist of the first order, the book is not easy to read, to master, or to appraise. An extremely wide range of problems, none of them simple ones, are dealt with in an unnecessarily small number of pages. Had the book been made longer, the time required for reading it with a fair degree of understanding would have been shorter, for the argument often proceeds at breakneck speed and repeated rereadings are necessary before it can be grasped. The book, moreover, breaks with traditional modes of approach to its problems at a number of points – at the greatest possible number of points, one suspects – and no old term for an old concept is used when a new one can be coined, and if old terms are used new meanings are generally assigned to them. The definitions provided, moreover, are sometimes of unbelievable complexity. The old-fashioned economist must, therefore, struggle not only with

* From *Quarterly Journal of Economics*, vol. 51 (November 1936), pp. 147–60.

new ideas and new methods of manipulating them, but also with a new language. There is ample reward, however, for the expenditure of time and attention necessary for even partial mastery of the argument.

## 1. *'Involuntary' Unemployment*

Mr. Keynes claims that the 'classical'[1] economists recognized the possibility only of 'frictional' and of 'voluntary' unemployment, and that a vitally important chapter of economic theory remains to be written about a third class of unemployment, for which there was no place in the 'classical' scheme of things, namely, 'involuntary' unemployment. The concept of 'frictional' unemployment relates to the inevitable loss of time between jobs, and presents no difficulties. 'Voluntary' unemployment is defined as the unemployment 'due to the refusal or inability of a unit of labor . . . to accept a reward corresponding to the value of the product attributable to its marginal productivity', but is used in such manner as to require the addition to this definition of the proviso that the money wage offered must not be below what the laborer regards as a proper minimum rate of *money* wages. If laborers refuse available employment at a money rate below this minimum, or if employed laborers refuse to permit a prevailing money rate to be lowered and unemployment results for themselves or for others from this refusal, Keynes would apparently regard it as 'involuntary' unemployment, but deny its possibility or probability. He defines 'involuntary' unemployment as follows: 'Men are involuntarily unemployed if, in the event of a small rise in the price of wage-goods relatively to the money wage, both the aggregate supply of labor willing to work for the current money-wage and the aggregate demand for it at that wage would be greater than the existing volume of employment.' (p. 15). What he seems to mean by this is that any unemployment which would disappear if real wages were to be reduced by a rise in the prices of wage-goods, money wages remaining the same or rising in less proportion, *but not falling*, would be involuntary. It is with 'involuntary' unemployment so understood, its causes and its remedies, that Keynes' analysis of unemployment is primarily – and almost solely – concerned.

---

[1] Used by him to mean the later economists, such as J. S. Mill, Marshall, Edgeworth, Pigou, who in the main were adherents of the Ricardian tradition; a usage which I shall follow here.

In Keynes' classification of unemployment by its causes, unemployment due to downward-rigidity of money-wages, which for the 'classical' economists was the chief type of cyclical unemployment and the only important type of secular or persistent unemployment, therefore finds no place. As will be seen later, it is excluded on the ground that resistance to reductions in money wage-rates generally does not involve a reduction in the volume of employment and is, if anything, favorable to employment rather than the reverse. The omission charged against the 'classical' economists is their failure to note the lesser resistance of labor to reductions in real wages if unassociated with reductions in money wages *per se*, and their failure to recognize the existence of a large volume of unemployment for which the former is an available and practicable remedy, but not the latter. Keynes' reasoning points obviously to the superiority of inflationary remedies for unemployment over money-wage reductions. In a world organized in accordance with Keynes' specifications there would be a constant race between the printing press and the business agents of the trade unions, with the problem of unemployment largely solved if the printing press could maintain a constant lead and if only volume of employment, irrespective of quality, is considered important.

The only clash here between Keynes' position and the orthodox one is in his denial that reduction of money wage rates is a remedy for unemployment. Keynes even follows the classical doctrine too closely when he concedes that 'with a given organization, equipment and technique, real wages and the volume of output (and hence of employment) are uniquely correlated, so that, in general, an increase in employment can only occur to the accompaniment of a decline in the rate of real wages' (p. 17). This conclusion results from too unqualified an application of law-of-diminishing-returns analysis, and needs to be modified for cyclical unemployment, as well as for the possibility that the prices of wage-goods and of other goods may have divergent movements. If a plant geared to work at say 80 per cent of rated capacity is being operated at say only 30 per cent, both the per capita and the marginal output of labor may well be lower at the low rate of operations than at the higher rate, the law of diminishing returns notwithstanding. There is the further empirical consideration that if employers operate in their wage policy in accordance with marginal cost analysis, it is done only imperfectly and unconsciously, and the level of wages they can be persuaded to establish is strongly influenced by the profitability of their operations as a whole, and not solely – if at all – by calculations of the marginal contributions of labor to output.

Keynes uses the term 'full employment' to signify the absence of any involuntary unemployment (p. 16). He describes it also as the condition which would prevail 'when output has risen to a level at which the marginal return from a representative unit of the factors of production has fallen to the minimum figure at which a quantity of the factors sufficient to produce this output is available' (p. 303). There are implied here several questionable propositions. The concept of diminishing marginal productivity is generally used in economics in a partial differential sense to indicate the diminishing increments of output which would result when some particular factor or group of factors was being increased, the remainder of the working combination being held constant. If all the factors are being increased simultaneously and in uniform proportions, it requires some such assumption as that of the general prevalence of external technical dis-economics from increased production if it is to be accepted that output and return per compound unit of the factors must be negatively correlated. There is also implied here the assumption that any increase in real wages (money wages remaining constant, or rising) will result in an increase in the amount of labor available. If, as widely-held opinion since the seventeenth century has maintained, and as Professor Paul Douglas's recent investigations for urban labor in the United States appear to confirm, the supply schedule of labor with respect to real wages is, for part of its range at least, negatively inclined, the volume of employment could conceivably be much greater when there was 'involuntary' unemployment than when there was 'full' employment, and Keynes' conditions of 'full' employment might be met at an indefinite number of levels of employment.

'Full' employment rarely occurs, according to Keynes, and the main immediate responsibility for the persistence of 'involuntary' unemployment lies with the persistence of interest rates at levels too high to induce employers to bid for all the labor available at the prevailing money rates of wages. An elaborate and strikingly novel analysis of the causes determining the level of interest rates leads to the conclusion that high 'liquidity-preferences' of savers, an excessive disposition to save and a low marginal productivity of investment are responsible for the absence of such a relation between the rates at which savers are willing to lend and the rates at which entrepreneurs are willing to borrow for investment as would result in an approximation to 'full' employment.

Mr. Keynes claims further: (1) that there can be 'full' employment only when entrepreneurs make investments sufficient to absorb any excess of income paid-out by entrepreneurs over expenditures on consumption by income-recipients; (2) that the amount of investment entrepreneurs are prepared to make, or their 'investment demand for capital', is governed by the relation of their anticipations as to the yield of additional investment, or what Keynes calls the 'marginal efficiency of capital'[2] to the interest rates at which funds can be borrowed; (3) that the amount which income-recipients are willing to spend of their current income, or their 'propensity to consume', a function primarily of the amount of their incomes,[3] determines the quantity of saving; and (4) the rate of interest is determined by (a) 'liquidity preferences' and (b) the quantity of cash available to satisfy such preferences. The quantity of cash is generally assumed to be a constant. I accept most of this as valid in its general outlines, but I am unable to accept some of Keynes' account of how these 'propensities' operate in practice or his appraisal of their relative strength.

## 2. The Propensity to Hoard
Keynes maintains that for centuries back the propensity to save has been so much stronger than the inducement to invest as to create a substantial barrier to 'full' investment. He finds fault with the 'classical' economists for their alleged neglect of the gulf between the desire to save and the desire to invest, i.e., for their neglect of 'liquidity preferences'. It was a shortcoming of the Ricardian wing of the classical school that in the face of strong criticism they steadfastly adhered to their

---

[2] 'Anticipated marginal efficiency of capital' would seem to me a more accurately descriptive label for the concept.

[3] It is, in my opinion, probably dependent appreciably also on anticipations as to the prospective trend of income, and is surely affected significantly by amount of accumulated wealth at current valuations as well as by current income. See infra, §4, for further comments on this point.

position that hoarding was so abnormal a phenomenon as not to constitute a significant contributing factor to unemployment even during a period of severe deflation. In static equilibrium analysis, in which perfect price flexibility is assumed and monetary changes are abstracted from, there is no occasion for consideration of hoarding. In modern monetary theory it is generally dealt with, with results which in kind are substantially identical with Keynes', as a factor operating to reduce the 'velocity' of money. There has been, I believe, common agreement among economists that when price-rigidities are important hoarding could present a serious and continuing problem, and that it is always a significant factor in the downward phase of a short business cycle. Keynes, however, attaches great importance to it as a barrier to 'full' employment at almost all times, and apparently irrespective of the degree of flexibility of prices.

There are several reasons why 'liquidity preferences' loom so large to Keynes as a source of trouble in the economic process. He takes it for granted that they are ordinarily so strong for the average person in control of liquid resources that a substantial interest rate is required to overcome them; and apparently that they cannot be overcome by *any* rate of interest if a still higher rate of interest is anticipated in the near future. He assigns to them the rôle of sole determinant (given the amount of cash available, which he treats ordinarily as a constant) of the rate of interest. He believes that the marginal productivity function of capital and therefore the investment demand for capital have little elasticity. Finally he assumes in general that nothing can satisfy liquidity preferences except that 'cash' whose quantity is one of the determinants of the interest rate.

We have almost no reliable information about the strength of liquidity preferences under varying circumstances, and in the absence of statistical information of a genuinely relevant character discussion must be based largely on conjecture. Nevertheless I venture to present a series of considerations which, in the aggregate, seem to warrant the conclusion that Keynes has grossly exaggerated the extent to which liquidity preferences have operated in the past and are likely to operate in the future as a barrier to 'full' employment.

(*a*) Keynes stresses the pressure which is exercised by the expectation of a rise in the interest rate on potential purchasers of securities, leading them to postpone their purchases in order to escape a capital loss. There are, however, in every country large numbers of investors who have been taught to buy gilt-edge securities on the basis of their yield to maturity and to disregard the fluctuations in their day-to-day market values. Even investors of a speculative type are ordinarily as anxious not to miss a 'low' as not to buy too high. There are many opportunities for investment which are – or seem at the time to be – of the 'now-or-never' type. There is a widely-prevalent aversion to the waste of 'dead' cash.

(b) Keynes seems to exaggerate the actuarial valuation of postponement of investment during a period of anticipated rise in interest rates. Rising interest rates are frequently associated with periods of greater confidence in the security of the investment, as far as payment of principal and interest according to schedule are concerned; or in the case of equity securities, with periods of more favorable anticipations of long-run yields. Hence periods of rising interest rates are often associated with periods of rising rather than falling prices of securities, especially for equity securities. Keynes seems to be in error also when he asserts that, abstracting from the risk of default on principal or interest, it will be equally profitable to hoard as to invest at par in a long-term security paying 4 per cent if the market interest rate is rising by 0.16 per cent per annum. In the first place, hoarding and investment in a long-term security are not the only alternatives. Let it be provisionally granted that hoarding and the purchase at par of a 4 per cent long-term bond would prove equally profitable at the end of the first year if the interest rate during that year had risen by 0.16 per cent. The purchase at the beginning of the year of a one-year maturity security paying anything over 0.16 per cent would then have been more profitable even if it had to be exchanged for cash within six months, and even if the short-term interest rate were also gradually rising by as much as 0.16 per cent per annum. Secondly, even a purchaser of the long-term 4 per cent security would have been richer at the end of the first year than if he had hoarded his cash, unless the security were a *perpetual* bond.

(c) Even if it be granted that liquidity-preferences are as strong ordinarily as Keynes indicates, their operation as a barrier to investment would necessarily be important only if it be assumed (1) that liquidity-preferences can be satisfied solely by the holding of non-investment assets, and (2) that the quantity of such assets does not automatically respond to the demand for them. Keynes takes care of this second qualification by his assumption that the quantity of money – in the assumed absence of a positive central monetary control – is constant. Here, indeed, he concedes more than is necessary, for if liquidity preferences are assumed to be stronger during depressions than during periods of business expansion, then the quantity of money, under such monetary systems as have existed in the past, varies inversely with the strength of liquidity preferences. But he does not give adequate consideration to the first qualification.

The satisfaction of liquidity preference on the one hand and of investment on the other, are opposite phenomena only if the range of assets which can satisfy investment demand corresponds with the range of assets which can satisfy liquidity-preferences, so that it shall be impossible to satisfy both by the same transaction. If liquidity-preferences can be satisfied by the holding of resources which are not identical with the 'money' whose surrender satisfies investment demand, the satisfaction of the former does not necessarily entail failure to satisfy the latter. Keynes explains liquidity-preference as a wish to retain one's resources in the form of money. There is no systematic examination of what is to be included as 'money' for this purpose, but incidentally to his analysis of one particular form of surrender of liquidity, namely, exchange of money for a debt, he states:

> ... we can draw the line between 'money' and 'debts' at whatever point is most convenient for handling a particular problem. For example, we can treat as *money* any command over general purchasing power which the owner has not parted with for a period in excess of three months, and as *debt* what cannot be recovered for a longer period than this; or we can substitute for 'three months' one month or three days or three hours or any other period; or we can exclude from *money* whatever is not legal tender on the spot. It is often convenient in practice to include in *money* time-deposits with banks and, occasionally, even such instruments as (e.g.) treasury bills. As a rule, I shall ... assume that money is co-extensive with bank deposits (p. 167, note).

If everything which satisfies liquidity-preference is to be

included as money, then money must be broadly defined so as to include not only demand deposits and time deposits, but also short-term securities, any other assets which are readily marketable without serious risk of loss through depreciation of value, and even the command over credit from banks or others. But the conversion of newly-acquired cash into any other form of asset either involves investment directly or transfers the decision as between hoarding and investment to a banker or other intermediary between the original saver and the ultimate borrower for investment. If the banker permits his investments to remain constant while his cash reserves are increasing, or if he maintains the same cash reserves for idle as for active demand deposits, or for time deposits as for demand deposits, or for deposits as for bank-notes in circulation, then the propensity to hoard which manifests itself in the maintenance of idle bank deposits does operate to check investment, but only with the connivance and support of the banking mechanism.

It may be objected that even if liquidity-preferences operate only, or in the main, to check purchases of long-term securities, they still operate as a check to investment; because the latter is and must be largely in durable goods, or in assets far removed from the stage of the consumers' goods. But the relation between the period of investment intended by the saver and that intended, or in fact resulting, by the borrowing entrepreneur is not a simple one of necessary equality. It is highly flexible and approaches to free variability at the discretion of the borrower. Every money market has an elaborate machinery for transmuting short-term loans into long-term investments and long-term loans into short-term investments, to suit the convenience of original lenders and ultimate borrowers. The typical entrepreneur will shift from long-term to short-term borrowing, or vice versa, even tho the time period involved in the particular operation is unchanged, or (as often) unknowable in advance. He may also be able to shift from long-term to short-term investment if the interest rate at which the latter can be financed is much lower than that at which he can conduct admittedly long-term borrowing. If savers have a 5 per cent per annum preference for cash over investment in 10-year bonds but only a $\frac{1}{4}$ per cent preference for cash over time-deposits or short-term securities, and if entrepreneurs want funds for 10 years and are unwilling to incur the sacrifice of their own liquidity which would be involved in the attempt to finance 10-year operations with say 3-month borrowings, middlemen will step in who are prepared to lend on long-term funds which they have borrowed on short-term. The modern money market is fortunately equipped to some extent with procedures for satisfying liquidity-preferences without providing genuine liquidity.

(*d*) The propensity to hoard exercises its influence as a restraint on investment through its tendency to raise interest rates. But in what seems to me the most vulnerable part of his analysis, his explanation of the determination of the rate of interest, Keynes assigns to the desire for cash for hoarding purposes a grossly exaggerated importance.

Keynes denies the validity of the 'classical' doctrine that interest is the reward for saving and is directly determined by the supply schedule of savings with respect to the interest rate and the investment demand schedule for capital, and his exposition leaves the impression that the interest rate is not dependent to any important extent on these two factors. He denies that interest is the 'reward' for saving on the ground that, if a man hoards his savings in cash, he earns no interest, tho he saves just as much as before (p. 167), and claims that, on the contrary, it is the reward for surrender of liquidity. By analogous reasoning he could deny that wages are the reward for labor, or that profit is the reward for risk-taking, because labor is sometimes done without anticipation or realization of a return, and men who assume financial risks have been known to incur losses as a result instead of profits. Without saving there can be no liquidity to surrender. The saver who has no concern about liquidity gets the same reward as the person who saved with liquidity as his initial objective but is persuaded by the interest rate to lend; and the return is granted for loans irrespective whether it is reluctance to postpone consumption or reluctance to surrender liquidity which keeps the supply of funds for investment down to the level at which borrowers are willing to pay the prevailing rate of interest for it. The rate of interest is the return for saving without liquidity.

Keynes explains the rate of interest as determined by the schedule of liquidity-preferences and the available quantity of money, the prevailing rate of interest being simply that price for the sacrifice of liquidity at which the desire to hold cash is equated with the quantity of available cash (p. 167). The rate of interest determines the amount of investment, given the investment demand for capital; but a change in the investment demand for capital will not affect the interest rate 'if nothing has happened to the state of liquidity-preference and the quantity of money'. (See especially the figure on p. 180, and the text on p. 181).

There have been previous attempts to discover a basis on which the interest rate could be held to be determined independently of the demand for capital, the level of wages, and other important elements in the economy, but the growing recognition of the basic interdependence of all the important economic variables has led to widespread scepticism that any such attempt could succeed. In Keynes' present attempt the fatal flaw is, to repeat, the exaggerated importance attributed to hoarding. In his discussion of liquidity-preferences Keynes distinguishes between the desire for cash for use in the current transaction of personal and business exchanges, and the desire for cash as a security against loss from unsuccessful investment. As I have already argued, the latter consideration should not operate as a barrier to short-term investment, and while it may induce a high long-term interest rate, it will be compensated for in part by a shift of borrowing to the short-term market. The pattern of behavior of the desire for transaction-liquidity is probably very largely the inverse of that of security-liquidity, or hoarding proper. As D. H. Robertson points out in his contribution to this symposium, the transactions-desire for cash is for cash to be used and not for cash to be held unused. It must therefore vary positively with the volume of investment, of income, and of expenditures for consumption. In so far as it consists of demand for cash from entrepreneurs for business uses, it is but a reflection of their investment demand for capital. In so far as it is a demand for cash from consumers who are living beyond their current income, it is the demand for consumption loans of older theory. Whatever its origin, demand for cash for transaction purposes is, dollar for dollar, of equal influence on the rate of interest as demand for cash for hoarding purposes. The demand for capital and the propensity to save (which is the reciprocal of the propensity to consume) are thus restored – tho, I admit, in somewhat modified and improved fashion – to their traditional rôles as determinants of the rate of interest.

While (to repeat again) relevant statistical information is

scarce, what we do know about the holders of cash balances in the United States points strongly to the importance of the transactions-motive for liquidity and to the relative insignificance in ordinary times of hoarding. It is the corporations, institutions, and governments that hold at all times the bulk of the cash balances, especially if savings deposits are excluded as constituting investments rather than cash. Moreover I suspect (I know of no data on the question) that at least in prosperous times the savers – those who add each year to their estates – who are supposed by Keynes to be a source of so much trouble because of their hoarding propensities, typically hold in cash a smaller percentage of their incomes, let alone of their total resources, than do the spenders. The former have investment habits, and abhor idle cash as nature abhors a vacuum. The latter hold cash until the bills come in for settlement. It would at least be interesting to know whether these are facts or fancies.

The importance of the transactions-demand for cash makes it easy to explain a whole series of historical phenomena which do not fit into Keynes' theory. Because the demand for cash for business use varies positively with the investment demand for capital, and the demand for cash for personal use varies positively with the level of income and of expenditures for consumption, there is no need for treating as a perplexing puzzle the facts, that business is active when interest rates are high and slack when interest rates are low, and that the quantity of money and the interest rate are historically correlated positively rather than negatively. There is an important stabilizing influence, moreover, in these circumstances. During a depression entrepreneurs and spenders release some of the cash to supply the demand of hoarders for security, and during an expansion of business the absorption of cash by business and by spenders, serving as it does to raise the interest rate, keeps the expansion from going beyond bounds; or, Keynes would say, from even approaching reasonable bounds.

# [FROM] SOME NOTES ON MR KEYNES' GENERAL THEORY OF EMPLOYMENT*
## D. H. Robertson

I am grateful for the opportunity to publish these notes in a setting which will make it plain that they are not an attempt to appraise Mr. Keynes' book as a whole, or to discuss properly the high matters of judgment and policy on which it bears – matters on some tho not all of which I am, I think, more nearly in agreement with Mr. Keynes than the reader of these notes might suppose!

After numerous discussions of this book and these notes I am in the usual difficulty – how to acknowledge indebtedness without compromising the acknowledgee. Especially from Professor Pigou, Mr. Henderson, Dr. Bode, Mr. Hicks and above all from Mr. Sraffa, I have derived much positive illumination and helpful criticism; but they are none of them guilty except – I mean not even – Mr. Sraffa. What follows should, at the least, be peppered with footnotes containing his name. The page references are to Mr. Keynes' General Theory, except where otherwise stated.

## I. *Effective Demand*

§1. There is a verbal obscurity in Mr. Keynes' exposition of his central apparatus (pp. 23–32) which may have troubled others besides myself.

Income (later called $Y$) is the proceeds which result from giving a certain amount of employment; aggregate demand price $(D)$ is the proceeds which are *expected* to result from giving that amount of employment; aggregate supply price $(Z)$ is the proceeds the expectation of which will just make it worth while to give that amount of employment, and for simplicity may be regarded as made up of factor-cost $(F)$ and associated profit $(P)$ (pp. 24–25).

* From *Quarterly Journal of Economics*, vol. 51 (November 1936), pp. 168–70, 175–9, 187–91.

Suppose we are in equilibrium, i.e. with $D = Z$, at a level of output $R$ entailing less than 'full' employment. Why is not output increased to $R+\Delta R$? Because if it were, then, since part of the increase in individual incomes would not be spent,[1] sales-proceeds would fall short of the sum which makes the production of $R+\Delta R$ worth while ( $\Delta Y$ would be less than $\Delta Z$). But suppose that entrepreneurs (perhaps having heard at their last Rotary Club luncheon a lecture on J. B. Say) expand output in the *belief* that $\Delta Y$ will equal $\Delta Z$. Their disappointment must surely not be represented, as is suggested in these pages, as due to a divergence between aggregate demand price and aggregate supply price; for in the case supposed these two are equal. It must be represented (as Mr. Keynes first discloses much later, on p. 78)[2] as due to a divergence between aggregate demand price and income. Mr. Keynes in fact oscillates between using 'aggregate demand price' to mean what he has defined it to mean, viz. what entrepreneurs *do* expect to receive, and using it to mean (p. 30, line 5) what they 'can expect' to receive, i.e. what they can legitimately expect to receive, because that, whether they expect it or not, is what they *will* receive. In a world in which errors of anticipation are common, the distinction is not unimportant!

§ 2. Suppose, for instance, that $\Delta Y$, while less than $\Delta Z$, turns out to be greater than $\Delta F$ – as will happen, e.g., if factors spend all their increments of income, and profit-receivers even a small fraction of theirs. Then $\Delta P$ is positive; the general mistake has promoted the general gain. $Z$, it is true, exceeds $Y$, i.e. for the representative entrepreneur marginal cost exceeds marginal receipts, and if he expects the situation to be repeated he would be wise to contract output. But he is doing better than he was; hope springs eternal; may not the mistake be repeated, and on a larger scale? If it is, $\Delta P$ will again be positive; indeed on these lines, even tho $Z$ continues to exceed $Y$, output will be in unstable equilibrium at any point short of 'full employment' in the consumption trades. But perhaps, as

---

[1] I am not here examining the conditions under which this is probable.

[2] The contrast here (rather suddenly) declared to be 'vital for causal analysis' is, indeed, not between aggregate demand price and income but between effective demand and income; but 'effective demand' is simply that particular value of the aggregate demand schedule at which aggregate demand price is equal to aggregate supply price (and in the real world therefore is something of a Cheshire cat?),

output grows, $Z$ will not continue indefinitely to exceed $Y$, for consumption breeds investment, as well as investment consumption. The mistake will turn out not to have been a mistake after all.

It is tempting to interpret along these lines Marshall's famous account of the automatic process of trade recovery, with its suggestion of the need for, and ultimate occurrence of, a sort of plot.[3] A precarious and dilatory process, perhaps, and one that we may well fortify by contrived investment. But in assessing so low the natural recuperative powers of the economic system, has Mr. Keynes taken full account of the potentialities, for good as well as evil, of that contrast between the realized and the expected which, at some moments 'vital for causal analysis', at others seems forgotten? . . .

### III. The Rate of Interest

§1. According to Mr. Keynes the rate of interest does not depend at all on the demand for loanable funds for use in investment. 'The schedule of the marginal efficiency of capital may be said to govern the terms on which loanable funds are demanded for the purpose of new investment, while the rate of interest governs the terms on which funds are being currently supplied' (p. 165; cf. p. 184). The rate of interest in turn depends on the state of liquidity preference and on the quantity of money (p. 168), liquidity preference being defined as a schedule relating the amount of money which people are willing to hold with the rate of interest prevailing in the market. Thus if we measure money along $OX$ and interest along $OY$, $OM$ is the amount of money which people will be willing to hold if the rate of interest is $MP$. For various reasons the curve $LL_1$, the locus of $P$, normally slopes downwards to the right.

§2. It will be convenient to examine this doctrine in connection with a particular series of events – the upward swing of

---

[3] *Principles*, p. 711. 'If all trades which make goods for direct consumption agreed to work on and to buy one another's goods as in ordinary times, they would supply one another with the means of earning a moderate rate of profit and of wages. The trades which make fixed capital might have to wait a little longer; but they too would get employment when confidence had revived so far that those who had capital to invest had made up their minds how to invest it . . . There is of course no formal agreement between the different trades to begin to work again full time, and so make a market for each other's wares. But the revival of industry comes about through the gradual and often simultaneous growth of confidence among many various trades.'

an expansion initiated by the monetary authority. A common sense account of this process may be given as follows: The authority[4] operates by handing out money, partly to persons who, at a lower rate of interest, i.e. a higher price of income-yielding assets, are desirous of *holding* more money in lieu of income-yielding assets,[5] partly to persons who, at a lower rate of interest, see a prospect of *using* more money profitably in their businesses. It is tempting to identify these two classes with those from whom the authority has bought securities and those to whom it has made loans respectively, but it seems probable that to do so would often be to exaggerate the importance of the former class. For instance it seems likely that the purchases of securities by the English banks in recent years have been largely made from business firms who were preparing to finance extensions of production by selling securities instead of by borrowing.[6]

If we take, as it were, a flash light photograph of the situation when the new money is still in the hands of its first holders, we shall, it is true, find Fig. I formally applicable. Both of the classes distinguished above are caught, so to speak, in the act of acquiring more money as a result of the fall in the rate of interest. But it is evident that in the case of the second class productivity conditions, as embodied, if we like, in a curve of declining 'marginal efficiency of capital', are exercising a dominant influence upon their actions, and therefore an important effect in determining the rate of interest which will be associated with a given emission of money. A formula which obscures this by lumping together in the same portmanteau those who desire to *hold* more money and those who desire to *use* it does not seem to me helpful towards clarity of thought.

§3. The situation so far considered is of course highly unstable. The second class of persons distinguished above stand ready to spend the money in their hands. The first class ex hypothesi desire under existing conditions to continue to hold it, but the fall in the rate of interest which they have cooperated in determining stands as an inducement to others to acquire

---

[4] I use this word to include not merely the Government or Central Bank but also the associated complex of 'member banks'.

[5] This, of course, is the point which Mr. Keynes has particularly illuminated.

[6] Economist, Banking Supplement, May 16, 1936, p. 9.

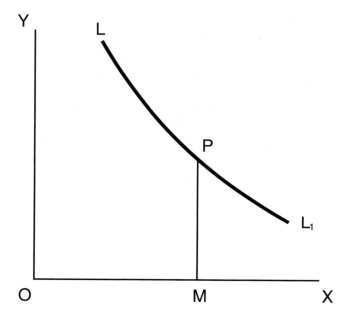

Fig. I

newly created money for use in their businesses.[7] Thus normally forces will be set to work to expand the stream of money devoted to the purchase of commodities. This will raise the schedule of profitability of funds devoted to business uses, by generating an expansion of the stream of sales proceeds which entrepreneurs expect to receive, without a corresponding expansion in the stream of money costs which they expect to disburse.

Meanwhile, however, the attractiveness of keeping any given

---

[7] See Cassel's formulation (Theory of Social Economy, 1st Eng. tr., II, 60). 'Capital goods are capitalized at too low a rate of interest, that is to say, their prices go up. Hence the production of capital goods seems to be particularly remunerative, and employers make free use of the purchasing power which the banks offer them so cheaply.' But there is no need to enter here into the relation between the 'cost' and 'capitalization' aspects of the situation, excellently discussed by Ellis, German Monetary Theory 1905–1933, pp. 415–421.

proportion of wealth or income idle in the form of money is being diminished by the expected depreciation of money, and dishoarding takes place. Further the expansion of real income and its redistribution in favor of entrepreneurs is likely on the whole to be leading to an increase in the flow of current savings[8] available for distribution between various uses. These two sets of forces are acting on the rate of interest in *opposition* to the predominant set of forces, namely that which is raising the schedule of profitability of funds directed to investment. So is the continued injection of money, if money is still being injected.

Subject to a complication presently to be mentioned, a photograph taken on any day in this phase will reveal the rate of interest in quasi-equilibrium under the influence of these various forces. And while the result depends of course on what level of activity we start at and how long we wait before pressing the button, the common opinion is that sooner or later in the expansion our plates will reveal that it has been substantially raised.[9] But whether this is so or not, it is evident that during this phase productivity conditions play not merely a part but a leading part in determining its level.

§4. The complication mentioned above is as follows. Owing to the imperfection of markets, and to inequality of foresight and bargaining power between borrower and lender, there is likely to arise a divergence between the marginal rate of return from productive assets and what, following Marshall, we may

---

[8] I do not enter here into the tangled question of which parts if any of these savings can usefully be described as 'forced' or 'quasi-forced'. But I may remark that in conceding (p. 124) that under the pressure of an expansion of investment there may occur a 'temporary reduction of the marginal propensity to consume', Mr. Keynes seems to me to go a long way towards readmitting that concept of 'some species of levy on the public' which he elsewhere (p. 183) dismisses as among 'the worst muddles of all'.

[9] Cf. Marshall, Money, Credit and Commerce, p. 257. 'The increase of currency . . . increases the willingness of lenders to lend in the first instance, and lowers the rate of discount. But it afterwards raises prices and therefore it tends to increase discount. This latter movement is cumulative.'

Among all his quotations from Marshall, Mr. Keynes does not, I think, in this book, include any from the famous passages of Evidence which were for many years in Cambridge the basis of exposition of this subject. See Official Papers, pp. 52 and 131, reproduced and expanded in Money, Credit and Commerce, pp. 75–76 and 254–257. The reader who wishes to retain a just estimate of Marshall's contributions to interest theory is earnestly recommended to refresh his memory of the whole of these passages.

call 'interest in the strict sense', viz. 'the payment which anyone receives during a given period in return for a loan'.[10] If, however, the former is rising, it is unlikely that the frictions will be so great as to prevent altogether the competition of borrowers from raising the rate of interest 'in the strict sense'. As Professor Fisher puts it,

> not only will lenders require, but borrowers can afford to pay higher interest in terms of money, and to some extent competition will gradually force them to do so. Yet we are so accustomed in our business dealings to consider money as the one thing stable . . . that we reluctantly yield to this process of adjustment, thus rendering it very slow and imperfect.[11]

> The money rate of interest, while it does change somewhat, does not usually change enough to fully compensate for the appreciation or depreciation.[12]

In view of these and similar passages, it is not easy to agree that Professor Fisher has made a 'mistake in supposing that it is the rate of interest on which prospective changes in the value of money will directly react' (p. 142), still less to understand why Mr. Keynes apparently believes him (ibid., bottom of page) to have argued that it is the rise in the rate of interest 'in the strict sense', and not its failure to rise further, which exercises a stimulating effect on the entrepreneur . . .

§7. According to Mrs. Robinson,[13] Mr. Keynes' theory 'has been developed mainly in terms of short period analysis'; but at times his purview extends over centuries, and it may be convenient to conclude by examining briefly the bearing of his 'liquidity preference' formula on the long-period problem of saving. This problem can be put in various forms, of which I choose what is, I hope, alike the simplest and the best adapted to bring out Mr. Keynes' points. Will an increased rate of saving which is not itself hoarding (e.g. which takes the form of an increased demand for securities), but which involves an actual diminution in the rate of expenditure on consumable goods, lead to a progressive shrinkage in total money income?

[10] Money, Credit and Commerce, p. 73
[11] Purchasing Power of Money, p. 57.
[12] The Theory of Interest, p. 493.
[13] Zeitschrift für Nationalökonomie, 1936, p. 74.

In one of his extremer passages (pp. 211–213) Mr. Keynes appears to invoke his formula in support of the view that such an event has *no* tendency to bring down the rate of interest nor therefore to stimulate the formation of capital equipment. For why, he asks, the quantity of money being unchanged, should a fresh[14] act of saving diminish the sum which it is required to keep in liquid form at the existing rate of interest? The answer surely emerges from the composite nature of 'liquidity preference'. If the event in question deprives the producers of consumption goods of income, it reduces by the same act their ability to hold money for 'transaction' and 'precautionary' purposes. It is only if they resist the switch in public demand by continuing to indulge in expenditure, to offer employment, and hence to hold (or cause to be held) money balances on the old scale, that 'liquidity preference' as defined will remain unchanged. Mr. Keynes' argument in this passage seems to be a repetition in disguise of his old argument that increased saving which is not itself hoarding is necessarily balanced by the sale of securities on the part of entrepreneurs who are making losses but are determined not to restrict the amount or change the character of their output. In so far as this argument is ever valid, it is as valid when employment is full to start with as when it is not – indeed, as Professor Hayek pointed out long ago,[15] it depends on the assumption that employment will be *kept* full at all costs: it is thus not easy to reconcile with Mr. Keynes' concession to the efficacy of Thrift under conditions of full employment (p. 112). So long as such a situation exists and is expected to continue, the rate of interest will, it is true, not fall nor the formation of capital equipment be stimulated, but neither, so far as the mere maintenance of income[16] and employment goes, is it necessary that they should. If such a situation does *not* exist, there is nothing in the doctrine of liquidity preference to invalidate the common

[14] I must take this, as explained above, to mean an additional act, for nobody has argued that with a given level of the demand for (new) savings, the maintenance of an existing rate of supply of (new) savings will bring down the rate of interest below its existing level. On this whole matter, see the illuminating discussion by Durbin, Purchasing Power and Trade Depression, especially p. 76 and note.

[15] Economica, February, 1932, p. 30.

[16] Other than that of the entrepreneurs primarily affected. For full discussion of this case see Economic Journal, September, 1933, pp. 403–409.

sense view that the increased demand for securities will tend to raise their price.

§8. There remains, however, a further point. Even tho the producers of consumption goods take their medicine, nevertheless, if there exists for the community as a whole a negatively inclined curve of 'liquidity preference proper' ($LL_1$, Fig. II [or Fig. I]), some part of the additional savings devoted by individuals to the purchase of securities will come to rest in the banking accounts of those who, at the higher price of securities, desire to hold an increased quantity of money.[17] Thus the fall in the rate of interest and the stimulus to the formation of capital will be less than if $LL_1$ were a vertical straight line, and the stream of money income will tend to contract. Liquidity appears on the demand side of the market for savings as an equal partner (tho no more) with Productivity, and as a potential source of damage.

It would, I think, be agreed by 'orthodox' writers[18] that this is a situation calling for a progressive increase in the supply of money.[19] That the task of the monetary authority, even regarded as a long run task, might under certain conditions become a very difficult one is certainly not a theoretical impossibility. In estimating its difficulty, however, three points must be borne in mind.

(1) According to Mr. Keynes, the liquidity schedule proper is a phenomenon of 'speculation', turning on the expectation of *reversals* in the downward movement of interest rates. It is not evident that it is right to attach much importance to it in connection with the long period problem now under discussion.[20] (2) On the other hand, it is usually

---

[17] This point was already made by Mr. Keynes, somewhat obscurely and much tangled up with the previous point, in his Treatise on Money, I, 145; was mishandled by me in Economic Journal, 1931, p. 400; and has since been brought out clearly by Meade, Rate of Interest in a Progressive State, pp. 110 ff. and Durbin, Problem of Credit Policy, pp. 151–152. I am glad of the opportunity to admit its theoretical validity and possible importance.

[18] E.g., I imagine, by Professor Pigou and by most at any rate of those continental writers who have written in terms of 'neutral' money and of making the bank rate of interest conform to the 'natural' rate.

[19] For there is (in my language) an increase in hoarding (increase in the Marshallian $K$), tho the 'propensity to hoard' is unchanged.

[20] Cf. Pigou, Economica, May, 1936, p. 130.

held[21] that there is *some* elasticity in the desire to hold resources in monetary form even for 'transaction' and 'precautionary' purposes, so that there will be a successive decline in the rate of yield equated in the minds of holders with the successive doses of convenience and security so obtained. Reflection however suggests that here, too, the rate of yield which money holders equate in their mind with any *n*th parcel of convenience and security is not likely to be arrived at by some kind of intuition functioning in vacuo, but rather to be influenced by the rate of return actually obtainable from investment. Thus, so far as the rate of interest goes, Liquidity in the long run appears perhaps rather as a kind of ghost or poor relation of Productivity than as its equal partner, and as likely to furnish a progressively less dangerous trap for savings as, with a successful process of saving, the normal rate of interest declines.

Finally (3) it will be recalled that Mr. Keynes sometimes invites us to reckon liquidity preference in terms of 'wage-units'. The logical extension of this line of thought, over periods in which the actions or inactions of the monetary authority have time to work their way right through the system, seems to lead us back into the 'orthodox' world in which the quantity of money, in the ordinary sense, becomes irrelevant, and an increase in hoarding works out its effect not on the rate of interest at all but on the level of prices and money incomes. It is, I think, as I have said above, generally agreed that the evils of progressive shrinkage would be so great that it should be the object of monetary policy to avert them. But if we are concerned for the moment with problems of 'comparative statics' rather than of 'dynamics', this line of thought should, I think, make us cautious about accepting the view that unemployment is likely to be specially great, or even the rate of interest specially high, in societies where 'liquidity preference' is high.[22] Only if the hunt for liquidity eventuates

[21] Cf. Pigou, *Essays in Applied Economics*, pp. 180–181. 'Thus the curves that represent the desire for resources to be used in production and in titles to legal tender respectively both slope downwards.'

[22] Still less does there seem any reason why a high prestige-value for *land* (p. 241) should make the rate of interest rule high. What it does is to keep the purchase price of land high, i.e. the net yield from buying it low, and to make the mortgage rate of interest seem high by comparison; but the mortgage rate (e.g. in India) is presumably *lower* than it would be if the land pledged had less prestige-value. Indirectly, of course, the opportunity to sell

in the successful devotion of resources to the acquisition of the precious metals will a high liquidity preference be inimical to an abundance of income-yielding instruments and to a low rate of interest. India, for instance, is less well equipped, and has higher rates of interest, than if she had not dedicated so much of her thrift to the acquisition of gold.[23]

As regards future trends in the West, the whole matter is, as Professor Pigou has said, highly speculative. I could wish that Mr. Keynes had found it possible to say his say about it without, as I think, cumbering our judgments with an apparatus which accords to Liquidity a unique position in the theory of interest to which, even in the short run, it is not, I have attempted to argue, entitled.

---

land at high prices or to borrow on it at relatively low rates may well encourage extravagant consumption and thus raise interest rates and retard the growth of wealth; but Mr. Keynes cannot be thinking of that, for it is an explanation which he specifically rejects (p. 242).

[23] Thus from a long period point of view it is not inelastic (p. 230) but elastic conditions of supply of the money metal which help to keep the rate of interest high.

# THE FUNDAMENTAL ASSUMPTION OF MR KEYNES' MONETARY THEORY OF UNEMPLOYMENT*

## Wassily W. Leontief

### I

The difference between Mr. Keynes' new theory of economic equilibrium and the 'orthodox' classical scheme is fundamentally a difference in assumptions, or rather in one basic assumption. While the two divergent points of view come to a clash more specifically in the discussion concerning the shape of the supply function for labor, the theoretical issue involved is much more general in its scope. In the present note I shall first of all try to redefine the contested principle in precise terms, then interpret its relevant theoretical implications, and finally make an attempt to examine the arguments which Mr. Keynes raises against the 'orthodox' solution of the problem and in favour of his own standpoint. I shall confine myself to the strictly theoretical problems.

The theoretical picture underlying the economic analysis of general equilibrium is that of the system of interrelated household and entrepreneurial units engaged in more or less continuous economic transactions. The quantity of each particular kind of commodities and services sold or purchased by each individual enterprise or household is considered to be a function of a number of different prices. On the basis of certain assumptions concerning the forces which are supposed to govern the behavior of business firms and individuals, economic theory is able to derive the general characteristics of these functional interrelations between prices and quantities.

One of these fundamental assumptions – that which Mr. Keynes is ready to repudiate – defines an important universal property of all supply and demand functions by stating that the *quantity of any service or any commodity demanded or*

* From *Quarterly Journal of Economics*, vol. 51 (November 1936), pp. 192–7.

*supplied by a firm or an individual remains unchanged if all the prices upon which it (directly) depends increase or decrease exactly in the same proportion.* In mathematical terms, this means that all supply and demand functions, with prices taken as independent variables and quantity as a dependent one, are homogeneous functions of the zero degree. In course of the following discussion, this theorem will be referred to as the 'homogeneity postulate'.[1] The term 'price' is used here in its general theoretical sense, i.e. it includes money wage rates paid for all the different kinds of services as well as commodity prices.

The significance of this theorem for the analysis of monetary influences within the framework of our economic system has been mentioned often enough. It is best expressed by the well-known hypothetical 'experiment' of doubling overnight the cash holdings of all business enterprises and households. Ricardo used this device to show that the prices of all commodities and services will undergo under this condition a proportionally equal change, and the quantities produced, traded and consumed by all individual firms and households will remain exactly the same as before. His conclusion is obviously based upon the homogeneity postulate. The practical implications which Ricardo was inclined to draw from this hypothetical case obviously imply also a second assumption, and an unrealistic one – that our economic system is absolutely free from any kind of frictions and time-lag effects; i.e. that it adjusts itself to any primary variation (in this case it is a monetary one) instantaneously.

In order to admit the possibility of monetary influences upon the quantitative, material set-up of an economic system it is necessary to sacrifice at least one of these two assumptions. The modern 'orthodox' monetary theory definitely dropped the second one, its analytical apparatus being dominated by more or less explicit introduction of time lags and frictions of various kinds. Mr. Keynes is ready to repudiate also the first, the homogeneity postulate. He does not in any way neglect

---

[1] The homogeneity postulate applies to the simple Walrasian type as well as to all possible kinds of 'dynamic' equations which include among the independent variables 'expected prices', derivatives of the given price changes, etc. It hardly needs to be mentioned that this postulate has nothing whatever to do with the controversial issue of homogeneous and non-homogeneous production functions.

time-lag phenomena; they definitely constitute an important element of his latest as well as his previous system. In analyzing the new theory, it is very important, however, to realize that the abandonment of the homogeneity assumption alone would suffice to make the automatically neutral behavior of the economic system toward monetary influences impossible.

Let us modify the set-up of the frictionless, lagless and 'homogeneous' economic system by assuming that one demand or one supply curve of any single household or enterprise is not homogeneous (in the previously defined sense). A proportional price variation with unchanged quantity relations becomes, under this condition, logically impossible; the new non-homogeneous household or enterprise would be induced by an all-round price rise or price fall to demand (or to supply) larger or smaller quantities of one or more particular commodities than before, while the amount demanded and supplied by all the other households and enterprises, still subject to the homogeneity condition, would remain unchanged. A discrepancy would arise incompatible with conditions of general equilibrium. This shows that *in a frictionless system with at least one or more non-homogeneous elements, the quantity of money ceases to be a 'neutral' factor.* On the contrary, the equilibrium amount of every commodity or service produced or purchased by *any* household or business unit must be now considered to be a function of this quantity.

The determination of the monetary maximum for the output of any commodity, or of the maximum employment of any kind of service (say labor) becomes a simple mathematical problem. It is, of course, very unlikely that the monetary optima computed for each of the many different kinds of goods and services would be the same. The quantity of money which brings about the maximum output of automobiles might be much smaller or much larger than that which would secure the greatest possible employment to some particular kind of labor. Monetary unemployment of any factor of production as well as the monetary underproduction (= underconsumption) of any and every commodity can be consequently defined as the difference between the theoretically computed monetary maximum and the actual figure of employment or production. On the basis of the non-homogeneity assumption, the interest rate becomes of course a function of the quantity of money (and vice versa) in the same way as are the employment and output figures of all industries. That is, the main point of Mr. Keynes' theory of interest follows as simply and directly from his basic assumption as his interpretation of monetary unemployment.

Summarizing the argument, we conclude that a monetary theory of unemployment, unless it is based on time-lag and friction phenomena, stands and falls with the non-homogeneity condition.

## II

Mr. Keynes assumes that the supply function for labor is non-homogeneous. Unfortunately for the present discussion, he does not commit himself to a precise, clear-cut statement of this basic postulate. In particular, it appears to be practically impossible to say which of his assertions concerning the behavior of labor are supposed to set forth the main thesis and which are used to substantiate its correctness.

If taken literally, all of Mr. Keynes' remarks concerning the behavior of labor in relation to prices and wages are compatible with the 'orthodox' homogeneity assumption. The assertion, for example, that 'in the event of a small rise in the price of wage-goods relatively to the money-wage . . . the aggregate supply of labor willing to work for the current money-wage . . . would be greater than the existing volume of employment' (p. 15) (the omitted part of the sentence deals with the demand for labor) expresses a widely accepted 'orthodox' theorem concerning the 'negative inclination' of the supply curve for labor. It is perfectly compatible with the classical homogeneity assumption. If we turn to another somewhat more general statement by Mr. Keynes, of the same idea, his view appears to be that the fact that a reduction of money wages might be accompanied by an increase in real wages (i.e. proportionally greater decrease in the prices of consumption goods) militates against some basic assumptions of the classical theory (pp. 11–12). By the use of the most 'orthodox' analysis it can be shown that within the framework of a classical Walrasian system this particular type of price variation can occur as easily as any other. The nearest Mr. Keynes comes to a precise formulation of the crucial issue is his assertion that the supply of labor depends not upon the 'real' but (also?) upon money wages (pp. 8–9).[2]

The homogeneity postulate is not introduced by the classical economists as an axiom; it is derived from a series of fundamental assumptions concerning the economic behavior of individuals and business firms. The most effective way of disputing their theory would be that of discrediting these initial assumptions. Mr. Keynes has not resorted to this method of attack but has attempted to show directly that the contested postulate itself is at variance with facts. In order to be successful in this endeavor, he would have to find a series of empirical situations in which all the prices which might exercise a direct influence upon the size of the labor supply, altho constant in their *relative* magnitude, would differ from case to case in absolute height. The non-homogeneity of the labor supply function would be proven if, under these conditions and in absence of friction and time lags, the amount of labor employed would change (in a significant degree) with the variation of the price level, instead of remaining constant as expected by 'orthodox' theorists. No demonstration of this kind is given in the pages of the *General Theory of Unemployment*. There is good reason to believe that in view of the scarcity of available statistical information and because of the presence of the great number of frictional phenomena, no direct demonstration could be made. Mr. Keynes' assault upon the fundamental assumption of the 'orthodox' economic theory seems to have missed its target.

These critical remarks are concerned with what appears to be the essentially novel contribution of the General Theory of Unemployment to the monetary 'theory of total output' – the attempt to modify one of the basic static assumptions of the 'orthodox' economists. The static character of the proposed innovation is somewhat obscured by the fact that in his endeavor to give a realistic analysis of economic forces and interrelations, Mr. Keynes has introduced into his theory a number of dynamic considerations, most of them in one form

---

[2] Mr. Keynes' interpretation of the 'orthodox' theory is liable to produce the false impression as if the dubious index concept of 'real' wages constitutes an essential element of this theory. As a matter of fact, if carefully stated, the 'static' 'classical' supply function does not include any other variables than the amount of labor, prices of the consumer's goods, the interest rate and the money wage-rates.

or another already incorporated in the apparatus of the modern monetary and business cycle theory.[3]

The essentially static foundation of the new theory of unemployment becomes quite obvious as soon as we try to visualize a stationary state with constant prices, unvarying output and perfect foresight. If Mr. Keynes' theory were correct, this economic system could and most probably would be subject to involuntary monetary unemployment.

Dynamic considerations are introduced into the General Theory of Employment mostly in connection with analysis of deflationary tendencies which are supposed to threaten the expansion of employment opportunities. This latter effect is inseparably tied up with the responsiveness of the economic system to monetary influences, which again leads back to the non-homogeneity of the labor supply. Thus it appears that Mr. Keynes' case has yet to be proven.

---

[3] The 'method of expectations' so ingeniously used by Mr. Keynes and interpreted by Mr. J. H. Hicks (in his review of the General Theory of Employment, Economic Journal, June, 1936) can be characterized as an attempt to simplify the analysis of dynamic phenomena by application of a static theoretical pattern. Instead of considering, as the 'orthodox' mathematical economists do, the expected prices and the expected rate of interest to be a function of the present or rather past price and interest rates, this method interprets them as independent data.

One cannot resist the temptation to cite in this connection, Mr. Keynes' ill-tempered remark directed against the 'pseudo-mathematical method' which 'assumes strict independence between factors involved' where it should not and 'allows the author to lose sight of the complexities and interdependencies of the real world'.

# [FROM] UNEMPLOYMENT, BASIC AND MONETARY: THE CLASSICAL ANALYSIS AND THE KEYNESIAN*
## D. G. Champernowne

### IV

Before considering in what sense it is still possible to believe that a rise or fall in money-wages is likely to result eventually in a similar rise or fall in real wages, we may revise what has been suggested already, by describing it in terms of different concepts.

According to our theory, the money-wage which a labourer demands to-day is that money-wage which would have given him a certain definite standard of life (i.e. which would have been a certain definite real wage) at prices ruling at some date in the past.

If the cost of living had been constant for a long time the labourer would demand that real wage which would ensure him that standard of life at present prices. If the cost of living has been recently rising, he will fail to take this into account and will demand a lower real wage than this: if the cost of living has been recently falling, he will demand a higher real wage than this. For convenience, we may refer to the real wage which he would demand if the cost of living had been stationary as the basic real wage. The basic real wage will obviously be different for different individuals.

Since the cost of living is not in fact always stationary, but rises and falls, there may at various times be men either in employment, receiving less than their basic wage, or men out of employment, although they would be able to obtain employment at their basic real wage.

In a corresponding manner we may state that in any given situation the amount of basic unemployment is the amount of unemployment that there would be in that situation if each

* From *Review of Economic Studies*, vol. 3 (1936), pp. 203–14, 216.

man demanded neither more nor less than his basic real wage. Then if the cost of living has been rising, we should expect actual unemployment to be less than basic unemployment, whereas if the cost of living had been falling we should expect basic unemployment to be less than actual unemployment. We may call any deficiency of actual unemployment below basic unemployment 'monetary employment', and we may call any excess of actual unemployment over basic unemployment 'monetary unemployment'.[1] On these definitions:

Actual Unemployment = Basic Unemployment − Monetary Employment

or

Actual Unemployment = Basic Unemployment + Monetary Unemployment.

Then the unemployment of the monetary-unemployed is due to the fact that they or their unions have overlooked a recent fall in the cost of living, whereas the employment of monetary-employed is due to the fact that they have overlooked a rise in the cost of living. In so far as these oversights are likely to be repaired eventually, the monetary-unemployed are likely to lower the money-wage which they demand, and the monetary-employed are likely to raise the money-wage-rate which they demand. We may express this by saying that a period of monetary unemployment is likely to cause falling money-wages and that a period of monetary employment is likely to cause rising money-wages. In so far as we can assume that rising and falling money-wages will respectively cause rising and falling real wages, we may conclude that a period of monetary employment contains the seeds of its own destruction in the form of a tendency for real wages to rise, whereas a period of monetary unemployment has in it the seeds of its own destruction, in the shape of a tendency for real wages to fall.

V

We must now return to the consideration whether it is still possible to believe that in any sense a rise in money-wages is likely to lead to a rise in real wages. For the second wave of Keynes' attack consists of a convincing demonstration that

[1] The concept of Monetary Unemployment is copied from Keynes' 'Involuntary Unemployment' (*General Theory*, p. 15), but differs from that concept.

there is no reason to expect that a rise in money-wage-rates is more likely to lead to a rise than to a fall in real wage-rates, unless the monetary authority takes the necessary steps (e.g. raises the rate of interest) to increase unemployment. He shows convincingly also that a lowering of money-wage-rates is no more likely to lower than to raise the real wage-rate, unless the monetary authority takes the necessary steps (e.g. lowers the rate of interest) to decrease unemployment.

There is no obvious flaw in this argument, and it follows that the demand of labour for a certain real wage can only make itself effective in so far as it influences the attitude of the monetary authority and its manipulation of the rate of interest.

Consider a position in which there is considerable monetary employment. After a time, money-wages must start to rise, and unless real wages also rise, in which case monetary employment will be reduced, the cost of living will rise in as great proportion. This must lead, after a further interval, to another rise in money-wages: this will be accompanied by another rise in prices and followed by yet another rise in money-wages. Under such conditions the bargaining power of the labourer will become stronger and stronger as he becomes more and more confident of his ability to raise his money-wage-rate, and the speed with which he will revise his demands in the face of increases in the cost of living will become greater the more accustomed he becomes to the danger of his real wage being reduced by the rise in the cost of living.

We see that a period of monetary employment will be accompanied not merely by rising money-wages and prices, but moreover by money-wages and prices rising at a rapidly increasing rate.

It is difficult to believe that such a process would continue for long without evoking a very violent protest from those classes of the community who stood to lose from a rapidly rising price-level; considerable difficulty would be experienced in adjusting the rates of exchange in order to compensate the effects of the increased labour-costs in the export trades; people would become alarmed lest there should be an inflation 'like they had in Germany'; in one way or another the monetary authority would be forced to put a stop to it.

The effects of the deflationary efforts of the monetary authority would be to enable labour to get its increase of money-wages without any further increase in the price-level but at the cost of considerable unemployment. Real wages would rise sharply, and unless the monetary authority had succeeded in applying the brakes very skilfully, not only would monetary employment be eradicated, but it would be substituted by considerable monetary unemployment.[2]

In any case, if the monetary authority was to check successfully the rise in prices, it would have to continue its deflationary policy until all monetary employment had been eradicated, for so long as monetary employment remained money-wages would continue to rise.

There are thus strong grounds for believing that monetary employment will never last very long without there being an intervening period of monetary unemployment. Unfortunately there are no grounds so strong for believing that monetary unemployment will never last very long.

However, there are some grounds for believing this: We know that a period of monetary unemployment will be characterised by falling money-wages and falling prices. This fall is likely to become accelerated as labour becomes more disorganised by the depression, and as employers get more desperate and more confident in their power to cut money-wages.

Eventually, it would be imagined, a point must come when the lunacy of the situation will be realised and the monetary authority will be urged to put an end to the process of deflation. In this case, the monetary authority will expand credit until prices start rising again, and monetary unemployment will be gradually exterminated.

But the operation of this check to monetary unemployment is by no means so certain as the operation of the check to monetary employment. For there is the significant fact that influential opinion is far more easily frightened by the thought of an inflation 'like Germany had' than by the prospect of a slump 'like they had in America'.

## VI

The argument developed in the last section suggests the conclusion that no period of monetary employment or of monetary unemployment is likely to last for very long. We should expect there to be alternate periods of monetary employment and of

---

[2] Because a check to rising prices checks industrial expansion and leads to a fall of prices later on.

monetary unemployment, so that the actual level of unemployment would oscillate above and below the level of basic unemployment.

There is some reason to suppose that the periods of monetary unemployment will be longer than the periods of monetary employment, since the forces tending to bring to an end a period of monetary employment act more swiftly than the forces tending to bring an end to a period of monetary unemployment.

Yet as a first approximation we may regard the trend value of unemployment as being equal to the level of basic unemployment, since we may expect the actual level of unemployment to oscillate more or less regularly about the level of basic unemployment.

If we are content to accept this degree of approximation, it follows that in order to study the trend value of unemployment, we may neglect monetary unemployment and monetary employment, and consider only the movements of the level of basic unemployment. In order to make this study, we may take over the ordinary tools of classical analysis, very little modified.

For, by definition, the amount of basic unemployment is that amount for which the supply price of labour is equal to the demand price for it, whereby the supply price of labour we mean the real wage which labour would demand (at any given level of unemployment) if its demands were not warped by any recent changes in the cost of living. It is on the assumption that the level of real wages and of unemployment are determined by the supply and demand for labour that the classical analysis is based; this analysis breaks down when we try to apply it to finding the actual level of unemployment, but if we neglect monetary unemployment and monetary employment, and examine only changes in basic unemployment, then the assumption is correct and the analysis is valid.

In so far as it is true that on the average monetary employment and monetary unemployment will balance out, we may neglect their effects also when we are considering the *trend* values of real wages, prices, the rate of investment, the rate of interest, etc., and make use of the ordinary classical analysis but slightly modified to discover the trend movements of these also.

## VII

In order to render this analysis simple we must make the usual assumptions.

We shall consider a closed system in which there is only one rate of interest. We shall treat money and labour and capital and product as though each of these were homogeneous.

Our method of finding the trend values of unemployment percentage, real wages, money-wages, prices, the quantity of money, the rate of investment and the rate of interest will be similar to the classical analysis of the stationary state. It will not be exactly similar, because the equilibrium which we wish to examine is a dynamic equilibrium in which investment is supposed to be taking place.

We may define dynamic equilibrium to be a state in which the demand for and supply of labour, the demand for and supply of saving, and the demand for and supply of money are all balanced. In order to make this definition precise we must define the six demand and supply functions more carefully.

By the supply of labour in any given situation we may mean 'the amount of labour which would have been forthcoming in that situation, if the real wage-rate, the price-level, and any other relevant conditions had been fairly constant about their present values for (say) one year'.

We may construct analogous definitions of the demand for labour, the supply and demand of savings and the supply and demand for money. In each case we suppose the relevant influences to have been fairly steady for some years.

In particular, we may define the supply of savings to be the amount of saving which would have been forthcoming if the level of (real) incomes, the level of real wages, and the rate of interest had all been fairly steady for some years at their present levels, and the demand for saving as being the amount of investment that would have taken place if the rate of interest, the level of employment, and the price-level and the level of real wages had all been at their present levels for some years.

Then, with these definitions, having described a position of dynamic equilibrium as one in which the supply of labour equals the demand for labour, the supply of saving equals the demand for saving, and the supply of money equals the demand for money, we may proceed to the analysis of the equilibrium position corresponding to any given situation.

Following the classical tradition and considering only basic unemployment (i.e. assuming the supply and demand for labour to be brought into equilibrium by movements of the real wage rate), we find that for dynamic equilibrium, the volume of employment and the real wage-rate are determined by the supply and demand for labour.

In other words, in any given situation, if at real wage $R$, the supply of labour (defined above) would be $N_s(R)$, and the demand for labour would be $N_d(R)$, then the appropriate values of the real wage $R$ and of the amount of employment $N$ are found from the equation

$$N = N_d(R) = N_s(R)$$

Having found the level of employment and the real wage, we may deduce from these and from our knowledge of the general situation the corresponding level of real aggregate income; from this we can estimate the supply of saving $S_s(r)$ (defined above), and the demand for saving $S_d(r)$, corresponding to any rate of interest $r$; we can then find the position of dynamic equilibrium for $S$ and $r$, from the equation:

$$S = S_d(r) = S_s(r).$$

Since we know now the level of employment, the real wage and aggregate income and the rate of interest we are in a position to estimate, on the basis of our further knowledge of the general features of the situation, the real value, measured in wage-units, of the amount of money which the public will require.

Let this real value be $H$, and let the amount of money supplied by the monetary authority be $M$, then we can derive the equilibrium money-wage-rate, $w$, from the formula

$$M = wH.[3]$$

It should be noted that our assumption that in considering trends only basic unemployment need be taken into account was based on the supposition that the monetary authority would never allow a period of rising prices to continue for long, nor allow a period of falling prices to continue for long, so that the supply of money can only be considered indepen-

---

[3] The equation $M = wH$ is the same in principle as the quantity equation $M = PH$, since real wages are 'given' and $w$ is simply a convenient index of prices.

dent of the demand for it within these limits. In the broader sense, the rigidity of the money-wage-rate determines the price-level and the demand for money determines its supply. However, granted that monetary policy must not be such as to allow the price-level to alter too much, it is then true that the supply of money $M$ tells us the money-wage-rate according to the equation $M = wH$, provided that we know $H$ from our knowledge of the amount of employment, the real wage, the aggregate income, and the rate of interest.

## VIII
The apparatus for determining the equilibrium position corresponding to any given situation can be described more simply by means of supply and demand diagrams.

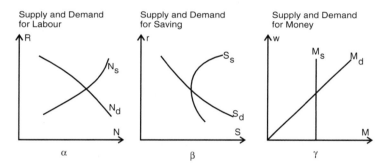

The procedure described in detail in the last section can loosely be set forth as follows:

(i) The level of real wages and the amount of employment are determined by the point of intersection of the supply curve and the demand curve for labour.

(ii) Given the level of real wages and the amount of employment, and hence, the aggregate income, the amount of saving and the rate of interest are shown by the point of intersection of the demand curve and the supply curve of saving.

(iii) Given the volume of employment, the real wage, aggregate income, and the rate of interest we can estimate the real value $H$ of the amount of money demanded; if the money-wage is $w$ the amount of money demanded is $wH$, so that the demand curve for money at different wage levels is a straight line passing through the origin. If we know the amount of money $M$ supplied by the monetary authority, then we can read off the money-wage $\frac{M}{H}$ from the point of intersection of the demand curve and the supply curve.

Thus we read off in turn, the real wage-rate and the amount of employment from the demand curve and supply curve for labour; having determined these we then find the amount of saving and the rate of interest from the point of intersection of the demand curve and the supply curve for saving; having determined these, we then find the money-wage-rate from the point of intersection of the demand curve and the supply curve for money.

This procedure is only justified if the approximation involved in assuming that, on the balance over a period of many years, the effects of monetary employment will cancel the effects of monetary unemployment, is close; only in this case may we consider the effects of basic unemployment alone, and act on the assumption that the amount of unemployment is not affected by the cost of living, but only by the demand and supply for labour at various real wage-rates.

IX

The conclusion to which our discussion has led is that if it were true that in the end real forces such as labour's demand for a certain real wage work themselves out, in spite of temporary disturbances due to monetary phenomena, such as unemployment or extra employment due to changes in the cost of living, then the classical analysis would be applicable to the examination of trends of real wages, etc. It is not, however, suggested that even under these circumstances Mr. Keynes' analysis would be invalidated: it is suggested that it would then predict the same result.

As a sequel to this discussion it may not be inappropriate to consider a formal comparison of the logical structures underlying some parts of the 'General Theory of Employment' and the classical analysis. This discussion does not pretend to be very new or very deep, but it may serve as a useful mnemonic to those who are slightly confused when comparing the two systems by the difference in the terminologies used.

There is one problem which both systems of analysis set out to attack: the problem shortly expressed is to determine the levels of *employment N, real wages R, real savings S, rate of interest r, money-wages w,* and the *quantity of money M,* given the general situation, from the fact that the demand and supply of labour must balance and so must respectively the demand and supply for saving and for money.

The two systems of analysis are only two of many possible systems each with its different conceivable set of hypotheses: let us consider the different systems of analysis which could be conceived.

Denoting by the suffices $_s$ and $_d$ respectively, the amounts of a factor supplied and demanded, so that $N_d$ means 'the amount of labour demanded', our problem is to derive values for *N, R, S, r, w,* and *M* from our knowledge of the general situation and from the six facts:

$$N=N_s=N_d; \; S=S_s=S_d; \; M=M_s=M_d.$$

From our knowledge of the general situation, we should ideally be able to find functions $N_s(RSrwM)$, $N_d(RSrwM)$, $S_s(NRrwM)$, $S_d(NRrwM)$, $M_s(NRSrw)$, and $M_d(NRSrw)$, where, e.g. $N_s(RSrwM)$ denotes the value that $N_s$ would have now if *R, S, r, w, M* had been steady for some time at the values given inside the brackets of $N_s(RSrwM)$.

Having found these functions, we should then be able to find the values *N, R, S, r, w, M* from the six equations:

$$N = N_s(RSrwM) = N_d(RSrwM)$$
$$S = S_s(NRrwM) = S_d(NRrwM) \dotfill (I)$$
$$M = M_s(NRSrw) = M_d(NRSrw)$$

This would be the most general method of finding the position of dynamic equilibrium corresponding to the given situation; it would take account of every conceivable cross-influence between any pair of the six variables. It would, for instance, take account of the effects of a change in the rate of interest on the supply of labour.

Now it is obvious that some effects, e.g. the effect of a change in the amount of employment on the demand for money, are more important than others, e.g. the effect of a change in the rate of interest on the supply of labour (*ceteris paribus*). For many purposes it is more convenient to use a system of analysis which concentrates attention on the important effects and ignores the unimportant ones than a system which indiscriminately considers all of them.

Accordingly, any economist is at liberty to choose a special case of the general system represented by the six equations (I), and to cross out some of the symbols within the brackets, and so concentrate attention on the most important relationships between the variables, e.g. by crossing out the symbol $r$ within the brackets of $N_s(RSrwM)$, we should clear our general system of analysis of any need to consider the reaction of changes in the rate of interest (*ceteris paribus*) on the supply of labour.

Both the modified form of the classical system which we described in sections VI, VII, and VIII, and the system of analysis described in the general theory of employment may be thought of as particular cases of systems obtained from the set of six equations (I) by erasing some of the variables within the brackets in such a way as to eliminate consideration from certain unimportant causal relationships, and to concentrate it on the causes which are economically the most significant.

## X

The system described in sections VI, VII and VIII will be referred to as the classical system: it may be represented by the six equations:

$$
\begin{aligned}
N &= N_s(R) &&= N_d(R) \\
S &= S_s(Nr) &&= S_d(Nr) &&\quad\dots\dots\dots\dots\dots\dots\dots (2) \\
M &= M_s &&= M_d(Nrw)
\end{aligned}
$$

and it is important to notice that the symbol $w$ has been erased from within the brackets of $N_s(RSrwM)$; this means that the system does not take account of the effect of changes in the cost of living on the amount of labour which will be supplied at a given real wage and amounts to a rejection of the possibility of monetary unemployment or of monetary employment, or to the assumption that all unemployment is basic unemployment.

The system suggested in 'The General Theory of Employment' will be called the Keynesian system: it may, I believe, be roughly described by the six equations –

$$
\begin{aligned}
M &= M_s(R) &&= M_d(rQ') \\
S &= S_s(Nr) &&= S_d(NrQ) &&\quad\dots\dots\dots\dots\dots\dots\dots (3) \\
N &= N_s(Rw) &&= N_d(R)
\end{aligned}
$$

where $Q$ and $Q'$ are certain influence such as general nervousness, the state of the news and effects due to the expectation of changes in the price-level, etc.: these influences are suggested as having a very significant direct effect on the demand for loans $S_d$ and on the demand for money $M_d$.

The six equations given above describe only that part of the Keynesian analysis which deals with the most significant direct effects; in order to take account of the other indirect effects which are discussed in the analysis, but on which less stress is laid, we should have to enlarge the equations to the form:

$$N = N_s(Rw) = N_d(Rw)$$
$$S = S_s(NRr) = S_d(NRrQ)$$
$$M = M_s(rw) = M_d(NrwQ')$$

and we should have to make them more comprehensive in order to take account of every less important indirect economic effect suggested in the book.

But we may concentrate our attention on the difference in emphasis shown by the Keynesian analysis as represented by the equations (3) and by the version of the classical analysis given by the equations (2).

## XI

The most important difference to notice is that whereas the classical system of analysis considers the supply of labour $N_s(R)$ as depending only on the real wage $R$, Keynes considers the supply of labour $N_s(Rw)$ to be influenced by the money-wage also.

In other words, Keynes takes account of 'monetary unemployment', whereas the classical economists assume that all unemployment is basic.

The second point to notice is that Keynes thinks of the supply of money $M_s(r)$ as being influenced by considerations about the rate of interest, whereas the classical economists regard the supply of money as a datum. Thus Keynes' conception of the banks 'doing nothing' would perhaps be that of the banks adjusting the supply of money in such a way as to keep the rate of interest constant, whereas the classical economists would regard the banks as doing nothing if they kept the quantity of money constant. On the classical analysis which we have been considering, it would be impossible for the banks to keep the rate of interest constant, because the rate of interest depends on the supply and demand for saving.

The third point to be noticed is that the classical analysis can only take account of the forces $Q$ and $Q'$ considered in the Keynesian scheme by super-imposing their effects on an equilibrium position already found.

Whereas the classical system of analysis was to deduce the levels of $N$, $R$, $S$, $r$, $M$, and $w$ by considering in turn the demand and supply of labour, saving, and money, the Keynesian system is just the opposite, namely, to consider in turn the demand curves and supply curves for money, saving, and labour.

As explained on page 208 [230], the classical scheme is to consider in turn the three diagrams $\alpha$, $\beta$, $\gamma$:

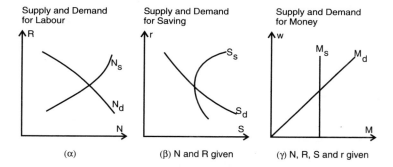

(α)  (β) N and R given  (γ) N, R, S and r given

but the Keynesian scheme is to consider in turn the three diagrams $\delta$, $\varepsilon$, $\zeta$:

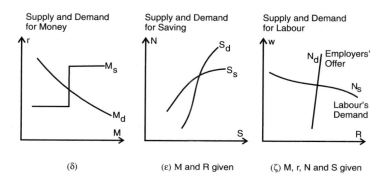

(δ)  (ε) M and R given  (ζ) M, r, N and S given

## XII

The contrast between the two techniques may be illustrated by applying them in turn to the problem of determining the effect of an increase in thriftiness on the part of the people of a country whose central bank keeps the quantity of money constant.

Let us apply the classical technique: Referring to diagram $\alpha$, we find that since neither the supply curve nor the demand curve for labour will have been affected, the amount of employment $N$ and the real wage will remain unchanged; hence, aggregate real income will remain unchanged. Turning to diagram $\beta$, we find that there is no reason why the demand curve for saving should have moved, but that since aggregate income has not changed, and there has been an increase in thrift, the supply curve of saving will have moved to the right; hence, the rate of saving will have increased and the rate of interest will have decreased. Turning to the third diagram $\gamma$, we find that the supply of money will have remained the same, but the demand for money may have risen slightly because the rate of interest has fallen (so that people will hoard money rather than securities), so that the demand curve will have moved to the right; hence, the quantity of money will not change but there may be a slight lowering of the price-level and hence, also (since real wages do not change), of money-wages.

Hence the classical analysis suggests that the results of the increase of thrift will be: A fall in the rate of interest and an increase in the rate of saving and a fall in money-wages and in the price-level, but no change in real wages, employment or the quantity of money.

Now let us apply the Keynesian technique to the problem. Referring to diagram $\delta$, we know that the supply curve of money is a vertical straight line which does not move; similarly, the demand curve does not move for any direct reason. Hence, the quantity of money and the rate of interest will not be directly affected by the increased thriftiness. Turning to diagram $\varepsilon$ we find that the demand curve for saving will not be directly affected by the increased thriftiness, but that the supply curve of saving will be shifted to the right; hence, if the curves have the slopes shown in diagram $\varepsilon$, there will be a fall in employment and a slight fall in the amount of saving. Turning to diagram $\zeta$, we find that the fall in employment is likely to have increased the marginal productivity of labour and the real wage offered by employers, so the demand curve for labour will have moved to the right; on the other hand, the fall in employment will have made labour more prepared to accept a cut in money-wages, so that the supply curve will have been lowered. There will be an increase in the real wage and perhaps a slight fall in the money-wage, and, hence, a definite fall in the price-level.

Hence the direct effects of the increase in thriftiness will be a decrease in savings and employment and a rise in real wages and a fall in the price-level, with no change in the quantity of money or the rate of interest.

Certain indirect effects remain to be considered. The supply curve of money will not be affected: but there will be two indirect effects on the demand for money. On the one hand, the fall in prices and employment will decrease the demand for money for business, but, on the other hand, the psychological effects of depression will be to increase the demand for money for hoarding. Let us suppose that the first effect predominates so that the demand curve for money in diagram δ is moved just a little to the left: we see that the rate of interest will be slightly lowered.

There will be two indirect effects on the demand for saving: the fall in the price-level may lead people to expect a further fall, this will lower the demand for saving by making investment less profitable; on the other hand, the slight fall in the rate of interest will increase the demand for saving. Let us suppose that the second of these effects predominates: then the demand curve for saving may move slightly to the right, so that the fall in saving and in employment may be slightly offset. As a result of this the fall in the price-level and the rise in real wages will also be slightly offset.

We find then that the result of the increased thriftiness will be a small decrease in the rate of interest, a fall in the rate of saving and in employment and in prices, and a rise of real wages.

These results may be contrasted with the results predicted by the classical analysis, namely, a fall in the rate of interest and in prices, but a rise in the rate of saving and no change in the amount of employment or the rate of real wages . . .

### XIV

It is not the purpose of the above analysis to suggest that the Keynesian analysis is merely an elaboration of the classical analysis. The purpose is to show just how much artificiality must be introduced into the conditions assumed in order that the Keynesian technique should lead to the same results as the classical technique: it is to bring out the point that the Keynesian analysis differs from the classical analysis in the fact that it picks out for emphasis different economic forces such as the stickiness of money-wages, which are evidently extremely important in the short run. It is also intended to show that in so far as there is a 'real' tendency which must make itself felt eventually for labour to insist in a certain standard of life, and for labour's bargaining power to increase as unemployment decreases, then provided that the monetary authority does not allow labour to be misled by too long periods of rising or falling cost of living, the 'real supply curve of labour' may be a useful concept for estimating the *trend* of unemployment and real wages of the rate of interest and of saving. If there is such a real tendency, then, when considering such trends, the *real* wage may be more significant than the money-wage in determining the trend level of unemployment. The Keynesian technique is then likely to yield the same results as the classical technique, and it may be simpler to consider the classical analysis direct.

This method will be of no avail if outlets for investment are so scarce or if the employers are so nervous of any increase in the supply of money that they hoard, and it is impossible to lower the rate of interest sufficiently to cause sufficient investment to keep prices and money-wages from falling. For in this case the monetary authority will not be able to prevent a constantly falling cost of living and there will necessarily be monetary unemployment constantly. It would be quite inappropriate to make use of the classical analysis in such a case.

In such a situation the most significant economic fact would be enormous monetary unemployment. The classical analysis is ill suited to deal with this because it can only treat it as an indirect effect caused by a lowering of prices raising the real supply curve of labour. In such a situation the Keynesian analysis is particularly convenient because it treats 'nervousness' $Q$ and $Q'$ as direct effects on the rate of interest and on the demand for saving, and regards the demand for saving as having a direct effect on the real wage, the money-wage and the amount of employment (basic and monetary).

It is only in a situation, if such can exist, where only basic unemployment matters, and where uncertainty and nervousness are not very important, that the classical analysis has the advantage over the Keynesian, because it treats the effect of real wages on the supply of labour as direct, and the effect of changes in the quantity of money on the price-level as direct. In all other situations the new technique would seem to be advantageous.

# UNDER-EMPLOYMENT EQUILIBRIUM*
## Alvin H. Hansen

Mr. Keynes's new book is much more than a treatise on business cycles. It presents a general theory of employment as a whole and raises the question whether it is possible for the economic system in advanced industrial countries, operating on orthodox lines, to give reasonably full employment, even in normal times. It challenges the thesis of classical economics that the system, despite periodic disturbances and maladjustments, tends towards an equilibrium at which all factors are employed.

The imposing edifice which Mr. Keynes had earlier erected in his 'Treatise on Money' (1930) is now abandoned. It had, under the damaging attack of his critics, become untenable. Not only had his first fundamental equation been shown to be wrong; it had also been pointed out that the disequilibrium of saving and investment, as there defined, merely reflected the prevailing maladjustments, and hence these concepts were incapable of throwing light on the causal factors at work. This theoretical structure gone, Mr. Keynes now finds the determinants of income, consumption, investment, and employment in: (1) the propensity to consume, (2) the marginal efficiency of capital (or the prospective rate of profit on new investment), (3) the complex of rates of interest on loans.

While the classical economists were primarily concerned with the theory of prices and distribution under conditions of full employment, Mr. Keynes attempts to develop a theory of underemployment equilibrium. The classical economists emphasized the virtues of saving (which indeed was consistent with nineteenth-century investment outlets), but in conditions of under-employment, Keynes argues, the propensity to consume must be encouraged. What may be appropriate policy under conditions of full employment, becomes a wrong policy under conditions of under-employment.

* From *Yale Review*, vol. 25 (June 1936), pp. 828–30.

All this is elaborated by the aid of mathematical equations into a closely reasoned and difficult analysis. Nevertheless, anyone who takes the pains to follow this analysis through to the end, will discover that the fundamental ideas are relatively simple. The wealthier the community, the weaker becomes the propensity to consume, which propensity may be measured by the ratio of consumption to income. Moreover, wealthy communities are supplied with such an abundance of capital that the marginal efficiency of new investment is low. In brief, wealthy communities tend to accumulate vast funds for investment, but the investment outlets are limited. In consequence, a part of the productive resources of the community is unemployed and the income is thereby reduced. Not until the community has been impoverished sufficiently so that the ratio of consumption to income has risen to a point at which individual savings no longer exceed new investment, does the decline in income and employment cease. At this point an equilibrium is indeed reached, but under conditions that preclude full employment.

Not all individual savings are invested because the rate which borrowers can afford to pay may be so low that hoarding (of a part of the savings) is preferred to investment. Investment at 2% or 2½%, risk considered, is not sufficient to offset the security of complete liquidity. But the preference for liquidity prevents full investment of all individual savings.

It becomes, therefore, necessary to take definite steps to raise the level both of consumption and of investment. The propensity to consume may be increased by a forced redistribution of income. The propensity to invest may be stimulated by monetary policies designed to increase the supply of money and provide the lowest possible rate of interest. At the point of full employment the rate of interest should indeed be raised to the marginal productivity of new investment in order to prevent inflation. But Keynes has no fear of inflation. Indeed, he does not believe that the all-around devaluation of currencies, and the easy money consequent thereto, will prove adequate to stir business enterprise to full employment of the production resources. Monetary policies must be supplemented by fiscal policies designed to redistribute income and stimulate consumption.

It is reasonably safe to predict that Keynes's new book will, so far as his theoretical apparatus is concerned, fare little better than did the 'Treatise'. In particular, his theory of interest will certainly be challenged. His theory of equilibrium at less than full employment is not tenable except upon the assumptions of an approach to a rigid economy in which costs are highly inflexible and supplies are monopolistically controlled, or else one in which there are relatively limited technological innovations. For when these assumptions are withdrawn, a progressive and flexible community is always busily at work raising the marginal productivity of capital and the rate of investment. It may indeed be true that, under conditions of relative stagnation of technical progress, the marginal efficiency of capital may fall below the lowest attainable rate of interest, and so prevent an adequate amount of investment. It remains to be seen whether we have, in fact, reached this state of technological stagnation. There is, at any rate, no inherent imperious law of the economic system that precludes full employment. Institutional arrangements are, however, being built up which make full employment difficult, but that is in line with accepted theory.

# NOTES ON THE AUTHORS

Adarkar, B. P. [no information]

Ashton, Thomas Southcliffe (1889–1968) Reader in Public Finance and Currency, University of Manchester. Economic historian specializing in eighteenth-century England.

Beckhart, Benjamin Haggott (1897–19?) Professor of Banking, Columbia University.

Butchart, Montgomery [no information]

Champernowne, Daviod Gawen (1913– ) Economist. Fellow of King's College, Cambridge.

Coe, Virginius [no information; might be V. F. Coe, author of article on trade in *Canadian Journal of Economics and Political Science*, 1935]

Cole, George Douglas Howard (1889–1959) Reader in Economics, Oxford University. Socialist and active in Fabian Society.

Douglas, Henry [no information]

Durbin, Evan Frank Mottram (1906–48) Economist and politician. Lecturer in economics at LSE. Later member of Atlee government, 1947–8.

Ensor, Robert Charles Kirkwood (1877–1958) Journalist and historian. Barrister. Active in Fabian Society.

Fordham, Montague [no information]

Franklin, Fabian (1853–1939) Journalist and writer. Professor of Mathematics, Johns Hopkins, 1879–95. Newspaper editor, 1895–1917. Author of popular economics books.

Hansen, Alvin H. (1887–1975) Economist. Professor at University of Minnesota. Specialist in business cycle theory. In 1937 moved to Harvard.

Hardy, Charles Oscar (1884–1948) Economist. Staff member, Brookings Institution.

Harrod, Henry Roy Forbes (1900–78) Economist. Fellow in modern history and economics, Christ Church Oxford.

Henderson, Hubert Douglas (1890–1952) Economist. Fellow of All Souls, Oxford. Member of Economic Advisory Council, 1930–34.

Hicks, John Richard (1904–89) Economist. Lecturer at LSE 1926–35, and Cambridge University 1935–8. Later Nobel Prize for work on general equilibrium and welfare.

Jay, Douglas Patrick Thomas (1907– ) Journalist and politician. Fellow of All Souls College, Oxford. Financial journalist at *The Economist*. Later member of Atlee (1945–51) and Wilson (1964–7) governments.

Leontief, Wassily W. (1906– ) Economist. Professor of Economics at Harvard University. Later Nobel Prize for work on input-output analysis.

Marquand, Hilary Adair (1901–72) Economist and politician. Professor of Industrial Relations, Cardiff. Later held series of posts in Atlee government, 1945–51.

Pigou, Arthur Cecil (1877–1959) Economist. Professor of Political Economy, Cambridge University. Served on Cunliffe Committee (1918–19). *The Theory of Unemployment* (1933) strongly criticized by Keynes in *General Theory*.

Plant, Arnold (1898–1978) Economist. Professor of Commerce, LSE.

Robertson, Dennis Holme (1890–1963) Economist. Reader in Cambridge University. Specialist in money. *Banking Policy and the Price Level* (1926).

Robinson, Edward Austin Gossage (1897–1993) Economist. Fellow of Sidney Sussex College, Cambridge.

Rowse, Alfred Leslie (1903–?) Historian. All Souls College, Oxford.

Schumpeter, Joseph Alois (1883–1950) Economist. Professor of Economics at Harvard University. State Secretary of Finance in Austria, 1919. Specialist in business cycles.

Simons, Henry Calvert (1899–1946) Economist. Professor at University of Chicago. Early advocate of monetary expansion to cure depression.

Stewart, Maxwell S. Published series of pamphlets on economic and other topics with Public Affairs Office, New York.

Taylor, Horace (1894–?) Professor of Economics, Columbia University.

Tilby, A. Wyatt (1880–1948) Journalist and writer. Publications include *The English People Overseas* and *Lord John Russell*.

Viner, Jacob (1892–1970) Economist. Professor at University of Chicago. Special Assistant to Secretary of US Treasury.

Williams, Francis (1903–70) Journalist. Editor, *Daily Herald*.

Withers, Hartley (1867–1950) Financial journalist and author of popular books on economics.

## Main Sources Consulted

*Dictionary of National Biography*; *Who Was Who*; *Who's Who*; *Who's Who in America*; *Who Was Who in America*; American Economic Association, Directory of Members (1938 onwards); D. E. Moggridge, *Maynard Keynes: An Economist's Biography* (London and New York: Routledge, 1992); Mark Blaug, *Great Economists Before Keynes* (Brighton: Harvester Press, 1986); Mark Blaug, *Great Economists Since Keynes* (Cheltenham: Edward Elgar, 1998); Roger Middleton, *Charlatans or Saviours: Economists and the British Economy from Marshall to Meade* (Cheltenham: Edward Elgar, 1998).

Question marks indicate a failure to find the information. Unless otherwise indicated, positions refer to those held in 1936.

# LIST OF REVIEWS OF THE *GENERAL THEORY* PUBLISHED IN 1936

Note: This list contains all the reviews to which I have found references, many of which I have not been able to check, and for which bibliographic details are incomplete. Many reviews were found in the Keynes Papers in King's College, Cambridge, in scrapbooks. Dates were normally provided, but page references were rare. I am indebted to Don Moggridge for invaluable assistance, though he bears no responsibility for errors and omissions that may have occurred. With two exceptions, where confident guesses can be made about their names (their names are placed in square brackets), reviewers who signed reviews with initials are listed as 'Anonymous', with the initials in parentheses.

Adarkar, B. P. Book review. *Indian Economic Review* 7, pp. 229–333.

—— 'The "General Theory" of Keynes.' *Servant of India* (2 July).

Allen, G. C. 'Unorthodox economics.' *Liverpool Post* (28 April).

Altair. 'An economist speaks out.' *Prosperity* (April).

Anon. Book review. *Times* (10 March), p. 11.

—— 'Employment and money: dilemmas of saving and spending.' *Times Literary Supplement* 10 (14 March), p. 213.

—— 'Mr J. M. Keynes on cheap money.' *Financial News* (4 February).

—— 'A book for the expert: economics according to Keynes.' *Morning Post* (4 February).

—— 'Down, down, down?' *Investor's Guardian* (8 February).

—— 'Economic theory attacked.' *Cambridge Daily News* (5 February).

—— 'Mr Keynes raises the dust.' *John O'London's Weekly* (15 February).

—— 'Mr Keynes on money.' *Financial Times* (10 February).

—— 'Mr Keynes's shocks for economists.' *Aberdeen Press and Journal* (10 February).

—— 'Mr Keynes attacks the citadel.' *Manchester Guardian Commercial* (14 February).

—— 'Mr Keynes and a new social philosophy.' *Birmingham Post* (11 February).

—— 'The future of interest rates.' *Investor's Chronicle* (15 February).

—— 'Progress of an economist.' *Scotsman* (27 February).

—— Book review. *Social Service Review* (March).

—— 'Keynes on unemployment.' *Times Journal* (Ontario) (12 September).

—— 'Output and employment.' *Glasgow Herald* (6 August).

—— Book review. *Progress.*

—— 'Mr Keynes on interest.' *Tablet* (30 May).

—— 'The new economics.' *Bookman* (Wellington, NZ) (9 May).

—— Book review. *Labour Research* (May), pp. 113–14.

—— 'Is the economic system self-adjusting?' *Anglo-Norwegian Trade Journal* (March).

—— 'The money mystery.' *British Weekly* (10 March).

—— 'Unfettering competition.' *Wall Street Journal* (19 March).

—— 'J. M. Keynes' book: significant volume.' *Toronto Star* (20 March).

—— Book review. *Sunday Worker* (29 March).

—— 'The new economics.' *Christchurch Star Sun* (24 March).

—— 'Why we are short of money.' *Vancouver Sun* (27 March).

—— 'Salute to Stalin.' *Church Times* (27 March).

—— 'Orthodox economics attacked.' *Adelaide Advertiser* (28 March).

—— 'Another eminent economist endorses Mr Ostrer's views.' *Sunday Referee* (1 March).

—— Book review. *Times* (14 March).

—— Book review. *Highway* (April).

—— Book review. *Draughtsman* (April).

—— 'Mr Keynes's challenge.' *Financial Post* (Canada) (April).

—— Book review. *Iron and Coal Trades Review* (3 April).

—— 'Keynes bridges an economic gulf.' *Christian Science Monitor* (8 April).

—— Book review. *Kingston Standard* (Toronto) (18 April).

—— Book review. *Listener* (22 April).

—— Book review. *Madras Mail* (16 May).

—— 'The old and new: a warning from Mr Keynes.' *Time and Tide* (25 April).

Anonymous (AMW). 'Keynes, the Einstein of economics.' *Christian Science Monitor* (USA) (15 April).

Anonymous (AWJ). 'Keynes's latest message.' *New Age* (26 March).

Anonymous (CH). 'British brain buster.' *New York Sun* (20 March).

Anonymous (CHB). 'Light in economic darkness.' *Egyptian Mail* (2 April).

Anonymous (FAL). 'An economic bombshell: Mr Keynes' cure for unemployment.' *Star* (4 February).

Anonymous (HCFH). 'And it comes out here.' *Branch Banking* (March), p. 160.

Anonymous (JFM). 'Employment, money and interest.' *Irish Independent* (3 March).

Anonymous (JHB). 'J. M. Keynes and free economy.' *The Way Out* (Texas) (July).

Anonymous (SW). 'Economics theory.' *Western Morning News* (3 March).

Arnold, Percy. 'Keynes on change.' *Stockbroker* (26 March), pp. 108–9.

Ashton, T. S. 'Mr Keynes bombards a citadel.' *Manchester Guardian* (24 February), p. 5.

Bacon, R. K. 'Economist and the future of capitalism.' *Yorkshire Post* (5 February).

Barger, Harold. 'Mr Keynes and the rate of investment.' *Nature* 137 (9 May), p. 761.

Beckhart, Benjamin Haggott. Book review. *Political Science Quarterly* 51, pp. 600–603.

Benvenisti, J. L. Book review. *Dublin Review* (July), pp. 197–99.

Burton, C. S. 'John Maynard Keynes on unemployment.' *New York Daily Investment News* (1 April).

Butchart, Montgomery. Book review. *Criterion* (September).

'Candidus'. 'Fixed interest versus ordinary shares.' *Investors' Chronicle and Money Market Review* (22 February).

Champernowne, D. G. 'Unemployment, basic and monetary: the classical analysis and the Keynesian.' *Review of Economic Studies* 3, pp. 201–16.

Coe, Virginius. 'Half-way house.' *Canadian Forum* 16, p. 26.

Cole, G. D. H. 'Mr Keynes beats the band.' *New Statesman and Nation* (15 February).

—— 'An important book.' *Manchester Evening News* (1–5 March).

Coyajee, Jahangir C. 'A revision of orthodox economics.' *Mysore Economic Journal* 22 (July), pp. 285–87.

Craig, J. I. 'Money and output.' *The Sphinx* (Cairo) (20 June).

Curtis, Myra. Book review. *Public Administration* 14 (April), pp. 206–11.

Douglas, Henry. 'What *does* Mr Keynes want – poison gas?' *Daily Worker* (8 April).

D'Souza, V. I. 'Mr Keynes's theory of employment.' *Hindu Educational and Literary Supplement* (2 April).

'Duplex'. 'The economics of prosperity.' *Time and Tide* (6 February).

Durbin, E. F. M. 'Professor Durbin quarrels with Professor Keynes.' *Labour* (April).

'Edmonton Reader'. 'A Daniel come to judgement.' *Edmonton Journal* (20 March).

Elliott, Courtland. 'An assault on orthodox economic theory.' *Board of Trade Journal* (April).

Ensor, R. C. K. 'Mr Keynes as Copernicus.' *London Mercury* (April).

F[lux], A. W. Book review. *Journal of the Royal Statistical Society*.

Fordham, Montague. 'The conversions of Keynes.' *GK's Weekly* (26 March).

Franklin, Fabian. 'Keynes's economics.' *Saturday Review of Literature* (4 April), p. 32.

Gifford, J. L. K. 'Loans without interest as an economic remedy.' *Brisbane Telegraph* (17 March).

Hansen, Alvin H. 'Mr Keynes on underemployment equilibrium.' *Journal of Political Economy* 44, pp. 667–86.

—— 'Under-employment equilibrium.' *Yale Review* 25, pp. 828–30.

250 Responses to the General Theory

Hardy, C. O. Book review. *American Economic Review* 26, pp. 490–93.

Harrod, R. F. Book review. *Political Quarterly* 17, pp. 293–98.

Henderson, H. D. 'Mr Keynes's attack on economics.' *Spectator* 156, p. 263.

Hicks, J. R. 'Mr Keynes' theory of employment.' *Economic Journal* 46, pp. 238–53.

Holdaway, N. A. Book review. *Adelphi* (May).

Jay, Douglas. 'Mr Keynes on money.' *Banker* (April), pp. 8–14.

Laski, Harold J. 'Notes on the way.' *Time and Tide* (15 February), p. 8.

Lederer, Emil. 'Commentary on Keynes.' *Social Research* 3, pp. 478–87.

Leontief, W. W. 'The fundamental assumption of Mr Keynes' monetary theory of employment.' *Quarterly Journal of Economics* 51, pp. 192–97.

Lerner, A. P. 'Mr Keynes' General Theory of Employment, Interest and Money.' *International Labour Review* 34, pp. 435–54.

Madhura, P. B. 'The new approach in economics.' *Indian Preview* (Madras) (September).

Marquand, H. A. 'Mr J. M. Keynes joins the heretics.' *Western Mail* (13 February).

Mormi, G. W. 'Mr J. M. Keynes defence of capitalism.' Post (6 June).

Mussey, H. R. Book review. *Books* (12 April), p. 4.

Mussey, Henry B. 'A landmark in economics.' *New York Herald Tribune: Books* (12 April).

Neisser, H. 'Commentary on Keynes.' *Social Research* 3, pp. 459–78.

Neumark, S. D. Book review. *Sunday Times* (Johannesburg) (12 July).

Northridge, R. L. 'Work or leisure.' *Social Credit* (10 April).

Ooms, C. W. 'One prophet who has already made good.' *Chicago Evening Post* (18 March).

Pigou, A. C. 'Mr J. M. Keynes' General Theory of Employment, Interest and Money.' *Economica* 3, pp. 115–32.

Plant, Arnold. 'A challenge to orthodoxy.' *Fortnightly Review* 145, pp. 369–71.

Randolph, James Lee. Book review. *People's Money* (Dec).

Reddaway, W. B. Book review. *Economic Record* 12.

Robertson, D. H. 'Some notes on Mr Keynes' General Theory

of Employment.' *Quarterly Journal of Economics* 51, pp. 168–91.

Robinson, Austin. 'Mr Keynes on the causes of unemployment.' *Cambridge Review* (21 February).

R[obinson], E. A. G. 'Mr Keynes on money.' *Economist* 122 (29 February), p. 471.

'Rocco'. 'Mr Keynes.' *Oxford Magazine* (7 July).

Rostow, Eugene V. 'Keynes' economics.' *New Haven Courier* (20 July).

Rowse, A. L. 'Mr Keynes and the labour movement.' *Nineteenth Century* 120, pp. 320–32.

Rukeysen, M. S. 'Spending doctrine.' *New York American* (12 March).

Schumpeter, J. A. Book review. *Journal of the American Statistical Association*, pp. 791–95.

Simons, Henry C. 'Keynes comments on money.' *Christian Century* 53, pp. 1016–17.

Smith, W. B. Book review. *Springfield Republican* (29 March), p. 7.

—— 'Keynes argues need of wide distribution.' *Union* (29 March).

Somerville, Henry. 'Mr J. M. Keynes' latest book reviewed.' *Catholic Register and Canadian Extension* (9 April).

Stewart, Charles D. 'Economist Keynes wades into theory of money and jobs.' *Milwaukee Journal* (12 July).

Stewart, Maxwell S. 'The mainsprings of capitalism.' *Nation* 142, pp. 185–86.

Taussig, F. W. 'Employment and the national dividend.' *Quarterly Journal of Economics* 51, pp. 198–203.

Taylor, Horace. 'Mr Keynes' General Theory.' *New Republic* 86, p. 349.

Tilby, A. Wyatt. 'A Daniel come to judgement.' *Observer* (16 February).

Viner, Jacob. 'Mr Keynes on the causes of unemployment.' *Quarterly Journal of Economics* 51, pp. 147–67.

Williams, Francis. 'Social control of investment essential.' *Daily Herald* (4 February).

Withers, H. 'The blunders of economists.' *Sunday Times* (23 February).

# INDEX